Quiet World
A Librarian's Crusade for Destiny

Quiet World

A Librarian's Crusade for Destiny

The Professional Autobiography of
Louis Shores

Linnet Books 1975

Library of Congress Cataloging in Publication Data

Shores, Louis, 1904-
    Quiet world: a librarian's crusade for destiny.

    Includes index.
    1. Shores, Louis, 1904-   I. Title.
Z720.S53A35   020'.92'4 [B]   75-2220
ISBN 0-208-01477-2

© 1975 by Louis Shores
First published 1975 as a Linnet Book,
an imprint of THE SHOE STRING PRESS, INC.,
Hamden, Connecticut 06514

All rights reserved

Printed in the United States of America

To my wife Gerry

                and
*to the next generation
with faith in our
profession of destiny*

Contents

I—LIFE

Introduction: *Once upon a Time*	3
1 In the Beginning	6
2 New York City	17
3 Southern Accent	27
4 In Love	40

II—ODYSSEYS

Introduction: *Comparative Librarianship*	51
5 Armed Forces	54
6 Fulbright Year	82
7 Mission Extraordinary	118

III—CRUSADES

Introduction: *Evangelisms*	151
8 One Race	153
9 Basic Reference	162
10 The Librarian as Encyclopedist	171
11 Library-College	195
12 Media Unity	211
13 Library History: *The Quest for the Constant*	224

IV—LIBRARY AND SOCIETY

14 Library Communities	239
15 Organization Librarian	252
16 Intellectual Responsibility	269
17 Library Education	277
18 Testament	294
Index	301

I Life

Introduction: *Once upon a Time*

I can think back to a terraced roof outside my second story bedroom where I used to play. My mother told me later that proved I was about two years old. Our family had just moved to Cleveland, Ohio from Buffalo, New York, where I was born about six months earlier. She, my father, and my older sister Frances told me also many times after that my big blue eyes always looked up at them in wonder. There was an older brother, too, and that comprised our family then.

Frances began bringing books to me from the public library in my earliest memory. As I recall, we had just moved to a two-story frame house on the corner of Cedar and 90th Street, which was then on the outskirts of the city. One day she took me with her to the Hough branch. It looked then like one of the fairy palaces with its dark stone front wall decorated by climbing ivy. I imagined all of the fairy tales Frances read to me and that I began reading for myself happened in this wonderful building. On that first day in the library I was attracted to a picture book, with a boy on the cover who had very long hair and even longer finger nails. With the children's librarian's help I made out and pronounced Rumpelstiltzkin, and became as captivated by the name as by the story itself. She introduced me to *Henny-Penny*, and I read along with her, and lingered over "cocky-locky" each time, until the sky finally fell for Henny-Penny though she never told the king.

The library became my other home. I worried my parents because I disappeared for a whole day at a time. The mere touch of books in the children's room induced a trance in which time disappeared. Mostly, I read fairy tales—Blue, Green, Red, and colors Andrew Lang had not found for his titles; English, Scottish, Irish, French, Norse, Chinese, Asian and American Indian—the nationalities meant nothing to me then. I identified with the good characters, and raged against the wicked ones.

That nameless children's librarian encouraged me. She brought out treasures she had hoarded especially for me. Sometimes she would read aloud to me in the story-telling alcove. Soon she was encouraging me to read aloud to her. I could not have been over five when she asked me to come to the Saturday morning story hour. I recall that first time, because it brought me my first library triumph. She told several stories in her inimitable way, and I sat there captivated, agonizing over the bad things being done to good little children, and the punishment that was finally meted out to villains. This sequence appealed to me then as now, and contributed to my lifelong aversion to realism in literature.

Toward the end of the story hour, my beloved children's librarian told the other children how much I had read in the last few weeks. I was pleased: and then startled when she asked, "Louis. How would you like to tell us the story you enjoyed most?" I came to the front and told the story of *The Tinder Box*. The name Hans Christian Andersen meant nothing to me then; but the dog with eyes as big as saucers who stood guard over the copper money awed me. I became the soldier marching along the highroad who met the wicked witch and, at her instruction, climbed to the top of the tree and lowered myself down the hole to the wonderful treasures guarded by the three dogs with the extraordinary sets of eyes. I discovered the secret of the Tinder Box, and conjured out of it all the impossibles I could dream up, but not necessarily the lovely princess, at my age. My animation apparently held the children enthralled. I became co-storyteller every Saturday morning thereafter.

When I started to kindergarten, school became the competitor of library. I recall, however, that library maintained a big advantage until I graduated into first grade. Mostly I did not like kindergarten because instead of reading we were forever being kept busy cutting and pasting. "Learning by doing" was already in the educational vocabulary, and I hated all of the activity somebody thought was good for us. I wanted to read, and hold books in my hands, while I dreamed of conquering ogres with the help of a kind fairy. What did I care about making things when I could imagine so many more beautiful dreams?

My second triumph (after library story telling) came early in the first grade. We had our readers open, and the teacher began by reading the first (very easy it seemed to me) sentence, haltingly. Then began the excruciating exercise of extracting a letter at a time from each pupil called on. Again and again the teacher repeated sounds for letters, waited patiently for each word to form on the child's hesitating lips. For the first time I felt myself jumping right out of my skin.

At last my turn came. Without waiting for the teacher, I poured out word after word, sentence after sentence, page after page. I enjoyed the astounded look on my teacher's face, the gasps from my classmates. The truth was that the reader was insultingly easy after the hundreds of books

I had read in the public library's children's room. I finished the whole story, reading extraordinarily rapidly as if in protest against this senseless (to me) reading exercise. I remember my teacher's words to this day:

"Louis. Where did you learn to read like that?"

"In the public library," I recall I answered with pride. This brought on advice from the teacher to the class to go to the public library. And I was called on to explain how a child could get a borrower's card.

As I advanced through the primary grades, school was second only to the public library in my time and devotion. Part of the reason was the tremendous advantage my insatiable reading gave me over my classmates. I am afraid I did show off a bit with my vocabulary, even though words came out almost reflexively, because I had met them so often in print. Where my strength showed up was in my rich background of allusions, and in spelling. In my elementary days, spelling bees were the thing. We remained standing until we missed a word, challenged at each of us as our turn came up. I was the last standing so often in my second and third grade days that on occasion my teacher would excuse me from participating, or ask me to act as teacher.

I could attribute to reading my good work in two of the Three R's. But I was just as puzzled about my success in the third "R" as were my teachers. For some unaccountable reason I enjoyed adding long columns of figures, rapidly and perfectly. This quirk persisted through my adult years. I recall startling my secretaries, when I was librarian at Fisk and at Peabody, and dean of two library schools, as we worked on the mechanics of preparing a budget. Often before they had begun on the calculator I had added the necessary sums and presented them with the totals that the machine later confirmed. Skipping to Florida State University, many years later, I recall that our administrative vice-president had just acquired a new electric calculator which he was proudly displaying to me. While he majestically punched the keys, high on his desk, I reflexively added the column and recorded the total on a pad. His answer was different. We rechecked and his ineptness with the machine had caused the robot to trick him.

I recount these youthful triumphs with some embarrassment, as I reread for typos. Now I understand one of the hazard's of autobiography, as I did not when we were developing criteria in book selection courses for library school. How can the autobiographer report faithfully some incidents in his life without considerable immodesty? I fear these exhibitions are going to occur fairly frequently, and for them I apologize at the beginning. But for each such incident there is a point I want to make for some developing concept about library and society.

In these early "Three R" triumphs, the seed was planted for some strong protests against the learning folklore to which my classmates and I have been exposed these many years. Specifically, I did not like what was being done about reading in the primary grades, and I dissented even more markedly from later trends to focus on the mechanics of reading rather than on enriching background in the literature itself. Much later, I fumed at the whole "readiness" approach, and joined the Essentialist movement in Education, during the 1930s, to fight against the capitulation to John Dewey's "learning by doing."

And so another apology is due at the outset. Perhaps it is essential for evangelism to be so committed to cause as to tend toward biases. But, as H. L. Mencken implies in his series of books under the title "Prejudices," anyone—or at least anyone who stands for anything—is likely to be little other than a collection of preconceived notions. Some rather strong advocacies may emerge as I take up dozens of professional crusades. But I hope that seen in the context of my life as a whole they will not appear as mere bias.

1. In the Beginning

Perhaps Reading will be blamed for my comparative impracticality. I doubt that. Actually, books and libraries helped me overcome some of my disdain for things, and a basic ineptness with manipulations. In the imaginary world of print, I discovered hope for perfecting man's imperfections; infinite solutions to the finite problems of existence. Not for one moment am I suggesting that I was probing this philosophical riddle in the years before adolescence. But I am convinced that I was comparing the world I *sensed*, with the world I *dreamed*, almost from the first moment I can remember on Earth.

After I had re-read almost all of the fairy tale books in the Hough Children's Room several times, my librarian opened the door to mythologies—Greek and Roman, at first, and then Norse. In the first two I sided with Hector in the battle with Achilles, and dreamed a reversal of the decision in my daily walks; travelled with Ulysses between Scylla and Charybdis; helped Hercules in his 12 labors for Eurystheus, including holding the heavens for Atlas during those 24 hours; saved Leander from drowning so that he might forever be with his Hero.

And then came Thor, with his wondrous hammer. Hercules had to move over to make room for the Norse god of thunder. I imagined myself in Thor's place, preventing some tragedies that occur in Norse mythology. Principally I wanted to foil the wicked Loki and rescue the beautiful Baldur.

My children's librarian asked me one day if I would like to earn some money delivering newspapers. She knew our economy at home was quite austere. So, at the mature age of nine, I began delivering the Cleveland *News* in our neighborhood. In addition to the modest pay, there was an additional reward. The paper route entailed over two miles of walking for about two hours each afternoon after school. Those were wonderful hours. I dreamed all sorts of episodes in which I was the hero, refurbishing many of the fairy tales and myths with my imagination. Anticipating Dr. Seuss, I saw what really happened on the Mulberry Streets of our neighborhood.

As my reading took other directions, my dream walks changed their settings. In succession I owned a horse like Black Beauty, temporarily lost him, and saved him from a terrible fate. I went with Heidi to her grandfather at the top of one of the Alps, and brought to them many additional comforts. One day, another boy let me read *Try and Trust*, exposing me to the world of Horatio Alger. It suited my ten-year old outlook, and filled many hours of dreaming on my newspaper route. Classmate Pierce Mallison had almost a full collection of Alger, and I read them all. But not one of the heroes matched the triumphs I dreamed on my newspaper walks.

A new set of heroes emerged from my reading of the sports pages. Many years later, Florida's intellectual Governor Leroy Collins put his finger on the attraction for me of that part of the newspaper: it contained the positive and happy part of the news. There was the aura of "once upon a time," and "they lived happily ever after" in the reporting of baseball and football games, and of boxing matches, my three favorite sports.

As early as 1913, when I was just nine years old, I became enamored with our Cleveland Naps, before they were re-nicknamed the Indians.

Louis Shores

To this day, the lineup persists in my memory: Leibold, center field; Chapman, shortstop; Jackson, right field; Lajoie, second base, etc. My newspaper walks had me successively leading the Naps to an American League pennant, through my extraordinary prowess as both a hitter and a pitcher. I pictured myself almost single-handed overcoming Cleveland's two principal nemeses—the Philadelphia Athletics and the Washington Senators. Trouncing the former was comparatively easy, because Connie Mack, their wizard manager, was one of my villains. But defeating the Washington Nats was another matter, because of their great pitcher, Walter Johnson, my earliest boyhood hero.

What a strange childhood you will say. My vocation—newsboy; and my avocations were library, school, walking and dreaming, occasionally interrupted by the action of playing baseball on our neighborhood lot, and learning how to box from an ex-pug who lived on our street.

We moved from Cleveland to Toledo in 1918, the last year of World War I. I started high school in September, and got a job delivering the *Toledo Blade* six afternoons a week. Besides the money, which I needed, there was the reward of walk-dreams. To provide stimulation I registered as borrower in the Toledo Public Library the first day we arrived from Cleveland. But this time I went first to the adult reading room, and second to the children's department. I spent my reading time between the two library divisions, and soon the librarians began to know me by name.

I was still reading Horatio Alger, as I discovered titles I had not read. In my browsings I became absorbed in two novels about girls. The first was Eleanor Porter's *Pollyanna*. One librarian who has made invaluable suggestions for this manuscript does not want me to admit that *Pollyanna* is still a favorite. But the optimistic heroine personifies one of my criteria in personal book selection—looking for good in people and things. The second novel about a heroine was Louisa May Alcott's *Little Women*. As a matter of sequence, I read *Little Men* first; then *Little Women* and finally *Jo's Boys*. Porter and Alcott reenforced my growing literary commitment to "once upon a time" and "they lived happily ever after." I read the "telling it like it is" kind also, and began comparing the relative courage of both kinds of literature, as early in my reading life as those first Toledo days.

World War I was winding up in the fall of 1918. Approximately a month before the November 11 armistice, one of the Toledo librarians who had complimented me on my reading absorption day after day, and sometimes late in the evening, asked me one afternoon, "How would you like to work in the library after school, for pay, as a page, shelving books?" I was excited. Yet I hesitated. She hastened to add, "You don't have to decide right now. Go home and talk it over with your parents. Several of us on the staff have been watching you read, hour after hour, day after day. Have you ever thought of library work as a career?"

I really had not. To this point I was convinced I was destined to be a great baseball pitcher, even greater than my boyhood hero Walter Johnson. But the real reason for my hesitation was the afternoon newspaper route and the opportunity for complementing my library reading with day dreaming. Yet there was never any doubt in my mind. That afternoon I informed my parents that I was giving up my newspaper route to work in the library—at a cut in pay. The Toledo Public Library paid its 14-year old boy pages, in 1918, per hour of work, eight and one third cents. For twelve hours a week I earned one dollar, when the dollar, of course could purchase so very much more than it can today.

Herbert S. Hirschberg was then chief Toledo Public Librarian. He was my idea of a librarian—quiet, modest, considerate of even us lowly pages. We pages in the Toledo Public Library, however, worked directly under Mr. Hirschberg's associate director, Jesse Welles, who had a marked influence on my library habits. A strict disciplinarian, Miss Welles kept after the boys to keep returned books shelved. From her I learned the habit of pushing books tight up against the left upright, and pulling each book out meticulously to the edge of the shelf, so that as one looked down the range of a library stack the books were as straight in line as we soldiers had to be in our rigorous officer training at Miami Beach some 25 years later.

Indeed so lasting was this habit of library neatness drilled into us by Miss Welles that I was lectured by my wife just the other day, after a visit to some friends for a cocktail. "Did you have to embarrass Mrs. Jones by straightening out her books in the living room right in front of all her guests?" Suddenly I recalled what I had done reflexively, almost as if the spirit of Jesse Welles was prodding me. As is my wont, I had begun to look over the books on Mrs. Jones' living room shelves. Subconsciously, I pushed the books on each shelf over, right against the left upright and pulled out to the front of the shelf.

One early November morning while it was still quite dark I was startled out of my sleep, as was every one else, by the sound of sirens, the ringing of bells, and great shouting and singing in the streets. World War I had just ended. I had begun to read about World War I, about our General Pershing, France's Marshall Foch, and above all, about Sir Douglas Haig, the British commander, who became my favorite. That started me reading English history on my own to supplement the American history I was studying in school. In my high school junior year, I elected the single course in English history. The Spanish Armada and Sir Francis Drake, Oliver Cromwell, Gladstone and Disraeli became my new absorptions. Shakespeare, Dickens and Tennyson began to enter my reading through high school English classes. Almost from the freshman introduction, Sir Walter Scott was a favorite, not only for *Ivanhoe* and *Kenilworth*, which were required, but for the other Waverly novels which I read on my own in the library, and above all, the rhythm of his poetry.

In some ways, *Lady of the Lake* was my gateway to poetry. I was charmed by those opening lines

> The stag at eve had drunk his fill
> Where danced the moon on Monan's rill

and by those climatic lines about the struggle between the hero and the villain, Sir Roderick Dhu, when

> *Breathless all, Fitz James arose*
> From Scott I went on to Burns
> A man's a man for a' that . . .
> That man to man, the world o'er
> Shall brothers be for a' that.

And now comes the hazard of cataloging my reading. I believe these are some of the poems that had an impact on my mind and spirit that somehow shaped the drive behind those professional crusades which began to form in these high school days. William Blake, Rudyard Kipling, Samuel Taylor Coleridege, Edgar Allen Poe, Longfellow, Arnold, Shelley, Wordsworth in no apparent logic—thrust poems upon me. I simply had to memorize because of compulsion, not from a teacher, but from inside. What was there about *Gunga Din*, for example, which impelled me to recite it at every school opportunity that presented itself?

Two incidents among many stand out. In my junior year, physics was most discouraging because of our textbook, and the teacher's method.

Quiet World / Life

Try as hard as I would, I could not understand what the textbook author was trying to tell me. Nor could my classmates, apparently. Day after day they sat in the classroom trying to adjust to his deadening method of recitation, by one pupil after another, of each paragraph in the textbook. Every one of us kept his finger in the book. As soon as a pupil was called on we surreptitiously opened the book and began reading the next paragraph so we could recite the words, if not the meaning, should the axe fall on us next.

Rebelling against this procedure, I decided to consult other books on the subject assigned for the next lesson. It happened to be magnetism. Under "M" in the index of a half dozen other books in physics I noted the pages. I read three references in as many different books, and a revelation began. The very exercise of comparison and contrast of treatments taught me more about the subject than I had been able to learn from my teacher and textbook.

It was an exciting class period in physics the next day. Contemptuously, almost, I kept my textbook closed. When I was called on, I arose and expounded on magnetism, rapidly, and with defiant criticism of our textbook author, citing my sources for refutations. Not only was my "A" assured in that class, but my classmates noted how often the teacher referred to me as "our physics authority."

The other incident occurred in the economics class I elected during my senior year. I knew nothing about the subject. The teacher was so young and pretty that I fell deeply in love with her, even before I enrolled in the course. Determined to make a good impression I decided to read an encyclopedia article on economics. That gave me an overview of the subject and enabled me to sit in the class with anticipation. If the teacher developed the subject as the encyclopedia had I nodded my head in approval; if she did not, I fought her intellectually, inside myself, or outwardly with citations from my library reading.

Both of these incidents contributed to what became the Library—College learning mode, part of one of my later major crusades. I believe, also, that these incidents awakened my interest in Reference Books generally, and in encyclopedias particularly.

College began at the University of Toldeo in September 1922. The campus then consisted of a single factory-like building on Nebraska Avenue about a mile beyond the city limits; and a downtown, delapidated old structure. The former housed classes for full-time day students in the college of arts and sciences; the latter, evening and late afternoon courses for teachers and business people. The main library was housed in a single large room on the Nebraska campus; smaller general, and law and pharmacy collections were maintained in the downtown building.

I loved college though I protested much of the content and even more of the learning mode. But even if the climate then had favored physical communication of dissent, as it does now, I had no inclinations in that direction. Identifying problems has always interested me very much less than innovating solutions. From my first Freshman day, almost, I set about dreaming an ideal college and an ideal society. Early I began to ponder the meaning of art and to worry about those ultimates relating to the meaning of death and of life, and how campus philosophy and church religion compared.

Almost as automatically as my high school credits admitted me to the University, my public library experience opened the door to a university library job. Mary Mewborn Gilham was the librarian then, and she considerately built on my previous experience, offering me increasing responsibilities. I abandoned paging for duty at the circulation desk, and simple reference work. Toward the middle of my college year I was promoted to increasing responsibility for the downtown law library, and so began my special library experience. In an elementary way, I could claim to have served in all four types of libraries—public, school, academic, special—by the end of my college sophomore year.

Although I needed the money to pay my way through college, by far the greater library compensation came from widening horizons. To begin with, the mere shelving of books gave me a fantastic association of authors with titles. Again and again I startled faculty and students with my spontaneous identification of books. My background in the library made me a favorite with faculty and students as I enjoyed helping them just as much when I was off duty as when I was being paid on the job. Inevitably such assistance brought me into association with the kind of faculty and students who stimulated me.

There was an older student named Martin Ross whom I met in this way, early in 1922. He was only a sophomore when I was a freshman. At age 26, which was considerably older than the average age of 19 for second year college, he was respected not only by students but by faculty. He was the best read man I have ever known. Besides that, he had had some extraordinary experiences between graduation from a Chicago high school and admission to the University of Toledo. For several years he had been a hobo, "riding the rails" from city to city, protesting society and the post-World War I "establishment," in that era's dimension of dissent with what his older generation had wrought.

I helped Martin, one day, locate both sources and information. He was impressed by my library know-how, first, and after that I felt we were drawn to each other sentimentally. Shortly thereafter he invited me to his home where he lived with his elderly parents. What struck me first, however, were the shelves of books—from floor to ceiling—in nearly every room. When he left me alone for a few minutes to pick up some refreshments in the kitchen I reflexively began taking books off his shelves and browsing. The section I was nearest seemed reserved for some of his favorite English novelists. In turn I opened novels that I had previously only shelved in the public library—Richardson's *Pamela*, Fielding's *Joseph Andrews* and *Tom Jones*; then Martin returned to the room.

"Do you like Fielding?" I remember he asked. I had to admit he was an author to be shelved in the "f's" on the fiction shelves in the library. He gave me that friendly musical laugh. "Louis, he is the greatest of the English novelists."

"Why just *English*?" I remember laughing back.

"That's plenty," he said. And so began his big brother counselling. I borrowed *Tom Jones* and commenced, that very afternoon, reading until late that night.

This was the beginning of a friendship that lasted until his death in the mid-sixties. In succession I borrowed Fielding's *Joseph Andrews*, and *Amelia*; Richardson's *Pamela*; Sterne's *Tristram Shandy*; and Smollett's *Roderick Random*. I kept on reading England's Big Four, captivated especially by Fielding and his *Tom Jones*. For my English literature class I wrote a term paper on the "parabases," those first philosophical chapters that start each of the "books" of the novel. (Much later, when the line formed clear around the corner to get into the movie theater, nearest to the Florida State University campus, for a "mature" audience version of this classic, I remarked to a middle-aged English instructor about my interest in the *parabases*. "Parabases?" asked this quite sophisticated lady. "Are they sexy?")

More important to me than Martin's books, which I could have borrowed from the university library, were his oral annotations. He was the most convincing and cultured conversationalist I had ever known. The English Big Four lived for me in his informal monologues much more vividly than in any of the university lectures.

Toward the spring of that freshman year, I reminded Martin he had said the four greatest novelists in the English language. Were there greater in other languages? Cervantes in Spanish, for example, *Don Quixote* had already moved near the top of my reading. Or in the French because Hugo's *Les Miserables* had stirred me as almost no other novel. Without hesitation, Martin pulled off the shelf Tolstoy's *War and Peace*. I began reading it right there; continued at home until the early morning hours. Day after day, night after night, in every spare moment, I read in a sort of frenzy, hypnotically drawn to the character Pierre Bezhukov, and his Christ-like self-subordinations. I liked Bolkonsky, too, for contrast; and Natasha, and some other characters. Morning after morning, red-eyed, I reported to my eight o'clock class after all-night reading of *War and Peace*, in a state of semi-trance. When I finished the novel I knew my outlook on life had changed. It was as though there had been a commencement, a graduation from boy to man.

I had begun keeping lists of the "ten best novels." Indeed I had developed one of my freshman themes around such a list, in which *Les Miserables* was number one; *David Copperfield*, number two, etc. After reading *Tom Jones*, Fielding's novel took over the number one spot. Just like teams in the Associated Press weekly football polls, *Tom Jones* dropped to number two when I closed the covers of Martin Ross' copy of *War and Peace*.

He was pleased when I reported my new list of "top ten." In response he handed me Dostoyevsky's *Crime and Punishment*. I read it with the same frenzy. There was a fire in the writing of these Russians that seemed to inflame me. I suffered with Raskolnikov all through the lacerations of his crime. And when I had finished with *Crime and Punishment* there followed *Karamazov*, and then *The Idiot,* and *Raw Youth*.

Turgenev was next with *Fathers and Sons*. My heart broke over the parents' devotion to a dying son. And then the final member of Russia's Big Four—Gogol. *Taras Bulba* carried me along in that frenzy of Russian fiction reading. But *Dead Souls*, with that macabre idea of selling dead serfs, shocked me more than it amused, as it did Martin. I went back to Tolstoy, read *Resurrection*, which I liked better than *Anna Karenina;* to *Kreutzer Sonata;* and to the short stories, like *How Much Land*, and decided that Tolstoy was the Beethoven of fiction.

Indeed I had been reading the Russian novels to the practicing of the Beethoven sonatas by my brother Manuel. And this was another great impact in my college days. From Toledo days I had begun the habit of reading to his practice. While I was reading *War and Peace*, Manuel was repeating passages in the first, *allegro assai* movement of the *Appassionata*. Beethoven matched the soul of Tolstoy and the two together helped me catch glimpses of eternity. When I started on *Crime and Punishment* Manuel had shifted to the *Waldstein*. I read through the novels of the four Russian masters to the accompaniment of two other Beethoven sonatas—the *Pathetique* (opus 13) and the tripping opening of Beethoven's *opus 2, number 1*. Manuel was a perfectionist. He repeated a passage fifty or more times, before he was ready to go on. No wonder I know, to this day, the piano literature so well that I have startled pianists by recognizing or humming passages in the middle of movements.

Perhaps I should turn away from the impact of music and from literature, to society. In my reading, and entirely independent of Martin's growing influence on my aesthetic appreciation, I discovered some social revolutionaries. Injustices I found everywhere—hard working families with barely enough for subsistence contrasting with wealthy indolents. This stirred rage. I was ripe for Upton Sinclair, who made me forget the English Four and Russian Four, for a while. I read *The Jungle* first; and then I was off through *King Coal*, and what he called the "Dead Hand" series of exposes.

Sinclair led me into a concentration on revolutionary reading. I met Marx for the first time in his collaboration with Engels on the *Communist Manifesto*; and then had to tackle the formidable three-volume *Das Kapital*, the last two of which had been published after his death by Engels. It was too much for me, and I contented myself with reading more about Marx than by him.

By my senior year, my disaffection with Marx had gone so far that when the Communist local in Toledo had challenged every civic club in the city to debate, without getting any takers, I induced my colleagues on the university debating team to challenge them.

For three years I had been a member of the University of Toledo varsity debating team. That year—1925/26—we had an undefeated team, including a proud victory over Purdue, considered the best in the Big Ten. The Communist team was headed by their candidate for mayor. Surprised by our visit and challenge, at first, they saw an opportunity to advance their cause, and agreed to the debate. But to our embarrassment the debating team was called into the university president's office and told, in no uncertain terms, we could not hold the debate on the campus. Apparently local business men had advised against a debate, which they feared would be a mismatch. Determined to go through with it, we offered to debate them in their own Labor Temple auditorium.

Never before had we worked so hard to prepare for a debate. Cockily, they offered us, free of charge, any of the Communist publications in their book store. With the help of our coach, a speech teacher, and the head of sociology, a socialist we organized our notes on 3 by 5 cards. The Communist team had chosen the three judges—a local jurist, a liberal pastor, and an acknowledged "fellow traveller" of a prominent family. The Communist team members were soapboxers, not used to time restrictions, but practiced in rambling nightly on street corners. Inadequately organized, their fifteen-minute periods were up before they could get to their points. We found it necessary to make their points for them in order to refute them.

Long before the rebuttals, it was quite evident the university team was winning the debate. In desperation, the older men began resorting to heckling and to disrupting tactics during our presentations. Almost frantically, and somewhat pathetically the communists started shouting their cliches: "you can't patch up the old pants" and "we don't want our pie in the sky but right here and now." When the judges decision was announced—"unanimous for the affirmative on the proposition *Resolved that the reform of capitalism offers a better way to the good society than does communism*"—pandemonium broke out in the Labor Temple auditorium. The morning newspaper which had failed to mention the debate, before, displayed an eight-column headline the next day:

UNIVERSITY DEBATE TEAM CRUSHES COMMUNISTS

In a certain way, it is still another example of the superiority of library learning to what takes place in the conventional classroom.

2. New York City

Travel had always entered into my dreams. The only two places I had ever seen were Cleveland and Toledo. Of course, I had been born in a third city—Buffalo—but since we had moved away from there when I was only 18 months old I had no recollection of it. Once I had crossed over into the bordering state of Michigan, as far as Monroe, and that excited my travel longing.

When an opportunity to work on a Lake Erie passenger boat occurred the sixteenth summer of my life, I grasped the opportunity. The *State of Ohio* excursioned daily to Put-in-Bay and Cedar Point, two popular resorts. Once a week it made an all-night cruise to Cleveland, coming back to Toledo the following night. I looked forward to these weekly sailings especially, because it gave me an opportunity all day Monday to revisit familiar places in Cleveland.

But above all, that Lake Erie summer aroused a love of the sea that persisted throughout life. I loved to look out on the water and meditate when I was off duty. Especially did I enjoy the all-night sailings to Cleveland, because the wide expanse of the water in the dark stirred some awesome recollections, it seemed to me, of the real eternity that I must have known before I was borne to this Earth. I hope you will believe that at sixteen these concerns with ultimates were integral.

Perhaps this summer on Lake Erie began my plans to travel the following summer. I wanted above all to see New York. My reasons were more than mere sightseeing, although the wonders of skycrapers and subways lured also. I wanted to hear the New York Philharmonic and the New York Symphony (separate then) orchestras, some piano recitals, and violin and string ensembles too; opera, perhaps, but not as much vocal solo as instrumental. Then, I hoped to see a Broadway play: to visit the Metropolitan Museum: and last, but certainly not least, to read in the famed New York Public Library on 42nd Street and Fifth Avenue.

That started me thinking. I could certainly not afford travel. Would the NYPL hire a lowly library page with experience only in the "provinces," as sophisticated New Yorkers then referred to the rest of the United States? Librarians in both the Public and University libraries of Toledo wrote letters in my behalf. Late in the spring of 1924 came a letter from Personnel in the NYPL offering me a job as page and assistant in the Economics Division. I walked on air during the weeks before the close of the University academic year, late in May, until my departure the very first day of vacation.

I had no travel money and decided to try the "hitch-hike," just coming into vogue then, and still quite safe for both hiker and motorist. I had never been away from home before. Since this is supposed to be professional and intellectual autobiography I must telescope my week's experience on the road by merely saying I learned a great deal about the ugly in life as well as the beautiful. Even if I were inclined to expand my descriptions I would hesitate to do so for a climate which is still committed largely to realism in literature. Philosophically, I began asking myself even then, who is the ostrich burying his head in the sand: the realist who describes minutely the physiologial functions imposed upon us by a primitive nature, or the dreamer who tries to look beyond the temporal realism for a glimpse of the infinite?

From the start, NYPL was familiarly "library" in climate: quiet, first of all: staffed by my kind of undemonstrative people, for the most part: filled with books I loved to handle. But there were differences, too. The sixty-four miles of shelves about which they boasted then, bewildered this page of limited experience in much more modest libraries. The Billings classification, with its strange letters of TLH, were so different from the neat Dewey numbers by which I had always shelved books before. I set myself to the task of identifying subjects with these letters, and comparing with Dewey, as I raced through the stacks filling bookslip requests.

It was a very hot New York summer. Before air conditioning, the NYPL could become unbearably suffocating during night duty. I ran along the stacks filling call slip requests for books, bathed in my own sticky perspiration. Nor was there any relief from the heat on the streets, after work: nor in the dingy little room off Harlem that I rented for two dollars a week. During the day, I strolled through Central Park, visited the Metropolitan Museum, rode the subway to points of interest. The most relaxing excursion of all was the Staten Island ferry, then just a nickel, and if one stayed on and did not get off on the docks, it could be a round trip, certainly the cheapest ocean voyage in the world. My love of the sea and of ships was nurtured in these Staten Island ferry excursions, which acted as sort of a rehearsal for that mighty 96-day Pacific voyage I was destined to take for Uncle Sam in World War II; and the transatlantic trips that came subsequently.

That summer sped by swiftly. After, I hitch-hiked back to Toledo and entered my senior year at Toledo feeling considerably matured. That last year in college, the inevitability of librarianship as a career virtually engulfed me. I became the downtown law librarian for the University, afternoons and evenings; continued to put in some hours at reference and circulation at the Nebraska Main; and read omnivorously under periodic provocations by Martin Ross, who had become an English instructor at the University of Illinois upon his graduation. But he came back to Toledo nearly every other weekend to be with his elderly parents, and to engage his violinist friend Raphael and me in lengthy trialogues on art, music, literature and current events. Sometimes these evenings went on until dawn. Afterwards, we would turn to the books we had been arguing about; read them to the accompaniment of either Manuel's piano practicing, or Raphael's violin exercises, depending on whether my activity was at home or at Raphael's.

June 1926 brought my Toledo bachelor's degree. The choice was between teaching English in high school, or in a small Ohio college that had indicated an interest, or going to New York. Music influenced my decision for the latter. My brother's teacher in Toledo, convinced of Manuel's promise, secured scholarship aid with the master teacher Henry Holden Huss in New York first, and then with the great Sigismund Stojowski. Like Raphael, Manuel went on to a concert career. To help make his study possible, my widowed mother, younger sister and I established an apartment home in New York. I took on two jobs: junior high teaching in an upper East Side New York City public school; and seven nights a week in the Newspaper and Periodical divisions of the New York Public Library.

For recreation, Manuel, who also worked in the NYPL, and I went to the symphony concert every Saturday afternoon. One week it was the New York Symphony, under the baton of Walter Damrosch; the next it was the Philharmonic directed by William Mengelberg. Sometimes there were famous soloists performing in violin and piano concertos, among them such names as Albert Spalding, Erika Morini, Joseph Hoffman, Leopold Godowsky.

I ponder the communicabilities of different kinds of music. In preparation for a major article on the Beatles, which *Collier's* was one of the first among comprehensive encyclopedias to welcome, I reenforced my personal collection of their recordings. Strain as hard as I may, I cannot achieve the ecstasies that apparently older as well as teen age enthusiasts evidence. I like *Yesterday*, and *In an Octopus Garden* most; perhaps *Michelle* next.

But even these cause no such stirrings as come over me when I listen to their contemporary, Anita Kerr's trilogy on *The Sea*. With my mystical fascination about oceans, I dare say that Anita Kerr communicates an extrasense of eternity that even Debussy in his famous *La Mer* did not quite achieve. I ponder further why such other diverse contemporaries as Harvey Schmidt in "Try to Remember" (*Fantasticks*): Kurt Weill's "Mack the Knife" (*Three Penny Opera*). Mitch Leigh "The Impossible Dream" (*Man of La Mancha*), among others, move me along the way to uplift of the Chopin and Rubinstein concertos, and the Beatles don't. Unquestionably, the receiver's stage of development has much to do with the response.

New York was affecting me not only musically, but educationally and sociologically. I taught six classes in English daily. Half of them were all boys; the others all girls; as the sexes were not encouraged to mix in learning, in Prospect Junior High, during the school year of 1926/27. The neighborhood was just a little less "tough" (in the meaning of that word then) than the lower East Side. Pupils were over-age in grade. Several of the boys who towered over their teacher bragged about a father or uncle in Sing Sing prison. I was fortunate to win my boys over by securing passes for the whole class to a baseball game in Yankee stadium. From that point I had no discipline problem with the boys.

The girls' classes were a different story. At age 22, this male teacher was no match for the fifteen-year old girls, who were mostly merely marking time until their sixteenth birthday, when they could drop out and go to work. Trying to teach them Longfellow's *Evangeline* was both the most hazardous and frustrating effort of my life. In the contemporary idiom they would have declared "Acadia simply isn't relevant." Even worse, their female advances were too sophisticated for a male teacher not enough years older.

I survived the strenuous 1926/27 year, attaining all of my three goals. Pay from the two jobs—school and library—although barely $2,000 for the year, helped support the New York home that enabled Manuel to further his piano study. I earned my master's degree with a double major in English and Education, writing a thesis for Dean Paul Klapper on the "Municipal College." At the time, there were nine municipal colleges in the United States. Both Toledo and City College of New York were examples. The College of Charleston was the oldest municipal college in the United States. Others entirely funded by municipalities included Louisville, Cincinnati, Akron, and Wichita. The history of these seven institutions stimulated my developing interest in library history, since their libraries played an important part in my study.

But the third goal was the most significant of all. I had hoped to save some money so as to be able to give up teaching and enter library school. When the idea first occurred to me, there was an accredited library school in the New York Public Library. During 1925/26 it combined with the school at Albany to reestablish the School of Library Service at Columbia.

When I entered Columbia's School of Library Service in September 1927, C. C. Williamson was dean; Edna Sanderson assistant dean. Both were personally concerned with my objectives throughout the year, although the enrollment in the school was very large by library school standards then. Indeed it was necessary to organize the 1926/27 class into four sections, which was done according to previous library experience.

Sections one and two, for example, were limited to entering students with little or no previous work experience in a library; sections three and four to students with several years of library work experience. By September 1927 my application showed eight years of library work for pay—four in the Toledo Public Library; four in the University of Toledo libraries; over a year in the New York Public Library, plus some school library weeks at Toledo Scott and New York Prospect. All of these jobs had been part time and had therefore been calculated together as eight full years. I was placed in Section Three.

Comparatively, that Columbia library school faculty had proportionately more good teachers than any other faculty of any of the colleges I had studied in to that time. Dr. Williamson was not a library school graduate, his specialty having been the social sciences in general, and economics particularly. His approach to librarianship was freshly different from that of the librarian practitioners. He encouraged me in my earliest crusade for teaching library use to students and teachers more effectively than it had been taught to us in high school and college. As a result of his encouragement, my series of articles for *Scholastic* magazine was published and later republished as a pamphlet.

Reference was taught to our third section by Mary Louisa Sutliff, an Albany graduate, with a love for Reference Books and an even greater devotion to her students. Conscientious beyond her call, Miss Sutliff could not omit a single title in Mudge's *New Guide to Reference Books*. We used the fourth edition, which already included several thousand reference books. The result was an overtaxing of our memory and the beginning of a hunch that not all of these titles were equally important in every day Reference, and that concentration on the most frequently used would be more beneficial to the beginning Reference librarian.

From time to time, the great and good teacher, Isadore Gilbert Mudge lectured to the combined sections. She whetted my desire to know more about these books that seemed to have no place in the many literature courses I had taken in bachelor and master concentrations in English. I recall that during one of Miss Mudge's lectures she told us about her famous sleuthing in George Eliot and Daniel Defoe. The query from a British scholar had asked: George Eliot refers to an edition of Robinson Crusoe that has a picture of the devil. In which edition does this picture appear?

Miss Mudge, proceeding on her knowledge of George Eliot as a realist—as a novelist who loved to write it as it is—decided to confirm her bibliographic assumption that it was the Exeter 1828 edition. Sure enough, back came the word that in the George Eliot library the Defoe edition was the Exeter edition. This long after I am a bit hazy about the details of the incident; but I am clear that another link in my Basic Reference chain was forged during that Mudge lecture. Just as Miss Sutliff had suggested the need for a study of frequency use of reference sources, Miss Mudge had, by this incident, aroused my desire to study the literature of reference *per se* in the way I had studied the literatures of poetry, of drama, of essay, of fiction, and other literary forms. A concept of Basic Reference was beginning to form during that 1927/28 Columbia year.

Although I was instantly drawn to Reference as a type of library work, I became extraordinarily attracted to the courses in classification and cataloging. Dr. Harriet Dorothea MacPherson, a Ph. D. in Romance languages, unusual for a woman in those days, influenced me greatly. Even without that degree, she would have converted me easily because of her depth, especially in her philosophical considerations of the classification of knowledge. I immediately related my college study of Epistemology, which she augmented, in after-class conferences with her to such an extent that I began reading on my own in the area of classification.

I became captivated by Melvil Dewey, his many innovations, his leadership in simplified spelling, and even his many personal eccentricities. I much preferred his DC to the Billings classification, with which I was struggling at NYPL; and I was unable to become enthusiastic about what appeared to be the rather unimaginative L.C. Because I orated on the creativity of Dewey's decimal concept as compared with the Meneleev periodic table for chemical elements, and the Linnaeus classification for biology, Dr. MacPherson asked me to prepare the affirmative on the proposition "DC is a better library classification than LC." I recall that even as early as 1927, considerable support for LC was developing in academic and special libraries. Nevertheless, Dr. MacPherson complimented my defense of DC.

The Columbia year confirmed my decision for librarianship. I was more excited than ever by the library mystique of quiet, because I observed daily that mankind had its noblest moments during library quests. But my Columbia days also embarked me on my first professional crusade.

All through high school I had been floundering for a learning method that would overcome some of the discouragement that came from classroom teaching. I had stumbled on the *overview* idea via encyclopedia; the *browsing* technique as taught me by my library work and reading. In college I earned better than average grades by increasing my time in the library, and strengthening my independent study habits. I was captivated when I discovered over a library arch those most quoted words by the prolific author *Anon*: "The half of knowledge is knowing where to find it." Why had not my schools and colleges spent more time teaching students that important half of knowledge?

In an early conference with Dean Williamson, I communicated my protest. Not in the idiom of the Sixties, when courage meant *identifying* problems and leaving the solution to the protestees. Rather, I described my idea for a text on *library use* for high schools and colleges. Dean Williamson challenged me to solve the problem I had so violently identified. I set about this during the spring of 1928. The finished product, toward the middle of that summer, was the manuscript for my manual *How To Use Your Library*. *Scholastic Magazine* accepted it; publishing it first as a series of four articles in successive issues (October 28-December 1, 1928, Volume 13, numbers 3-7) and then as a reprint pamphlet with a lengthy foreword by the Editors. The *Scholastic* series really began that quantity of crusading publication that earned me the questionable "number one" ranking among librarians with subject doctorates in volume of published writings, (*College and Research Libraries*, 1966.)

Columbia clinched my life-long commitment to librarianship as a profession. That year aroused my desire to communicate the "half of knowledge" in schools and colleges, and to the out-of-school population as well, and perhaps to indoctrinate teachers and researchers in information sources for their respective missions.

In that Columbia year was born the *Basic Reference* concept. Two elements specifically emerged. First came the idea of determining which among the 10,000 or more Reference titles in the world were most frequently used to answer questions in all four library types. Next, I was stirred by Miss Mudge's lectures on literary searches and my own major in English to establish a place for the liberature of Reference comparable to the recognition given by English departments to other literary forms like Essay, Drama, Fiction, Poetry. These became further professional crusades.

As commencement approached in the spring of 1928, all of us without jobs became feverishly concerned about placement. Another crusade emerged from my decision between two jobs for which I was recommended. One was the librarianship of Battle Creek College in Michigan, with the added inducement of being near to the job of one young lady who had been a fellow student assistant in the University of Toledo library. The other position for which I was recommended was the librarianship of Fisk University in Nashville, Tennessee.

Partly because I had never been in the South, but mostly because of the challenge of serving in what was then described as a "Negro University," I accepted the offer, made after our Columbia interviews, by President Thomas Elsa Jones. Instrumental in my decision was Ruby Ethel Gundiff, a Columbia classmate, who had served at Fisk for a brief period.

From Columbia commencement in June 1928 until the beginning of my terminal August vacation I continued my night work in the Newspaper Division of the New York Public Library. Lou Fox was Chief, and both an exacting boss and a sympathetic friend. When I told Mr. Fox I had accepted the Fisk position, he was more than casually interested. A liberal, concerned with the reform of society, he enthusiastically dialogued about solutions to discriminations against Jews, Negroes, Catholics, Chinese, Indians, Puerto Ricans—the principal victims in New York, then. In those days to spell *Negro* with a capital *N* was an evidence of tolerance, and symbolized the racial pride now expressed by *Black*. Mr. Fox was that kind of liberal White, and he concurred in my selection of three librarians, above all, with whom I wanted to talk before beginning at Fisk.

The first of the three I had already met, since she was librarian of the NYPL Harlem Branch. As soon as my Fisk appointment had been confirmed, I rode the subway out to 135th street. Miss Rose set everything aside to give me some two hours of advice. Those who remember her know how committed she was to fighting prejudice. She poured fuel on my flames of indignation when she described discriminations not only in the South but right there in New York City. I admired what Ernestine Rose had done in the Harlem Branch, not only with the beginnings of the Schomburg Negro Collection, but especially in her brand of adult education for a disadvantaged section of the city.

Without telepathy it is impossible today to be sure how little or how much bias humans have toward other faiths, ethnic and national origins. I believe I have always liked some individuals more than others, and as I make up a list of the people for whom I have had deep intellectual and personal affection I note there are among them Jews; Catholics, and Protestants of the Christian faith; Moslems, Buddhists, a Shinto, an atheist, a Jain. There are Blacks, Yellows, Reds, and many shades of white in the skin colorations of the individuals who have meant so much *in my life*. Nor have their political differences affected my affection. Several communists, as well as conscientious objectors, and even an avowed anarchist have worked their way into my heart at times.

Speaking of communists, during my Columbia year, Whitaker Chambers served at the Newspaper Division reference desk with me. He was a communist then and he stirred my interest in Karl Marx. Many years later when he became disaffected he accused Alger Hiss, a U.S. Department of State officer, of being a communist traitor and published his best seller book *Witness*. After fierce interrogation by a young congressman named Richard Nixon, Hiss was convicted of perjury. There were other communists like Scott Nearing, and socialists like Upton Sinclair and Norman Thomas who affected me. In those days it was especially hazardous to admit such associations because the nation was in the throes of one of those perennial "red scares."

But the second of the three librarians I had decided to see before undertaking my Fisk job influenced me the most. In 1928 Edward Christopher Williams was librarian of Howard University in Washington, D.C., then the great federal Negro University. E. C. had been the first Negro to serve on the faculty of the white Western Reserve University before moving to Washington. I wrote and asked if I might confer with him after August one, when my NYPL terminal vacation began.

He wrote back immediately to invite me to stay at his home during my Washington visit. "Mrs. Williams is away; we will have the house to ourselves, and if you can put up with my cooking and house keeping you can make our home your Washington headquarters for as long as you care to stay." E. C.'s letter touched me so deeply that I found myself counting the days on my calendar until I should take off.

As I had already learned to do, I hitchhiked the 240 miles, and reported to the Howard University library first. There began nearly two weeks of dialogue that had a profound effect upon both my professional librarianship and my philosophy of human relations. As a library school professor at Western Reserve, E. C. had developed that art of communication that is the mark of a great teacher. From Acquisition through Reference he augmented my Columbia perspective so excitingly that I could hardly wait to begin at Fisk. Even more profoundly he introduced me to a race relations dimension that almost opposed Ernestine Rose's. I pondered this, in between the meals we prepared together in his home during those two weeks, and at night before I retired to that neat and well ordered bedroom he had assigned to me. Here was Ernestine Rose, a militant white, almost vindictively trying to compensate for the injustices people of her skin coloration had inflicted on people with darker colorations. And here was E. C. Williams, a Negro, no less aware of the suffering he and his people had known, yet suggesting that conciliation might be more effective than confrontation. If there is any doubt about what was E. C.'s pride in his race one need only read E. C. Josey's fine biographical sketch of E. C. Williams delivered before the A.L.A. American Library History Round Table and subsequently published in the *Journal of Library History*.

I have always recalled the two weeks in E. C. Williams' home. During the day he went to work at Howard, and I made my rounds of Washington libraries, beginning with the Library of Congress. E. C. fixed breakfast in the morning for both of us, and we had early talks, mostly about professional library matters. At night we cooked dinner cooperatively, washed and dried dishes, tried to maintain the neatness about the house that Mrs. Williams had left with us. And then would follow a long night of conversation about books and libraries, about national and international problems, and, inevitably, about the discriminations I would be meeting for the first time when I entered the South. He also told me about the third of the three librarians I had chosen to interview before going to Fisk—Florence Rising Curtis, whom he liked very much. I recall that my departure after these two weeks together included a very long hand clasp and a tear in my eye.

I then hitch-hiked to Newport News, Virginia, from where I took the ferry to Hampton. Miss Curtis met me and took me out to the Hampton Institute. In my full day there, my education in librarianship and in race relations was further augmented. From the start of our dialogue it was apparent that Miss Curtis, though white, was more inclined to E. C. Williams' rather than to Ernestine Rose's approach to race relations.

From my first introduction I noted her personal concern with each student. In subsequent years this was reenforced by observation of her visits to graduates on their jobs, and an extraordinary memory for incidents relating to each of them. When I began my very long professional life as head of two library schools I believe I carried Miss Curtis' picture in my mind.

In preparation for my Fisk job she alerted me to the kinds of segregations I would meet, as a Northerner, probably for the first time. Following in E. C. Williams' footsteps she cautioned me that confrontation might retard the integration that true liberals of all colors and faiths wanted for mankind. I pondered this admonition as I raged inside at my first experiences with separate drinking fountains and toilet facilities for Whites and Blacks.

3. Southern Accent

The moment came to board the Nashville train for the beginning of my career as a fully trained professional librarian, and above all, as the head of a library, for the first time. I recall my trepidations rather vividly and humorously. Always before I had worked under someone's direction, carrying out orders. Now I would have to direct a staff, give orders, decide what was to be done and what was not to be done. It made my heart palpitate every time I thought about it.

Humorously now, I recall the vivid pictures I painted for myself on that train, tickety-tocking over the rail ties in the lovely, rolling country of Kentucky. Just as I used to conjure visions up for my daydreams when I was delivering newspapers in Cleveland and Toledo, I pictured myself being taken into the Fisk library for the first time by President Thomas Elsa Jones. I saw him sit down and say to me, "now librarian Shores, let me see how a professional librarian libraries."

I kept asking myself, just what does a professional librarian do first, the first day on the job? Walk to the card catalog, pull out a drawer, start fingering the cards, wrinkle one's brows so as to convince watchers that some profound contemplations are going on? Or perhaps display some other outer manifestations as one walks along the reference shelves much like a general inspecting his troops?

I recall I was roused from my revery by the conductor's call: "Nashville."

Novelist Alfred Leland Crabb, whose best known novel *Breakfast at the Hermitage* had been the start of a series about the South, also wrote a non-fiction book titled Nashville: Personality of a City, (Bobbs-Merrill, 1960) which opens

> Creation day dawned bright and fair in that particular area of the universe which in the long passage of time was to become Nashville country . . .

Had those words been published on the 25th day of August 1928 I would have been certain of their truth, as the chugging L & N train approached the outskirts of the city. Furthermore, I might have dreamed that somewhere in God's plan he had conceived Nashville as the setting for a librarian to begin his career in surroundings of natural beauty and gracious, friendly people. What was not part of God's plan, I am sure, were the two uglinesses that jarred me a little later. In those days, a soft coal smoke smog shrouded the city during the cold days of the year. Segregation of Blacks from whites was even more pronounced than I had experienced in such separations, for the first time, in Hampton, Virginia.

On that 25th day of August 1928, red lettered on my calendar, I proceeded by taxi directly to Jubilee Hall on the Fisk campus. My preparation homework had already acquainted me with the famed Singers for whom the hall was named. I was greeted by the director of the Hall, a lady with a lovely, soft bronze colored skin, perhaps in her middle thirties:

"President Jones has not yet returned from his summer vacation but he left instructions. This young man will take you to your room in the Faculty men's house, and from there to the library. Meals are served in the Jubilee Dining Hall precisely at seven, twelve, six for breakfast, dinner, supper, respectively." She rang a bell, and the young man arrived to help me with my luggage and escort me.

I expressed my pleasure over the end of my journey, and especially the homey feeling about the Fisk campus. "This is the faculty men's bachelor quarters," he observed.

"Are they all bachelors?" I remember I naively asked.

"Just you and two others," he answered. "The others are married, have children, but simply do not want their families exposed to the segregation of the South. For example, the great chemist, Dr. St. Elmo Brady, has a very dark black skin. He knows the humiliations his wife and children would have to put up with here. So he maintains a home for them in Washington."

I remember the gloom that depressed my buoyant feeling about Nashville and Fisk; but I tried not to show it as we entered the house. My room was on the second floor. "The room to the left of yours is Dr. Brady's; to the right is Professor Currier's, of History; a white man. (I recall a jarring sense of apology I felt for the colorlessness of my skin.) Beyond, Ray Francis Brown, Music, director of the *a capella* choir, also white, is in this room. Upstairs is the famous anthropologist Paul Radin, a Jew. You will meet them all when they start coming in after the first of the month."

I unpacked only my suits to unwrinkle them on a hanger in the closet. Then, at my prompting, we proceeded to the library. My escort gave me the master key in a sealed envelope. We entered through the back door leading into the librarian's office. There it was. *My* private office; *my* desk. I looked about quickly, my heart pounding furiously, as I recall. Then I pushed open the door and saw a passage way past the circulation desk into the reading room. Excitedly I almost ran around inspecting with quick darts the loan desk, the public catalog, reference books, of which there were few indeed, on the shelves, almost choked by surrounding musty volumes of theology.

I began itching to get started, Columbia notes swirling in my head. Ruby Ethel Cundiff had told me there had never been an inventory of the collection. That was near the top of my priorities. I asked my escort if there were any students around who would like to work in the library. He volunteered, and suggested there was a girl who worked in the library as a student assistant who had just arrived. I arranged to have them both come in the following morning.

Then I proceeded to check the Reference shelves, according to my own system. Beginning with dictionaries, I noted fairly old editions of each of the two U.S. unabridged—Webster's *New International* and Funk and Wagnalls *New Standard*—plus a few miscellaneous abridgeds. Supplementary specials were scarce. In order, type by type, I checked encyclopedias, yearbooks, biographical and geographical sources, and right down the basic list I had begun to conceive in my mind. I began putting wants on order cards.

Then I turned to the three fundamental records. The accession book and the shelflist showed Ruby Ethel Cundiff's recent influence. But the dictionary catalog still had many handwritten half cards (1/2 by 5 instead of 3 by 5). I examined the circulation records quickly, comparing with those I had known in the libraries where circulation was my chief duty. Last, I quickly inventoried my own office: my desk drawers were clean except for some stationery and a pack of blank order cards. The shelves had an assortment of uncatalogued pamphlets and old books.

Outside, the sun had sunk to a point that reminded me Jubilee supper hour had arrived. I locked up, walked briskly to the dining hall, rejoicing that I had been so busy it would have been a pleasure to have President Thomas Elsa Jones watching me *library* on the first day.

The next day began with a professional tragedy that taught me practically what the Columbia classes had suggested only theoretically. I removed the rod from one of the shelflist drawers, took out a handful of cards and showed the two students how to inventory by checking cards against the Dewey-arranged books on the shelves. Crash! The boy dropped the tray and the first hour was spent refiling the shelflist drawer. I recalled what my Columbia teacher had taught. We tied string through the holes of packs of 100 cards so that if they dropped they would not fall out of place. It was a lesson for me as well as for the student assistants, although not a deeply professional one.

I was determind to shape Fisk's library to the standards I had been taught at Columbia as quickly as possible. With youthful impatience,

I began devoting eighteeen hours a day for seven days a week. Moving on a half dozen fronts simultaneously I drove myself and my staff relentlessly toward library school theoretical perfections. But libraries involve people, and no professional school can teach what a librarian must know about fellow members of his species.

A crate of new books arrived from Krochs in Chicago. When we opened it we found there was no library order for the titles; but there was an invoice to the library for several hundred dollars. The books were all in the field of Anthropology. My assistant librarian said quickly, "Dr. Radin must have purchased them."

"With library authorization?" I asked.

"Of course not," came back the response. "Dr. Radin always order his own books."

I responded rather angrily, "He may order his own books, but not out of the library budget."

My assistant observed, "Dr. Radin is the best known faculty member on the campus. He has special privileges and he orders his own books."

"Not with library money." I turned to my secretary and dictated a letter to Kroch's telling them that since the Fisk library had not ordered these books they could not be paid for out of the Fisk budget.

Part of Dr. Radin's special treatment was to report late for the academic year. I was aware of his famous books on the American Indian, and of the fact that Fisk valued the reputation this distinguished scholar gave to the campus. Nevertheless, I was determined to maintain control over the library budget.

Late one November afternoon, the telephone rang and the President's secretary asked that I report to the office at once. She had already become my friend during orientation into Fisk regulations, and she now added, "Dr. Radin has just arrived on campus and I have overheard him shouting your name. Better hurry over. He has just left the President's office and I have never seen him so mad."

Charge it to the impetuosity and rebellion of youth. Along the way I stopped off in my room, hastily packed my belongings into the one valise I had brought, and then crossed the street into the administration building where the president's office was at the end of the main hall. The secretary quickly showed me in.

Without waiting for the President to say a word, I began, "Mr. President, you have my resignation, if you want it."

Thomas Elsa Jones, a Friend, kindly and tolerant, looked at me and asked, "Why? It's about time someone on the Fisk faculty stood up to Dr. Radin. You are absolutely right. I hold you responsible for the library budget. How can I hold you responsible if any faculty member can spend from it without accountability to you?"

I was so ashamed of my approach that I apologized, rather painfully. To relieve my apparent discomfiture he asked me a great many questions about the library. I talked rapidly about our needs and about my plans and procedures. I could see he was pleased. He ended by indicating some sources for financial help on the horizon. First, he had been told by the Rosenwald Fund (established by Sears, Roebuck to aid Negro education in particular) that they would supplement any library dollars Fisk obtained from other sources, and had indicated that Fisk was high on the list of colleges to receive aid from the million dollars appropriated by the Carnegie Corporation to help colleges build their book collections. In addition, the Rockefeller General Education Board had responded to his request for a new library, to replace the present Carnegie structure, with a $250,000 matching grant, which Carnegie and Rosenwald had already indicated an interest in. I walked out of the President's office and up into the sky. My staff was excited when I told them the news.

As if completely to reverse the doom with which the afternoon had opened, Dr. Radin himself came down to my bedroom in the faculty house. His own bedroom was just above mine, but it had been unoccupied since my arrival. He introduced himself, and then opened, "You apparently have more influence with the President than I have; and I thought I had a lot." He then asked me about myself; told me about his field work in Mexico during the summer, asked to walk over with me to Jubilee for supper. After this show of conciliation I could do no less than tell Dr. Radin the crate of books was still in the library unopened. If he would care to check the shipment I would approve the invoice, provided all future orders followed library procedure. He agreed, adding "It's sure good to have a professional librarian at last. I've been urging the President to hire somebody for a long time."

The confrontation with Paul Radin was only part of an idea for Fisk library book selection. From Columbia instruction and my own meditations about the place of the library in higher learning I had come to a plan. There was too much evidence in the collection Fisk then had of condescension of some white folks somewhere saying "Any books at all will be more than the Negro has had." That was not good enough, and I was determined that the Fisk collection should stack up against the ivoriest of the eastern colleges, which at that time were tops.

Almost from the first day on the job I set about creating a "want" file on three by five order cards. As I had been taught at Columbia, I began checking *Publishers Weekly* "Weekly Record" systematically, marking the margin with the word "biology" or "economics" or "English" as each entry suggested a departmental relationship. Other titles I marked "library" as relating to Reference or technical processes wants, or to my own peculiar interests relating to what should go into the serendipity part of a college student's learning experience.

Then began what I called "operation bookcheck." In personal conference I involved nearly all of the faculty in the idea of checking our library holdings against their instructional and research needs. There was a bit of promise and challenge in my approach. I told them about the President's contact with the three foundations and that we should be ready in case a sudden windfall happened. As the months went by the 3 by 5 drawers in my office filled with hundreds of "want" cards, which I periodically took to the President, and he would occasionally take some funds from elsewhere to satisfy the demands of individual professors and me. Nor did I limit these wants to faculty. A student request box was placed in the reading room next to displays of new book announcements.

Then the first big break. Carnegie Corporation announced one million dollars to strengthen the collections of a select group of colleges and universities. When the list was published President Jones' promise to me was substantiated. Fisk was on the list. To make the expenditures as worth while as possible, CC also announced the development of a basic list of books for a college library under the editorial direction of Charles Shaw of Swarthmore, and the overall chairmanship of Dr. Willian Warner Bishop of the University of Michigan.

With the impatience of my youthful 24 years I thanked President Jones and asked him to request an immediate release of funds for Fisk because of our dire needs caused by the discriminations against Negroes. The President tried, but CC was firm that Fisk would have to wait like all the rest of the colleges until the Shaw List was ready. The President could take that "no," but I couldn't.

At the next ALA I cornered Dr. Bishop, of all places in the convention hall elevator. Perhaps my earnest admiration of this great librarian permeated my pleading words. Dr. Bishop listened to me for several minutes after we got off the elevator, and concluded "I shall be in Nashville next week and will come by to see your library at Fisk."

Dr. Bishop kept his word. After showing him about our dilapidated old Carnegie building I brought him back to my office and went over my want file with him. Obviously impressed, he asked, "Where did you learn to compile a want file on cards like that?" But when it came to money he was firm about waiting for the Shaw list. I must have thanked him very sadly because he patted me on the hand and said, "Louis, don't take it so hard."

Three weeks later the President's secretary, my devoted advocate, phoned: "The President wants you in his office at once." My heart pounded all the way over as I wondered what crisis would follow the one with Radin. As soon as I opened the door President Jones held a letter out to me. I glanced at the heading "Carnegie Corporation" and plunged into the words "Dr. Bishop was so impressed with your librarian's 'want file' that we have voted to make an exception for Fisk and release $10,000 immediately; the remainder of your university's allocation when the Shaw List is published." It was the largest appropriation for books Fisk had ever had.

There were comparable triumphs in each of the four major divisions of library work. The card catalog was overhauled, replacing the half cards with standards, and the hand-written ones with typed or printed entries. More careful attention was paid to the other two records—shelflist and accession book, which I persisted in defending for reasons of library history even when it became professionally fashionable to dispense with an accession book. We reconstructed our circulation system which student assistants were proud to assume responsibility for.

If I was partial to Reference, it was because of my professional love for the information function; my attachment to Reference Books because they had opened the door to a whole new ball game in learning, and because the germ of the Basic Reference idea had begun to infect me. Using my own system of categorizing by types I took them in order—dictionaries, encyclopedias, atlases, etc., and reserved a generous portion of the CC $10,000 for non-departmental library expenditure. And that was not all. When the Shaw List finally appeared, the Carnegie Corporation announced the allocation of the million dollars among the U.S. colleges and universities. Lo and behold, Fisk led all the rest with the largest single grant—$50,000. A very large amount went into reference works—dictionaries, including the expensive O.E.D. which began making its appearance; encyclopedias for which we had only ancient imprints; and special reference sources that ran into the kind of money Fisk had never been able to afford.

From Ernestine Rose's Schomburg collection in the Harlem 135th street branch I got the idea of starting a "Negro collection" for Fisk. Over the years the idea developed into a separate division, with special funds, and an earnest bibliophilic quest for rarities. Eventually, we added Arthur Schomburg, himself, to our library staff.

The triumphs were many at Fisk. I watched the Library take on a professional profile with only less satisfaction than I felt the penetration of the library into the bloodstream of Fisk's higher education. Specifically, there were at least a half dozen experiments and innovations that were certainly not standard operating procedure in academic libraries in 1928.

But the payoff was with the students. I introduced, for the first time, a library use course. Before the first semester was over I had converts to my prolific author "Anon," credited with the words, on so many library facades: "The half of knowledge is knowing where to find it." I had them outbubbling their teacher as they discovered for themselves the reference books they had been passing by, before, without even a friendly nod. Many good and several outstanding students enrolled in my library use class. Among them was Eliza Atkins, who went on to become distinguished librarian Eliza Atkins Gleason.

Outside of class there were many more informal instructional victories. Let me call the student Hall. He was about six feet three, over two hundred pounds, a sophomore at the time. The coach considered him a whiz end on the football team. A rabid fan all of my life, I had been attracted to him at games. Several times I had talked with him at Jubilee Hall meals. His means were even more meager than those of most Fisk students. I asked him how he would like to work in the library for pay. He responded, "I need the money professor, but . . ."

"But what?" I asked.

"But, I've never read a book through in my life."

"So what?" I tried to reassure him. "I need you for some heavy work—like unpacking crates of books, carpenter jobs, things I never could do with my hands."

He took the job. In between work assignments we talked—mostly football, a subject for which I have always been a pushover. One day he unpacked the 15-volume *Pageant of America* which Yale University Press published that year. Volume 15 is the "Annals of Sports." I saw my chance. Partly it was contrived, but partly true.

"Hall," I said several days later, "I need your help. It's a little different job. You see this volume 15? I've got to review it for the phys ed department—your coaches and the others. What I don't know about football would fill a whole library. I've never played it like you. Could you give me a few pointers on how I should review this book tomorrow so I won't make a fool out of myself." Hall offered to take the book home.

Next day he greeted me, "Prof, you tricked me."

"How so?"

"You remember how proud I was that I could go through two years of college and four years of high school without ever having read a book through. You spoiled my record. I couldn't put it down and read the book from beginning to end."

When he asked me for something else in sports, I gave him Burnett's *Iron Man*, about a boxer. Then followed my most triumphant ladder list. It led up to a history major, a master's degree, and an eventual college instructorship. Hall was only one of perhaps a hundred students I worked with individually during my five years at Fisk.

Library contacts with students lured me into several extracurriculars. Football was easy. The head coach, Tubby Johnson, himself a Fisk alumnus, and a fabulous running back in his own undergraduate days, appreciated having an "academic" faculty member take an interest in football, at a time when some Ivory League graduates were denouncing intercollegiates as if they were variations on the disease leprosy. I went to practices when I could, and never missed a Saturday home game.

The Friday nights before a game thrilled me. In Jubilee Dining Hall, where Miss Jefferson enforced dignity and culture at the tables, restraint was lightened. Each table had seven students and one faculty member. The subject of the table I hosted was probably too often, for some of my Ivory League colleagues, football. On Friday night it was all out, especially as the team walked in together to their training table. I recall the musical yells, quite distinctive from the usual college variety. *Hold that line, oh hold that line* was chanted to a tune with Beethovenesque dimensions. Few marches exhorted more inspiringly than the stirring intonation of *Keep Fighting FU*.

To come back from my football weakness, a number of players

became my reading disciples, as I worked my "ladder" techniques, starting always with their keenest interest, whether it was bookish or not. I began to enjoy reading guidance above all. Discussions with students stimulated ideas for several innovations.

First, it occurred to me that there was need for some informal dialogue between faculty and students, somewhat less formal than that imposed by the restraints of classroom. The idea for the *Wranglers* was born—a men's group necessarily, because I proposed to hold the Wednesday night sessions in the faculty bachelor men's house. It broke a precedent, because the line between faculty and students in those days was as marked as that between officers and enlisted men in the army.

The Wednesday nights were memorable. Modeled after the Briar and Java group of my own University of Toledo undergraduate days, the men smoked, drank coffee, and wrangled over issues of all kinds, nearly always within a Black-White climate of segregations. We invited men from town, liberal whites who would be willing to dialogue as with peers—ministers from some of the liberal churches, a federal judge, an atheist, an authority on fallicism, a "queer" philosopher who was segregated in town even though his skin was "white." One time a YMCA secretary came. He wanted to say the right thing, but it came out with "segregation overtones" and the men took him apart and reduced him to sobbing tears. After, every one was so sorry for him that we went overboard to apologize. Discussing it later that night with St. Elmo Brady we understood how prejudices against race and religion were brainwashed into children by their parents, neighbors and climate.

We could not have the co-eds in a bachelor home in those days when co-visitation in dormitories would have been considered unspeakable. Instead I organized a co-educational group interested in reading and writing poetry. We called ourselves *Penchanters* and we published a little magazine titled *Pen-Chant*. I enjoyed student activities most of all and I believe both barriers—between faculty and student and Black and white almost disappeared in these common enterprises.

Perhaps the most dramatic of all my student involvements began when I became coach of the Fisk intercollegiate debate team. If the university had engaged in such forensic competition before, I could find no records to assist me. Modeling on the Toledo coaches' plan I held tryouts, and staged intramurals in the chapel before considerable audiences of students, faculty, and townspeople. The men proved better than the women and this was fortunate from the standpoint of travel when we began our intercollegiate efforts.

Two of the men were particularly outstanding and made their mark in the academic world. One was John Hope Franklin, now a history professor and a distinguished scholar who wrote the major article on the *Negro* in *Collier's Encyclopedia* for me, many years after. The other was Lawrence Dunbar Reddick, later curator of the Schomburg collection. Both were excellent speakers, fortified with solid reading background in history and the social sciences.

We were successful from our first intercollegiate debate. After successive victories against about a half dozen Negro colleges, both at home and away, the team encouraged my desire to see how we compared with some of the white debating teams. We realized it would be impossible to meet any of the Southern white institutions and so I proceeded to correspond with some of the northern universities against whom my Toledo team had debated in my own undergraduate days.

Two northern schools accepted—New York University and Northwestern in Evanston, Illinois. After campus conferences we decided to make two trips, one to the east and one to the midwest at different times during that spring. Our first trip to New York University included debates with Virginia Union and with Howard University in Washington. We were successful in both of these. As exciting as the debates themselves was the trip. I had purchased a new Chevrolet, the first automobile I had ever owned, in the days when owning an automobile was something. I drove my team proudly from Nashville to East Tennessee and over the Great Smoky Mountains.

Upon our return we began preparation for our midwest trip to Evanston. A new subject for us was proposed by Northwestern. The Volstead Act was still law but there was foment nationally to repeal so that freedom to drink might return to those American people who enjoyed alcoholic beverages. Bootleg and speakeasies had developed into a national scandal with many fatal poisonings from wood alcohol. What Northwestern proposed was that we debate the repeal of the Volstead Act. On the surface it looked like they were offering us the popular side of repeal. Sentiment in the United States however was turning against prohibition. We, therefore, prepared our case with confidence. But the Coach failed to recall, if he ever knew, that Evanston was the headquarters of the Women's Christian Temperance Union, a particularly militant prohibition force.

A packed audience greeted us, and as the teams walked on the stage rounds of applause followed introductions of the participants, the coaches, and the judges. Northwestern opened with its defense of Prohibition, their first speaker receiving warm but lady-like approval from a front row of women: obviously leaders in the WCTU. I watched them with deep concern. I knew only too well the eloquence of my lead-off man—Lawrence Dunbar Reddick—a brilliant mind with a flair for oratory and witty repartee. Above all I feared his repetitive line timed with telling devastation. After describing the horrors of blindness caused by wood alcohol, for example, Reddick would insist that if we repealed the Volstead act, "At least we would have good liquah."

The decision was inevitable: unanimous for the affirmative. Evanston's climate then would not permit the repeal of the Volstead Act. It was a sobering experience for us as a team, perhaps a bit overconfident from success.

Losing a debate was the kind of failure I could live with. But—aside from the omnipresence of segregation—my years at Fisk were wonderful, and my library work a success which never tempted me to relax. Perhaps my Operation Bookcheck would be taken for granted now. But how can I tell you the thrill of having faculty members coming in to push me for wants in their sections of Dewey, to bubble over some new book or journal, to argue with me about an economic issue, the philosophical validity of the scientific method as an approach to value, romanticism versus realism in the quest for an answer to what is art. I glowed because the Fisk Library was becoming the center for learning not only about sources, but about the subjects themselves. Faculty members were pushing each other and me and being pushed, intellectually and spiritually, in the Fisk library climate.

Louis Shores

4. In Love

On November 19, 1931, in Chicago, I married Geraldine Urist, a school teacher. As I write this we are approaching our 43rd anniversary. Gerry is and has been the meaning of my life, for two thirds of it. I am more in love with her than ever.

But she has not been the only woman in my life. I fell in love, first, with my mother. At least as far back as when I was three I told my mother I wanted to marry her. I was afraid of my father who frequently forgot to spare the rod and in between frightened me so by just a word or a look that I sought shelter in my mother's arms.

My next love was my sister. She was sixteen and I only six when I fell in love with her. I hoped some day to be able to marry her. She had taken me to the public library branch, helped me obtain my first borrower's card, and brought home books to read to me. When I could read to myself I loved to do so when Frances was practicing those Chopin nocturnes and waltzes she played so sensitively. When she combed her long, beautiful auburn hair, in my presence, I recall, I had a strange stirring that helped me love Frances more tenderly than ever.

There were several little girls in school, I remember, who made me fall in love with them. This is supposed to be a professional autobiography and not a transcript of confessions on a psychiatrist's couch. Nevertheless, in a profession so dominantly feminine there is some point to a male's report on the women in his life. Perhaps three little girls he recalls most readily, and the teacher and librarian of his boyhood, will account for what one critic of this manuscript called the author's "Victorianism."

I confess to an old fashioned reverence for women. My mother and sister first influenced by romanticisms which were reenforced by fairy tale readings in which the beautiful princess was rescued from an enchantment, a wicked stepmother and jealous stepsisters, or an ogre, by a Prince Charming whom I always tried to imagine myself in my walk-dreams.

The first of the little girls I loved had golden curls and sat on a little chair opposite me in kindergarten. One day she accidentally exposed herself and that compelled me to ask my mother why little girls were different from little boys. Ours was a strict home in which I cannot recall sex was ever mentioned. After my father died there was no one at home to turn to on the subject.

Several reasons impel a librarian to devote some space to sex in an autobiography. In the first place librarianship is one of the few occupations in which a male finds himself in the minority. It is imperative that he consider how to get along with the majority. In the second place, there has been the inference that male librarians tend to be effeminate. In *The Public Library Inquiry*, for example, psychologist Dr. Alice Bryan reported in her volume on *The Public Librarian* that in the personality test known as the Guilford-Martin Inventory of Factors Gamin "The median score of the women librarians is a step closer to the feminine end of the scale than is that of their male colleagues to the masculine end." (1952, p. 41-42)

In the third place, the two subjects that have caused our Committee on Intellectual Freedom most problems in the "Freedom to Read" vigilance have been Marx and the four-letter words relating to sex. Whether the librarian can pass on obscenity in literature, or not, may be decided by his own moral upbringing. Perhaps this librarian has suffered from what the contemporary liberated would describe as "the Puritan Ethic."

If so, this Victorianism can be accounted for only by some sex autobiography. It is now generally agreed that children are aware of sex far earlier than grown folks around them admit. As I think back I am certain I had sex feelings as an infant when my mother rescued me, dripping, from my father's punishment. I was stirred sexually when the little kindergarten girl accidentally exposed her difference to me for the first time.

I was sexually stirred during a spelling bee in the fifth grade when a very pretty girl and I were the last to remain standing. I suffered over Mary Lou's tension as she awaited her turn. I recall how her pretty little legs twisted and moved nervously under her attractive jumper skirt. When the teacher gave the difficult word Mary Lou stood there for a few moments petrified. Then there was an explosion inside her and a cascade of water between her legs.

As the teacher led her from the room, dripping, and to a chorus of titters and cruel remarks from some of the other children I had a strange double feeling. Compassion was dominant. I wished I had missed a word so that Mary Lou could win. And there was a strange stirring that I now know was sex.

Of the other women in my life before I met Gerry, that first children's librarian in the Cleveland Public Library who introduced me to books; that high school economics teacher for whom I had an adolescent's crush; and a few other women whom I worshipped, story book fashion, were only dreams. I did not date during high school; never danced because of ineptness and reluctance; and suffered from shyness in the presence of girls. I was frightened by the information boys conveyed in four-letter words, yet intrigued and extremely curious.

My first serious love affair occurred in college. The co-ed who worked in the library at my side was the most beautiful girl I had known to that time. I felt at ease in her company and we talked about everything—books, music, recipes, football, and even girls and boys. One day we ventured to discuss sex. I believed I loved her and would one day like to get up the courage to ask her to marry me. But that day never came. She probably only liked me.

I met several young women thereafter, but only one other before I met my wife entered into my marriage considerations. She was on the Fisk faculty. I was deeply in love with her. But Tennessee law prohibited miscegenation in 1930, and although I was determined to defy the law, her greater maturity prevented a potential tragedy.

Shortly thereafter I began graduate study at the University of Chicago Graduate Library School. Through Martin Ross and his wife I met her niece Gerry.

They had tried to bring us together the summer of 1928 when I was in Chicago en route to my Fisk job. The best they had been able to accomplish was a telephone conversation, because she had a date with a handsome Texan, of whom I became properly jealous. It was not until the following summer that I met Gerry. I felt something at first glance. But it was not until several months later that I began to realize the inevitable. Nashville was 500 miles south. I could manage to drive up to Chicago only once a month. A quarter's leave from Fisk, however, for graduate work hastened the day.

In the summer of 1931 I was a visiting professor at the University of Dayton, only 200 miles from Gerry's Michigan farm. I managed to spend nearly every weekend with her. In my Pontiac coupe we toured the lovely lakeside country, talking books, our jobs, comparative outlooks of a country girl reared on a farm and a city boy who had never seen a cow milked until he watched Gerry do it, and conclude by feeding her little kitten by directing the stream.

Gerry's parents had a fruit farm on which apples were the main crop. She had three brothers, two of whom were in medical school, the third in college at Ann Arbor which they had all attended. All summer I had weekend instructions in agriculture in between driving about the countryside, sampling Michigan small town restaurants and getting to know each

Quiet World / Life

other. By midsummer we were holding hands and I had gathered enough courage to kiss her. I began wondering whether I would have the courage to ask her, and how I would feel if she said "no."

Late in August we drove back to the farm about midnight after a very full evening of dinner, movie, countryside drive in the dark, and talk that seemed to melt all time. We were parked behind the farmhouse's back screen porch. I asked her with my heart in my mouth. She did not keep me in suspense. It was a direct affirmative. We kissed and began planning immediately.

Next day we told her family. I wrote my mother. She came to meet Gerry's family. When I returned to Toledo my mother introduced me to a jeweler in Toledo she knew. With her help I selected an engagement ring and a wedding band. I couldn't wait to drive the 200 miles to the farm to show it to Gerry.

That fall I commuted the 500 miles between Nashville and Chicago nearly every weekend. Gerry was teaching school in Chicago with only warrants for salary. It was the depression. Chicago did not pay its teachers for 15 months. Some places accepted the warrants at face value; most stores discounted them up to 25%. My own Fisk salary was only $200 a month. Fifty of that went to my widowed mother; another twenty-five to pay back tuition debts due Columbia. One weekend in Chicago Gerry said she did not have bus fare for Monday morning to go to her school job. I handed her ten dollars. She refused at first and then insisted she would take it only as a loan and on interest.

Indignantly I exploded "Is that the way to insult your husband?" She finally dubiously consented with a promise to pay me.

When we married on November 19 in Chicago Martin Ross and Gerry's aunt were witnesses and had a small party for us. Gerry and I spent the evening at a Chicago Symphony orchestra concert. The Mozart Kochel #40 is a sentimental part of our disc collection. Our wedding night was spent in a northside hotel. The following day together was all we could afford before I drove back to Fisk.

During our courtship that fall I had brought Gerry to Fisk for one weekend. President and Mrs. Jones had put her up in the President's home. One night our date extended way past the President's bed time. The house was dark and Gerry was locked out. We rang the bell, determined that our relations would continue perfectly proper.

After our marriage, Gerry continued teaching in Chicago till the close of the year. We arranged to meet every other week-end at a half way point—Evansville, Vincennes, or Terre Haute. Twice I saved enough money to bring her to Nashville. Then the faculty men did an extraordinary thing never before done—a woman was permitted to sleep there with her husband. Gerry was very popular with them. She entered into their bantering with rare good humor.

One of the Nashville trips was paid for by Berea College. I was employed as a consultant and using my travel expense and fee I drove up to Chicago first, picked up Gerry and brought her to Berea with me. Robert Maynard Hutchins' father was Berea president then and he offered us the guest bedroom.

Trying to play the married couple maturely we came down to breakfast very dignifiedly. We had just given each other a complimentary look on how well we played the long-married couple when President Hutchins with a twinkle in his eye said very kindly, "I should guess you two have been married about a month."

Forty-three years married and at least a year and a half before that for courtship must add up to the most important part of two people. Writing as one of them I can say Gerry has come closest to answering my haunting question "Who Am I?" She has done that by stirring a love so deep that at times I seemed to hover over the solution to the riddle of the universe.

This is only my appraisal. I will show it to her shortly as I have all of my writing and work these many years. I am certain I have failed her at many points. Probably the Lib ladies would disown me as a chauvinist.

My romanticism insisted that she give up her well-paying Chicago teacher job. I wanted to be the sole wage earner, even though at that time it meant cutting our income in half, and both of us still had heavy commitments to our families and education debts. Except for two brief periods during the war when she resumed school teaching briefly, in Miami and in Washington, she gave in to my male "chauvinism."

But from the start she took over our finances. I warned her about my dislike of money matters, and my total incompetence when it came to personal finance. The proof was in my bank account which hovered around the overdrawn mark every first of the month. To my amazement we began showing a balance from the first month she took over. We had agreed on joint accounts for everything—checking, charge accounts, property. It has worked perfectly, and as I have joked, she has paid me my allowance regularly. I am convinced I also married a treasurer extraordinary. Her household books are models. She can tell me how much we spent on almost any day of our 43 years.

Any doubt that homemaking is at once the most scientific and humanistic profession of them all can be dispelled by visiting our home now or at any time before. She manages our home in a way to make an efficiency expert for industry drool. Once she employed an interior decorator from a bonus I had earned for editing, and with help from Gerry, the interior decorator redid our master bedroom so as to reflect the ethereal sense my wife seems to have about truth and beauty around a house. So much for shelter.

When it comes to clothes I have never seen a dress modeled more charmingly or seductively than when Gerry comes home from a shopping pilgrimage and gives her husband a fashion show. It has been a marriage tradition—these modelings. Early, however, she agreed to my one stipulation—that I be permitted to select ten percent of her wardrobe—and from my clothing allowance. (I hate to shop, and especially clothes for myself.) Occasionally when I go shopping with her I see something I want her to try on. On such occasions it fits perfectly and she falls in love with it. I have certain biases—I prefer vertical to horizontal accents in her hats; love to see her in suits; had to overcome her early resistance to pants. I kept after her. One day she came back from her afternoon of bridge and announced "I was the only girl without pants." She had to put up with her husband's usual poor jokes: "Gerry, every respectable girl when she goes out should always wear pants." I persisted and she now loves and wears pants on shopping trips, at bridge, to football games.

Food, even more than clothing and shelter, is Gerry's devotion. Together we have gathered a library of some 500 cookbooks on every continent during our travels. Her creative ideas are restrained by her husband's idiosyncrasies. Given a choice of soup or steak he will choose soup every time. She prepares both delectably. Neither of us can bear to look at meat that drips blood; so we shock connoisseurs by "medium to well," except that she tells her girl friends "My husband likes his steak cremated." I have been writing up her appetizing menus for a cook book I hope we will some day publish together.

We read out loud to each other at least once a day. Each of us in turn discovers passages we wax enthusiastic about. We argue heatedly about our differences on education, literature, music, politics, national and international affairs, philosophy, and almost everything. She is very critical about my writing, forcing me to defend my position, sometimes to excruciating lengths. Time passes excitingly. Like the time on the drive all night to my extension teaching in South Florida when she challenged the essence of my Library-College idea—independent study. Three hundred miles raced by as each of us documented our positions, sometimes furiously.

We have travelled together completely around the world. Each time I have seen things through her eyes that no photo or even master painting could possibly reveal. Everywhere her light observations evoke hilarious laughter. The more dignified some academicians attempt to be, the less they are once her contagious laughter permeates some of those pontifical essays to impress.

This chapter title is "In Love." Our library has a considerable number of books. I began collecting during adolescence to document the four-letter-word reports of conquests I heard, starting with adolescent boys, and later supplemented by college men, army troops, middle-aged lusties who bragged about their cave-man approaches. There are anatomy volumes by physicians. One of the first was by a woman physician—Dr. Marie Stopes—on *Married Love*. Martin Ross introduced me to what he called the classic—August Forel; and then to Havelock Ellis.

But as activist "liberation" spread, our library was augmented first with statistical surveys that featured declining virginity among college co-eds, and variations on sexual intercourse. Erotica classics like Boccaccio, and two of Chaucer's "Tales," which offered no language obstacles even to the dullest middle English undergraduate, became tame as modern "mature" audience movies, plays, and novels swept a "liberated" national mind of former inhibitions.

Former taboos on orgies, swinger swapping, deviations, homosexuality, incest were contemptuously repealed. The pill, apparently, liberated women, although it did nothing for the mounting VD menace. We read and talked about this new literature. Despite our Victorian upbringing, we did not find it all bad. Perhaps something good was accomplished by such a best seller as *The Sensuous Woman*, written by a woman; and by *Everything you Want to Know About Sex* written by a physician and his wife. Both contributed to dispelling the undocumented superstitions about a heretofore unmentionable—masturbation.

Perhaps there was a mean between Victorianism and "anything goes." We agreed in our talks about sex. The Puritan Ethic was not all bad. Existence appears to be a struggle between order and chaos. Part of this struggle seems to be the disciplining of appetites, of physical desires by the soul's innate longing for perfection. Nor was the liberalizing of sex all bad. Part of the struggle of existence seemed to be an opportunity to experience the appetites and desires so that the soul might contend with them and so develop. Sex, we agreed, was one of the most challenging and we accepted that challenge.

I write for one half of the family: these forty-three years together have given the most meaning to existence. The failures in our marriage have been mostly attributable to me. I delayed having children, for example, until too late because of a doctoral dissertation and war. The successes have been due entirely to the extraordinary girl who said "Yes" one midnight behind her farm home.

II Odysseys

Introduction: *Comparative Librarianship*

At Peabody, in 1933, where I joined the faculty as Library School Director and College Librarian I first heard the Goethe quotation, "To know thyself, compare." One of my new colleagues was the great Russian scholar Michael Demiashkevich. In his course on Comparative Education he quoted again and again Goethe's provocative words.

I had three courses with Demi, as he insisted we call him out of consideration for American difficulty with pronouncing Russian names. Toward the doctoral residence requirement I took Demi's remarkable Philosophy of Education course which dared to dissent with the great John Dewey. Subsequently Demi published his *Introduction to the Philosophy of Education* which contained a 150-page critique of Dewey, Pragmatism and the "Activity" school.

It was a daring thing to do in the 1930s when almost every book in education was either dedicated to or filled with acknowledgements to Dewey. Hardly had the book appeared than a Dewey disciple reviewed it devastatingly under the title "The Greeks had a word for it," in *Progressive Education*. Demi responded with an essay "Traditionalists Before a Progressive Tribunal." I was drawn into the struggle between traditionalists and progressives not only because of my friendship for Demi but because of what I feared Progressive Education was doing to books and reading. From the first we were attracted to each other. He was a lonely man in his forties then. He had been forced to flee from Russia because he became disaffected with the Bolshevik Revolution and became a White Russian. He was compelled to abandon his family, his fiancée; live in Paris for a while; then London; and finally emigrate to the United States.

In the fateful summer of 1938, Demi was a visiting professor in Berkeley. The previous two summers he had lectured at Harvard. Increasing concern about his family in Russia and overwork on his book had resulted in a mysterious illness hospitalization failed to diagnose. Despondently Demi began his Berkeley visiting lectureship, had an attack in one of his classes, and was forced to abandon his teaching. In an effort to regain his health he retired to his Maine cabin on Penobscott Bay.

Gerry and I could not wait for our Peabody summer session to end.

On August commencement day, we were packed and started the four days drive. We arrived at supper time and were shocked by Demi's appearance. From a normal 180 pounds he was down to 130, sallow and cadaverous looking. Gerry was determined to shop and begin feeding him back to health with all of the delicacies he liked and which he had taught her to cook. On the drive to Maine we had reminisced about the many evenings together in our home. He would come by my office at the end of the day and ask, "Let's take a walk?" We'd walk and talk for an hour about international relations and Hitler; about Peabody; and about Comparative Education, whetting my appetite to travel, and to initiate a counterpart study of Comparative Librarianship.

After the walk we shopped at Zager's delicatessen and brought home the makings for a proper bowl of borscht, as Demi taught it. Once Gerry made the borscht, trying to follow Demi's directions. He complimented her, but with one reservation, "It lacks that certain nuance."

We recollected in tears. As we returned with groceries to Demi's Maine cottage that Saturday morning after our long drive from Nashville, the cottage seemed strangely quiet. Gerry went in first, opened Demi's bedroom door slightly, called to him and then to me with panic in her voice.

I went in to his bedroom. The revolver was resting on his chest. The bullet hole was in his right temple. The shock numbed us, not only that day during the sheriff's inquest, but the entire distance; Demi's impact on me was deep. It started my Comparative Librarianship.

Demi, more than any one, spurred my incentive for comparatives. To this point, my comparisons had been restricted to domestic issues—ethnic and national origins, variations in faith, ranges of economic and social opportunities. Demi opened world comparatives, and whetted my longing to travel, compare with other nations, and work toward world understanding and peace.

Before Peabody, my Great Lakes boundaries were extended modestly at first, to the Eastern seaboard and then into the South. I had never been outside the United States except for one day when I went through the tunnel from Detroit to Windsor, Ontario in Canada. Everywhere I went I made comparisons—of similarities and differences. Over and over I sought for conciliations, for all of the attributes that made us part of the one human race.

As war clouds darkened with each Hitler aggression, beginning in the Sudetenland, and continuing with Austria *anschluss* to the inexcusable violation of Czechoslovakia, I became convinced that libraries, of all man's institutions, had the greatest potential for promoting comparatives, that out of these comparatives people would get to know themselves better and understand others.

My Comparative Librarianship crusade, born in Demi's Peabody Comparative Education course, was nurtured by four major odysseys and several minor ones. My first opportunity to go abroad was offered by Uncle Sam. In 1942 I enlisted in the U.S. Army Air Force to restrain Hitler from his savageries. I was assigned instead to the China-Burma-India theatre to fight Hitler's Japanese ally. In the course of four years I lived not only in India for two years, but went around the world going to and from my theatre of war. I was able to pursue my comparatives in between my military duties, not only in India and what is now Pakistan, but in Africa, Latin America and some island outposts.

My second opportunity came in 1951/52 through a Fulbright exchange in the United Kingdom to study British Reference. During that year two full months on the continent provided comparative opportunities in France, Switzerland, Germany, Austria, The Netherlands, Belgium, Spain, and especially in Italy. After a Christmas holiday in Rome, a challenge developed for the spring when Italy's Fulbright officials arranged with Britain to borrow me for a three weeks series of seminars on American library methods to be held in Rome, Florence and Naples.

The third major odyssey occurred in the summer of 1961. At the end of a year and a half leave to direct a major revision of *Collier's Encyclopedia*, as its editor in chief, I was asked to study comparatively British encyclopedia production and distribution. Again continental comparatives were added in France, Germany, Italy, Netherlands, and Belgium. It was a summer highlighted by our sharing a floor in a London apartment building with Aldous Huxley, novelist extraordinary, and seeing much of publisher Boni, and renewing associations with British librarians in Chaucer House, the Midlands and elsewhere.

The fourth great odyssey was the most dramatic of all. In a 76-day, 43,000 mile flight around the world for *Collier's Encyclopedia*, to augment our international coverage and perspective I met and spoke with librarians and scholars in other disciplines in nine nations, extensively, and in some others in between on four of the world's five continents.

The crusade for world understanding was dramatized by the decision to deposit all of the original manuscripts of the articles in the encyclopedia relating to the nine countries, magnificently bound, in the respective archives. Two major confrontations, in South Africa over *apartheid*, and in Australia over censorship, tested the library approach to world understanding.

The story of these four major odysseys follows.

5. Armed Forces

Had a 1940 oracle predicted I would enlist in the U.S. Army rather than wait to be drafted, my growing interest in precognition would have been blunted. Although my rage over what Hitler was doing made me an active interventionist, I had no confidence in my soldiering. Except for a beebee gun I had fired a few times, I was woefully inept with firearms. I had never hunted; disliked violence except in movies—westerns and who-dun-its—in the days when the hero always won. Yet before the next year was half over I was in.

On December 6, 1941, we dedicated the new Joint University Library building. With funds from the three foundations—Carnegie, Rockefeller, Rosenwald—a milestone in cooperation between the two institutions of higher education located on opposite sides of the street—Vanderbilt University and George Peabody College for Teachers—was accomplished.

That Saturday night's public convocation closing a week of educational conference scheduled concurrently with the formal dedication of the new Joint University Library building featured three distinguished speakers: Robert Lester, executive secretary of the Carnegie Corporation; Dr. Louis Round Wilson, distinguished director and dean of the University of North Carolina libraries and School of Library Science; Dr. Charles Harvey Brown, director of libraries, Iowa State University, Ames, pioneer apostle of the scientific method for predominantly humanistic librarianship.

All three of them were guests in our Nashville home that night following the dedication ceremonies. All three of them were scheduled to depart on 3:00 AM flights, and so from the 11:00 PM close of the dedication ceremonies until takeoff Gerry and I entertained the three distinguished visitors with a midnight buffet. The conversation that surrounded the refreshments was both socially light and professionally deep, but strangely as I recalled afterward, neglectful of the war.

All three—Brown, Wilson and Lester—were in rare form that night. The conversation sparkled with professional news and philosophy; with social amenities; with hilarious wit and repartee; as a kind of celebration at the conclusion of a week's dedication ceremonies. My wife and Dr. Wilson who began that night their many years of teasing each other had a misunderstanding. As the three visitors and their wives moved into the dining room, my wife called out to me "Louis, bring another chair in." Dr. Wilson, a much older married man than I, responded more promptly, "Yes ma'am." and brought the chair in. Later my wife kidded Dr. Wilson about his new Chicago "sinecure—six months on, six months off," because the University in order to attract Dr. Wilson for the GLS deanship agreed to let him divide the year between Chicago and North Carolina.

Shortly after 2:00 AM, we all repaired to the Nashville airport for the plane departure. It was three before we returned home, and four before we had washed the dishes and put the house in order. Then we turned in.

Very tired, we were both aroused out of a deep sleep by the loud and persistent ringing of our telephone. I dashed downstairs in my pajamas, picked up the phone, and heard Otis McBride's anguished voice, "Quick, Louis, turn on your radio." Because of a certain unnatural urgency in his agitation. I turned the knob: PEARL HARBOR BOMBED. WE REPEAT PEARL HARBOR BOMBED. THE UNITED STATES HAS BEEN ATTACKED BY JAPAN. PEARL HARBOR BOMBED.

I had been a fierce interventionist ever since Britain had entered World War II. Even before, Hitler's savageries against the Jews, and then the violations of the Sudeten, Austria, Czechoslovakia, and Poland, had stirred me to oppose the isolationism that permitted Nazis aggrandizement. In 1940, for example, I was chairing a weekly "Nights at the Round Table," on Nashville's powerful WSM radio station. Perhaps the chairman did expose his conviction in a series of forums on the war. It brought an angry telegram to the President of Peabody from a professor at Vanderbilt, strongly isolationist, demanding my resignation.

On the Monday morning after Pearl Harbor, Otis McBride and I joined the line in front of the post office of men waiting to enlist in the U.S. Army. Otis felt the way I did. He was 37 at the time; I was one year older. He had already become my closest friend. We had met at Peabody, where

I was head of the Library School and he director of alumni affairs and placement. I had been attracted to him from the first meeting because of his positive optimism, his rare sense of humor, and his manual talents. I have never known any one who could do more with tools.

When we finally reached the sergeant and he looked at the blanks we had filled out. "Sorry, we're not taking old men yet." Both of us were 3-A in the draft. But as the upper age limit was 38 neither of us was in immediate danger of being selected. Otis had a better chance, not only because he was one year younger, but because he was then unmarried.

In the early spring he was drafted. His assignment was in the Signal Corps and he went for his basic to Camp Crowder in Missouri. There, Gerry and I visited him several times. Each time I was more anxious than ever to join him, to the great concern of my wife.

She knew as well as I my ineptness with firearms. When several army library jobs were offered me, she encouraged me to take leave at Peabody and accept. But I stubbornly persisted in my intention to fight Hitler. My chance came through something the army instituted in the spring of 1942 labelled "VOC" (Volunteer Officer Candidate). The draft was not providing enough men. Our fortunes in the war were low. The Philippines had been taken as well as all of the Pacific islands strategically pointing to a possible conquest of Australia. Britain with its back against the wall, not only at home but abroad in India, Burma, Singapore, Africa; and France all but eliminated left the United States on the brink of disaster.

That was when the telegram arrived from the War Department ordering me to active duty. I was permitted to finish summer school teaching at Peabody. Then in mid-August I reported to Fort Oglethorpe in Georgia for induction and was given 10 days to settle affairs at home. We had already sold our home. I watched Gerry, with tears in my heart, dismantle our Nashville home, the first we had been able to buy and not rent. How cruel husbands can be. My stubborn insistence on fighting Hitler was destroying our home. I knew, as well as she, because of my age I would probably never be drafted, and I could better help win the war by teaching and keeping our home together.

The Army shipped our belongings to the Michigan farm house we had bought. There our good friends Ed and Minnie Wight went with us for a final reunion. Ed would take charge of the Library School in my absence. I had induced Frances Neel Cheney to give up her Reference librarianship in the Joint University Library to join the Peabody Library

Quiet World / Odysseys

School faculty and take over the editing of "Current Reference Books."

The 40-acre farm we had purchased and named Gerry-Lou had an old farmhouse, a small apple orchard, and a few pear and peach trees. Its post office was Fennville, and its location was near beautiful Lake Hutchins. There we spent our summer vacations and could visit with Gerry's people on the farm nearby where she had been reared. To that farm came my sister and brother-in-law for a final reunion as he prepared to enter the navy. Sitting in my favorite apple tree, Steve and I speculated about the future—our possible war assignments. He went with the fleet into the Pacific.

My assignment began with a brief 10-day basic as an enlisted man, which was interrupted by a telegram ordering me to officer training in Miami Beach. In August of 1942 when I arrived there, some 70,000 men were undergoing the most rigorous of all drills for war. In that class, which included Clark Gable, the movie actor, among some other celebrities, were many business, professional, and government leaders who, like myself, had waived their draft status to enlist.

We were stationed in various Miami Beach hotels taken over by the Army. Our day began at 0445, which was army for before dawn at a quarter to five AM. By 0600 we were marching, up and down Collins avenue, learning infantry drill regulations: falling in and falling out; squads right and squads left; to the rear march; by the numbers, etc. As the sun came out, perspiration blackened our khaki. Fat bulks melted away under the footpounding of the pavement, hour after hour. Colonel Siegfried, the tough wing commander, swore he would make us so tough Hitler would be sorry he ever let Uncle Sam get into it. One part of being tough was to stand at perfect attention for an hour and a half. Officers walked up and down the lines giving demerits for even twitching an eyelash. And enough demerits could mean washing out, and back to the ranks.

Standing at attention was easy for me. I returned to "once upon a time" and wove the most fantastic fairy tales about my own utopia. Or I would sketch an article or a story I promised myself I would write when this war was over. Frequently my reveries were interrupted by a thud, followed by a stretcher carrying a soldier out who had fainted. "One beer too many," Dougherty, on my left, whispered.

He became my life saver. A retread from World War I, he was the most disliked soldier in my flight. Forever he was comparing the soldiers of World War II unfavorably with the troops of World War I. His favorite start was, "Call this an army. Now in World War I. . . ." Some men declared openly they hated Dougherty's guts. But Dougherty patiently taught me soldiering, because I was the only one who listened to him.

Frighteningly grim for me was the beginning of firearms instruction. We began with the .45, which I could at least lift. The first day at target practice the sergeant separated us into three groups; experts; some experience; no experience. Quickly I joined the third group. Following instructions on grip and aim, miraculously I scored three bullseyes. Came an angry cry close to my ear, "Who the hell ya think y'r kiddin'; get the hell over there with the experts." I soon disillusioned him.

The old Springfield rifles were a different matter. They were heavy for a five foot, seven, 130-lb, small-boned college professor—a tyro with firearms. Target practice was scheduled for Baker's Holover, north of Miami Beach. Dougherty advised, "Leave those professor's rimless glasses in your barracks. The kick on this old Springfield will shatter them. Wait till your steel-rim GI glasses arrive. In addition, put a Kotex on your shoulder so it won't feel sore for a week after target practice."

When we arrived at Baker's Holover, many of the men who openly disliked Dougherty's bragging hoped he would do badly in target practice. Their hope was realized in an unexpected way. My target was 26, next to Dougherty's which was 25. We took five shots on the first round. When the sergeant went forward to score my target he and I both looked at it in amazement. No bullseyes, not a bullet in any of the rings. The target was clean, completely missed by my aim. The contemptuous look on the sergeant's face said clearly, "With soldiers like that Hitler has nothing to worry about."

Then the sergeant stepped over to score Dougherty's target. Out of five shots, Dougherty had *SEVEN BULLSEYES!* It was obvious to me that without my glasses my near-sightedness had led me to mistake 25 for 26. Poor Dougherty. He never heard the last of it. The men mimicked: "call this an army. Why in World War I we made seven bullseyes with every five shots."

My Reference librarianship helped in the officer mess course. The instructor asked each of us to prepare menus for a week. I went to the public library, consulted some of the basic cookbooks I had taught my Reference classes, and put together a week's menus that gave me the top grade.

Next day there was a blue slip in my P.O. box ordering me to report to the CO. Knees quaking, heart pounding, I recalled that such slips us-

Quiet World / Odysseys

ually meant wash out of officer training, I held my salute until recognized, and repeated as I had been taught: "Sir, Cadet Officer Shores, 0-916719, reports as ordered."

"At ease," he responded with his releasing salute. "The instructor tells me your work has been so outstanding in the mess course that I shall order you to duty, upon graduation, as a mess officer." I was not overjoyed. But this promise was countermanded by the Pentagon. It appeared I had been preempted as a cryptographic officer.

Graduation came in September's last week. Our faculty adviser had pleaded with us not to celebrate, even though he sympathized with the tension we had been under. One young Nashville attorney who, like me, did not drink, unlike me was encouraged by some heavy drinkers. The result: he was placed under a shower in the morning, dressed by his fellow cadets, and propped up in the graduation line. We had made it—we were lieutenants in the U.S. Army Air Force.

Daub was the code name that hid our overseas destination. The importance of secrecy in those early war days was driven home again and again as U-boats took tolls at sea. My assignment in cryptography underlined the significance of security. It was even then known that our ability to crack the Japanese code had enabled us to win at Midway. In the next few weeks I was to learn about the crypto craft.

Upon Miami graduation seven of us were sent to crypto school at Morisson Air Force Base in West Palm Beach. The move was most pleasant. It meant that our tropical shorts and summer khaki as well as pit helmets of Miami would continue to be in uniform. Our wives, who had been allowed to join us in Miami Beach just before graduation accompanied us. We speculated among ourselves and with our wives. Because we had been studying Spanish we hoped it was somewhere in Latin America. We also had bases in Spain. The more pessimistic guessed Africa. The apartments were somber that night. The wives fixed a "last supper." The men poured their liquor rations into a huge punch bowl. Before the dinner Gerry and I took our last ferry ride round trip to Palm Beach. We had romanced many a twilight after I returned from Crypto school at Morrison, holding hands, looking down at the water and across at the twinkling lights. Wherever Daub might be, or whatever operation this word cryptically described, some one in the Pentagon undoubtedly understood, but not the seven green lieutenants involved.

A force of impatient urgency had been underlined in our orders by requiring that we arrive at our destination, Fort Hamilton, in New York City's Long Island suburbs, 24 hours before their issue. Then followed what some GI's referred to as the Army SOP (standard operating procedure). We loafed in the barracks for a full week, engaging in daily drills, presumably to keep physically fit.

On the sixth evening at Fort Hamilton, Dave and I decided to risk AWOL and go into the big city, primarily to experience the Metropolitan Opera. He had never been. As soon as we arrived at Times Square we went to the USO to purchase discount tickets. The opera that night was *The Barber of Seville*. Quickly, I introduced Dave to the Automat for a time-saving supper, and then we walked through the bright lights to the old Metropolitan on 40th street.

As we handed our tickets to the doorman, a gentleman in evening clothes addressed us. "Do you mind if I substitute better seats for you? Mr. and Mrs. J. P. Morgan are desirous that two service men occupy their box this evening in their absence." When we arrived in our seats we both gasped with wonder. High up in the horseshoe our overview of stage and audience made me think of Balboa as he looked out on the Pacific for the first time from his promontory.

I never hear the music of the *Barber of Seville* that I do not recall the sad joy of that evening. On only one more occasion after that was I to see Dave alive. After the performance we both rushed, for some strange reason, to catch the Long Island train back to Fort Hamilton.

The moment we entered the barracks the other five pounced on us excitedly. "The CO is raving mad at you two. We seven are to report on the double." Without stopping we briskly marched in formation to HQ. There was a stern look on our commanding officer's face as he acknowledged our salute. Then with no preliminaries he held out seven strips of paper. "Draw one," he ordered us. Mine was the shortest. He turned to me. "You first. Move out. Transportation is waiting to take you to Pennsylvania station. Your train departs at Oh-two hundred, due Hampton Roads, Oh-six hundred. Report upon arrival there to POE [port of embarkation]. You others will depart later in the order of the length of the strips you drew."

So there it was. All the way to the station I kept saying to myself, there was no longer any doubt. I was going overseas. But where? Where and what were DAUB? I was on the train and in the tunnel and felt my heart beating over that question. I admitted to myself that I was afraid. Crane's

Red Badge of Courage kept thrusting itself into my recollections. I did not and could not sleep as two thoughts kept intermingling—Death and *Her*. Reason told me I was the least equipped soldier in Uncle Sam's army, and that my chances for survival were the worst possible risks any insurance company could undertake. But strangely, there was also a faith that death was not yet meant for me. To dissuade my reliance on that belief I recalled that somewhere in my reading someone had said it is a human belief that death is meant for others.

Even more haunting was the ever-present vision of the suppressed tears in her face when I asked her to sign the papers authorizing me to waive my draft status for volunteer enlistment. "Why?" every feature, every line in her lovely figure seemed to be asking, without a single word being said. But I had undertaken to say, "Because I can't live with my conscience, if I do not help prevent the awful things Hitler promises for mankind."

That very night I had a long distance call from a student of mine who was a college librarian in a neighboring city. "I have been dismissed, because I am a conscientious objector," he told me. "I am taking the midnight bus and will be in Nashville about four in the morning."

"Come right to the house," I ordered him, and we will talk it out." I picked him up at the bus station, drove him to our home, fixed some light refreshments, and talked with him without waking my wife.

"I am against war. It is senseless," he began. Then followed almost the identical words we heard from those who marched against our Vietnam involvement.

I recall I responded, as I have on many occasions recently. "Can you imagine me or any one being *for* war, except the few who stand to profit from it? I am as opposed to war as you. But it takes at least two sides to make war. I am opposed to Hitler's side even more." Then I watched his eyes almost leave their sockets as I informed him I had enlisted. But I closed, "Each of us must respond to conscience with mutual respect."

The train pulled into Hampton on time. I proceeded to the POE by military transport. Reporting in military style to the Major in command of troop movements, I waited for some clue as to my mission and destination. About the first, he informed me. "You have been assigned as security officer to the *Penelope Barker*. She is a liberty ship that will join a convoy in about two weeks. Loading has begun and I want you there now. Keep your eyes and ears open. We suspect Nazi and Fascist sabotage. Some funny things are going on around those Norfolk docks.

You will be the only Army personnel aboard. The rest of the crew consists of the merchant marine and a Navy gun crew. The ship's captain is a German. He's been checked out, and I think you'll agree he is on our side. The assistant Chief engineer is an Italian. We think we've checked him; but we'll count on you for a recheck. Any questions?"

"Yes sir. Destination?"

"I'm sorry. Classified." Then, "Lieutenant, you have been assigned BOQ quarters at POE. But I would rather you start bunking on board, at once." I unpacked my gear, and began my round of the ship, from bow to stern, up the portside and down the starboard. My lake boat terminology was coming back in the conversation with crew members, as I relearned to say aft and to discover where the "Head" was located. There was indeed, some "funny business" as the troop movements major had warned. That very morning, the first of the four 80-ton locomotives to be placed on the deck plunged into the sea when a crane cable that had been obviously tampered with gave way. Later, that first night on board, a fire broke out in the hold. It was discovered and extinguished in time to prevent the damage that had clearly been planned.

I remained on board instead of returning to the BOQ each night. It was a good decision. The men began to know me and I them. I had sensed a climate of suspicion from the moment I boarded. There were some feuds going between the Navy and Merchant Marine crews. A gob got to the heart of the matter with me. "We get thirty bucks a month; they get the union scale. They have bonus ports for which they get extra pay because these ports are in the combat zone. We go to the same ports, have to protect the merchant marine, for the same thirty bucks." I listened, and then I listened to the Merchant Marine side. But I learned to listen, and speak only when I was asked a direct question, as I was by one of the deckhands. "Are you a real doc?" I answered, "A doctor of Philosophy."

"A lot of good that'll do us on this voyage." He grumbled, "They promised us a real doc."

I looked forward to mess with the Captain. Only the officers, including the Ensign, the mates, the engineers, "Sparks" (the radio operator), and I shared the private dining table. My first lunch began very dignifiedly, with considerable silence. By the end of the meal we were all talking animatedly and even hilariously. That set the mood for meals throughout the voyage.

On the eleventh morning, the Captain gave me the word. I returned to the BOQ. for the first time, and found the other six in our mysterious mission all there. Dave briefed me. "It seems each of us has been assigned as a security officer on a ship with some unusual cargo. All of our ships are to join a convoy out there somewhere. Loading of these ships was staggered, for some reason, beginning with yours. That's why we drew strips of papers."

"Dave, what is our destination?"

"DAUB, wherever that is. I still don't know any more about that than is on our orders. Give the army credit. It has to be one of the better kept secrets."

Over and above the words I felt as if Dave were holding something back. I left and reported to the Major at POE. He interrogated me at some length about the *Penelope Barker*, confirmed that she would sail the next morning at six for the convoy rendezvous. He knew destination was on my mind and before I could ask again he said sternly "I can't tell you any more. You are to report immediately for your 'short arm' inspection. You now have the Army's authorization to talk with your wife."

"But I don't know where she is. You know I have been prohibited from communicating with her."

"The Army knows where she is. There is the signal now in that booth. Pick up the telephone." I hesitate to write in this anti-romantic, oh-so-realistic literary climate of ours exactly what I felt when I heard her voice. I have never had a sharp knife jabbed into my stomach, but I imagine the feelings are comparable. To my bewilderment her response came from a Chicago hospital. The surgery had been successful. She was convalescing.

"Surgery? What surgery?"

"Now, for sure, we will never have any children of our own," she said tearfully. I had to wait between sobs for words. The Army let us talk as long as we wanted to, and Uncle Sam paid the telephone bill that had always limited our long distance conversations before. And finally we said good bye. I reported for my inspection, wandered back over a circuitous route to let the tears dry a little bit. Dave was waiting for me.

"It's all arranged, Louis. Troop movement has agreed to let us swap ships. Mine is due to sail for rendezvous three days later than yours. That will give you time enough to fly to Chicago, see your wife in the hospital and get back in time for my later sailing."

I was touched by Dave's concern. Something compelled me to ask for time to think it over. I did not sleep that night. I was up and dressing at my army 4:45 AM. As I shaved and looked into the mirror I told myself I was deciding rationally rather than emotionally. The surgery had been successful. She was convalescing. There was nothing I could do to help. Going through another parting would be painful to her. Besides, I knew my ship and the personnel as Dave could not. I thanked Dave and said I had decided to stick with my ship.

We sailed out of Hampton Roads Sunday morning. I heard the harbor pilot call out "Steady as she goes." Ominously, protruding above the sea level was the bow of one of ours, sunk by a U-boat. Oh, yes, I repeated to myself, bitterly, the broad blue Atlantic would protect us, as the isolationists had contended to keep the U.S. out of this war. We sailed north along the coast furtively watching for that dangerous periscope somewhere out there on the horizon. We reached the rendezvous just outside New York harbor. There the huge convoy could be seen assembling, our Dutch commodore out ahead. Navy corvettes were sailing around the convoy's perimeters, reminding me of pictures of bloodhounds smelling out the victims for their hunters.

I learned something, and I surmised our destination from what the Captain shared with me. The convoy before ours had lost 33 out of 36 ships in a U-boat attack near Murmansk. Our orders had been changed from the North Atlantic to the South Atlantic. In 24 hours the convoy majestically began its hazardous journey by retracing as far as opposite Hampton Roads, and continuing south. It was apparent our cargo was destined for the Soviet Union, where the Red Army was magnificently battling the Wehrmacht around Stalingrad. It was easy to piece together our mission and destination when the Captain called me in to entrust me with the personal belongings of General Faymonville. I knew he was our liaison in the USSR.

I am not sure of the details. Somewhere along the Florida coast we were attacked by a U-boat wolfpack. Later, I learned we had lost 33 ships out of the hundred in the convoy. Among those 33 ships was David's, the one I would have sailed on had I accepted his generous offer to swap. I would change that favorite movie's title to "Fate is the Haunter." I have been haunted by the "if's" ever since. Was my decision an accident, or "was it written" as some in the orient have declared?

The disaster brought a decision from the high command to abandon convoy and send each ship off on its own. We proceeded in what was left of the convoy to Guantanamo, our U.S. base in Cuba. As we sailed more cautiously than ever, the navy corvettes moving along the convoy's perimeters, seemingly with their bloodhound noses deeper in the sea than ever, I shared the tension of the men.

Sunday came. At church service I faced a packed attendance. Every one who was not on duty, in both the Merchant Marine and Navy crew was on hand. I asked the preacher in the crew to help me with the services. He was pleased. I led the opening prayer. The Captain read from the seaman's *New Testament*; the Ensign preached a brief sermon; and I offered the closing prayer. The U-boat hazard had drawn us together. The suspicion that had hung over the ship like a cloud was beginning to melt.

I had begun to type the news as it came over the radio, and shape it into a daily newspaper format. The three carbons I made were for distribution at the morning mess in the three separated dining quarters: Navy, Merchant Marine, Officers. After breakfast, I was free to make up my own schedule. The Major had told me, proudly, "You are the Army's only representative on board. You are an officer. Don't let anybody put a mop in your hand."

As an officer I made my own decision. We were all in this perilous voyage together. I would do anything I could that was necessary. I began by asking the Captain to assign me to regular watch on the bridge with the other deck officers. He was very pleased. Then I set myself to meeting and talking with as many of the men as possible. The Captain especially appreciated this morale building effort. My major responsibility was to guard security, and to decode messages from BAMS, the allied naval command.

We reached Guantanamo at last. The route had been changed again. U-boat infection of the South Atlantic had dictated another shift, this time through the Panama Canal and across the South Pacific to the west coast of Australia, and beyond. The stories at night by the seamen who had experienced a sinking by submarine struck new terror into the hearts of all of us. One of the black gang (as those who belonged to the crew in the hold were referred to, long before *Black* took on its current issue-meaning) especially, took almost a macabre, if not a sadistic delight in detailing the screams of men overboard, drenched in oil from the tanker, becoming human torches. I suffered considerably, but I looked with even greater apprehension at my young bunk mate, the 17-year old cadet on his first voyage. Sure enough, that night I was awakened by a wild scream from the upper bunk. "No, I don't want to die. Save me. . . . ." Ted had had a nightmare: the *Penelope Barker* has been torpedoed; one of the oil drums on deck had split and covered him with oil. He was wedged in, and on fire, burning.

And in fact, our decks looked more hazardous than ever. Like most Liberty Ships rushed into service, we were overloaded by a third. The four eighty ton engines—two forward, and two astern—loomed especially ominous. Oil drums, airplane parts, and other military equipment, tucked into every deck nook and cranny, compelled the erection of cat walks so flimsy that even a moderate wave would wash walk and walker overboard. I peered out to sea like every one else. Every wave looked like a torpedo heading for us.

After what seemed like many days of terror-filled sailing, a shout was heard from above. We looked up and a formation of P-38 Lightnings, those World War II fighters with the double rail-like formats so distinctive then for aircraft identification. And on the sea ahead, our flag flew from the masts of a flotilla of warships. We were approaching the best guarded of all U.S. holdings, the very vulnerable isthmus of Panama. It was about noon when we began our entrance into the Canal. We were having our midday meal in the Captain's cabin. A Navy crew member entered, saluted the Ensign and reported, "Sir, the Marines have boarded and taken over our guns. They have ordered us to leave."

I was sorry for the first Engineer's effort at humor. "Golly," he mimicked seriously. "I took this assignment because I was told I would be protected by the Navy. And when I saw the Navy had sent a six foot four football star to protect me I felt safe. Now I'm not so sure. If a little Marine sergeant can take the gun right out of the hands of a big football Ensign, I'm not so sure I want this job."

We anchored in Colon, on the Atlantic side, and as the only Army Air Force personnel aboard I was able to spend two nights at France Field. There I ran in to two of the seven, and learned of Dave's fate. In deep gloom, the three of us decided to spend the first night in the city. It was a depressing experience for me. I was introduced to a "Blue Moon." It was my first experience in one of these seamy night clubs, where you were supposed to buy a drink for a girl. I found out later it was just some colored water, for which the customer paid about three dollars, half of it going to the girl. I tried to talk with the girl, but there wasn't time. She'd dash down her drink and expect another or go to another customer. The sights in the back, narrow streets were even more depressing: mothers selling their little daughters.

Quiet World / Odysseys

On the third day, the *Penelope Barker* was cleared to proceed through the Canal. It was a thrill to see the mightiest ocean for the first time. Her calm seemed to welcome us. But had I known then what she had in store for us I might have restrained my romanticism some. The crises began that first afternoon as I went to the bridge to take my watch. The third mate and a seaman were excited and worried. A B-24 approached us ominously, apparently uncertain of our identity. They were challenging us with the Allied code for that hour, and not seeming to get the desired response. As I mounted the bridge the bomber swooped very low. Suddenly the pilot seemed to spy the Air Force patch on my left sleeve and we could see his smile of recognition as he clasped his hands and shook them in friendly greeting.

That began a 45-day voyage during which time we never saw land. The voyage proceeded routinely for the first twelve days and nights. Each morning I checked the latitude and longitude as reported, consulted the charts and the little atlas I had brought with me. Our Liberty Ship was averaging eight knots, about 200 miles every 24 hours. I noted that we were passing west of the Galapagos Islands, and still the journey remained calm and peaceful. During the day I typed up my copy of the ship's newspaper with dispatches I picked up on the radio. To that I began adding ship news, about members of the crew. They liked to see their names in type, and to read about their fellow crewmembers. The Captain said my little paper was drawing the men together. I enjoyed varying the makeup, bringing my brief newspaper experience to bear. I talked with many of the men, listened to their concerns about loved ones at home, about the course of the war, which was not going well.

My fourth watch had ended at midnight. I turned in and slept soundly until I began to experience a groaning and creaking that I thought at first was part of a nightmare. Then I sat up in my bunk. The groaning and creaking was for real. But the sight was even spookier. Our linen drawers had opened by themselves and were stretched as if by the hands of ghosts. A stool and some loose racks were careening crazily. We were rocking and rolling, pitching and trembling. The cadet tumbled out of his upper bunk. I remembered my lake boat experience. We were in a storm, I told myself; slipped on more clothes, and shoes; and we both left our cabins. Some oil drums on deck had broken loose and were rolling toward us. We dodged them and caught a glimpse of a dark angry Pacific lunging at us with fury as if protesting our invasion.

Blackie came toward me. "Jesus, we've got it. Force eleven for sure." We helped him secure the drums and make the rounds, precariously, battening down and tightening wherever necessary. I caught a glimpse of the Captain, grimly directing seamen and officers. Blackie showed us how to use our sea legs as the ship pitched and rolled. There was no sleep for any of us that night.

The storm continued without abatement for 28 days, according to my recollection of the log. Our speed was cut to half. Day after day we tossed and rolled, listened to the creaking and groaning. At night, most often Blackie and I shared the watch on the bridge. His language was healthily salty, without the vindictive self-righteousness of our liberated literature of the Sixties. His swear words were sexless Goddams, Sunnavabitch, To hell with it. There was a bit of Eric Hoffer philosophy in his observations about men, luck, Scots, the war, ships and the sea. He repeated the sealore of the albatross: the white ones were the souls of the deckhands, the black ones of the crew in the hold. When they began to appear, later, the crew were careful to toss food to them, always with a kind of mystical reverence. I noted their 14-foot wingspread with awe, and felt an eerie look behind those beaks. Out there in the black night the ocean was like some mythical monster that could devour ship and men at any time.

Day after day and night after night the ship creaked and groaned, and tossed about like a pebble in a shaker. My cadet bunkmate became violently seasick, as did some members of both crews. The strain of the storm was beginning to tell on the nerves of the men. Frightening reports about Liberty Ships that came apart in such storms were circulated. Since these ships were put together rapidly, not with rivets, but welded, for the first time in the history of shipbuilding, it was rumored that welds would not take the strain.

Towards the 20th day of continuous storm, a violent lurch sent us scampering. The steering had been damaged. There began a frantic effort by the engineers and their men to repair. We were being tossed helplessly by the Pacific, circling carousel fashion, crazily at times. The Captain told me grimly we could not last 24 hours, unless they could come up with at least a temporary repair. The sturdy, five by five Scot, all fun at the mess, was suddenly gaunt in appearance. All of us wanted to help, but there was little we could do but stay out of the way and wait. About twilight, news of success reached us. We were sailing again.

The storm abated gradually. We resumed our former eight-knot speed. Another crisis had served to bring the ship's crews closer. There was now an air of comraderies we had never known. Good natured joshing was the order of the day and night. I came in for my share, especially when they found out accidentally that I was a librarian in civilian life. That occupation seemed to awe and captivate them, because it was so foreign to their way of life. But at last, we left the Pacific and entered the Indian Ocean, south of Australia; there was a general feeling we had made it. This was confirmed shortly when we had our first sight of land in 45 days. Soon we were entering Fremantle where we were scheduled to put in for repairs.

I can describe only to those who have been at sea for a comparable length of time and under similar conditions the feelings in my legs as I stepped off the gang plank on solid earth. My legs ached. I teeter-tottered as if I were still at sea, using my sea legs. The Captain told me we would have to remain for ten days, and that I was free to do what I liked. I determined to take the train to Perth, only 25 miles away. And what do you think I did first? Visited the Perth Public Library, met the librarian, who arranged for my lodging at his Weld Club. Australian hospitality was overwhelmingly gratifying.

When I returned to the ship, several days later, there were boxes of apples for the crew delivered by the good Australian people, who knew we had had no fresh fruit for so long. Our gear had been repaired, and we were ready to lift anchor again. We sailed out of Fremantle harbor, into the Indian Ocean and continued the planned course to the Arabian Sea, the Gulf of Oman, and the Persian Gulf. In these waters, I recall, I was captivated by the phosphorescent light in the water at night.

And then came our last and almost disastrous crisis. We entered the Persian Gulf at about twilight. As we sailed toward our port of debarkation, a British cruiser suddenly appeared on the horizon. It blinked the Allied challenge for that hour. We blinked back. Apparently our blinker was not strong enough. The huge cruiser raised its mighty guns and blinked the challenge again with the threat of no responses received they were opening fire. The irony of it almost caved in my spirit. To have come all the way to our destination and then to be sunk by one of our own. The Captain thought quickly. He ordered the response blown on the ship's whistle. We waited with our hearts surfacing to our mouths. They had sensed that something was wrong. They blinked, "stand by." It became darker and our signal man continued to blink the Allied response. Then came their acknowledgement. "Stand by." It became darker and our signal man continued blinking the Allied response. With increased darkness our blinker carried the distance, and the Cruiser responded. "What is your name?" Our blinker responded, *Penelope Barker.* Again a suspenseful wait while they checked. And then it came, "Proceed Barker." That was not all. We were to proceed under escort, the Union Jack ahead assuring us we were safe from U-boats under the protection of the Cruiser's formidable armaments.

We anchored at last in the Persian Gulf port of Basra, Iraq. As we approached anchor at about midnight, the Captain informed me that a British tender was coming along side to pick me up. I was packed and ready at Oh-One Hundred, as directed. I felt strangely sad, leaving my home, the *Penelope Barker,* named for that valiant Revolutionary war heroine. Quietly, I slipped out of my cabin, intending to depart as inauspiciously as possible. As I reached the side the men of all the crews appeared. A little speech was made by the preacher seaman, by the Ensign, and by the Captain. They handed me a framed sketch of me done by the crew's artist. Knowing our shortages I was aware how they had scraped to find the glass, the frame, the crude art materials. It hangs on my wall to this day, one of my most sentimental treasures. Below my portrait, these words:

> Our voyage together now is ended
> And your in a foreign land
> You've pitched a fighter's tent
> In a field of burning sand
> But when the war is over
> And guns are still once more
> We hope we'll meet again
> With our friend, Lt. Shores
> Officers, Ships Crew and Gun Crew
>   S.S. Penelope Barker

Oh, what's the use hiding, even from our callous sophistication. I was glad it was dark. The tears were bathing my cheeks and dampening my military collar and tie. I went over the side and aboard the tender, wiping my eyes with my sleeve so that the British seamen might not see a sentimental Yank, as from the Penelope Barker came the men's loud voices,

Quiet World / Odysseys

> Hip, hip,
> For he's a jolly good fellow . . .

China Burma India. I believe I was the first librarian to reach there and therefore, probably, the first to equate that CBI with Cumulative Book Index. It has been claimed many times since, even by soldier-librarians who never served in that theatre.

I did not really know for certain that was my ultimate destination. A funny thing happened on the way. The big brown envelope that had been guarded unopened so long in the Captain's safe over that 96-day voyage of 18,000 miles had the secret. As per instructions, I carried it unopened into U.S. Persian Gulf HQ. It's a small world. The sergeant who welcomed me was my own good Peabody graduate. I was shown in to the commanding officer, who greeted me and opened my brown envelope. There was nothing in it. He smiled. "That's a break. All you have to do now is wait this war out." But they radioed my POE in Hampton, Virginia, and despite the fact that there had now been a complete change of personnel there my orders were transmitted.

My military assignment began in New Delhi's Willingdon Airport in earnest. Six hours on, twelve hours off, around the clock, the cryptographers, radio operators, maintenance personnel performed their duties. I began encoding and decoding messages. Most of them were departure messages for aircraft. No pilot ever flew alone. So many of them had paid tribute to AACS that all of us in the Army Airways Communication System took particular pride in our various responsibilities.

An AACS station like Willingdon had, first of all, a radio range. This emitted continuously to the pilot the Morse code letters *dit-dot* (A) and *dot-dit* (N). The pilot was supposed to hear a continuous *dot* if he was on course. If he heard either *dit-dot* or *dot-dit* he was straying off the beam and had to adjust his course.

But the radio range was only one of the 22 facilities AACS maintained and operated to keep our planes and those of our Allies flying. Our radio operators, manually, received and transmitted coded messages, *point-to-point*, that is from station to station; and *air-ground*, that is between AACS stations and aircrafts aloft. Critical facilities were the control towers, not only because they directed takeoff and landing, but because they were most exposed to enemy bombers. A vital facility was D/F (direction finding), which enabled a lost aircraft to locate itself by signalling an AACS facility. Later, GCA (Ground Control Approach) was added, a most dramatic radar means for talking a pilot into precise landing when fog or night prevented seeing the runway. I never ceased to marvel over the assurance in the calm voice of the AACS ground controller (picked for his level-headed qualities, as well as for his technical know how) as he reassured the blind pilot: "You're doing fine. Touchdown in sixty seconds."

Mostly, we cryptographers were coding flight messages. Plane departures had to be communicated to destinations, as well as to AACS points along the way, with departures and ETA (estimated time of arrival) in code that could not be broken by the enemy. The encoded message then went to a radio operator who Morse transmitted the encoded message to be decoded by the receiving AACS station. It was not as routine as it sounded. Security alert without relaxation strained the work effort. We knew that somewhere enemy cryptographers were constantly at work to break our codes. Unless one has worked under comparable conditions it is not possible to indicate the shifting tactics and strategies to thwart the enemy. Our naval victory at Midway was accomplished largely through the breaking of the Japanese code.

The days and nights sped by at Willingdon. During the winter months the work was bearable. But with the coming of March the heat became increasingly worse. The midnight shift was most trying. The temperature was over 100, and the lack of any wind made it necessary to leave the suffocatingly close crypto hut for a gasp of fresh air. Each time it was secured, with my eye always on it. I would squat on the ground, keeping my mind off the heat by watching a scorpion or two in what looked like their backward motion.

On off hours, I slept in our army tent, with mosquito netting over my bunk. We had a mongoose tied to the center pole as a protection against snakes. Once, in a stroll past a vacant field I witnessed a battle between a cobra and a mongoose. The cobra struck; the mongoose lighteningly dodged the strike; and as the cobra recoiled before it could strike again, the mongoose had it by the neck, and it was all over.

When I was not sleeping, I went into the city of New Delhi. In 1942-44 it was very new indeed, with but few structures. All of the government buildings were impressive, however, and the streets comparatively wide and clean, in contrast to old Delhi. Among my regular places of call were two libraries: the special one maintained by the British government; and USIS, or its forerunner. One of my favorite shrines was the

Birla Temple, of the Jains, which contained statues of deadly creatures, such as the boa constrictor. The Jains do not believe in destroying any life, no matter how harmful to man we may consider it.

In old Delhi I visited the public library first. It was difficult walking through the crowded streets lined with merchants selling their wares. The congestion and poverty were only less depressing than the unsanitary conditions. Food exposed for sale was covered with flies. There was continuous stench in the air that seemed to be dominated by urine. Some men strolled naked and were taken for granted. When I finally reached the public library, I introduced myself to the librarian. He was not trained in the American sense, but had acquired considerable self education. Above all, he introduced me to the religion of Islam by taking me with him to the Mosque in Old Delhi, reading to me from the Koran, in English, and dialoguing with me, one day: "We accept all of your prophets—Old Testament and New. Why do you not reciprocate by accepting our Mohammed?"

My most stimulating CBI associations were with British personnel. When I first arrived in CBI, a theatre under the British command of Lord Mountbatten, only one third of the forces were GI; two thirds BOR (British other ranks). It was amusing listening to the two English accents and idioms blend. The GI was forever shouting "Get on the ball." It wasn't long before the British soldier was converting to "Get on the bloody ball." But I liked their "Get crackin' " even better. An Anglophile, already, I took to their mature acceptance of success and defeat with much less show biz than we Americans. Once we won a modest clash with the Japanese, and the G.I.'s were jubilant; but a BOR merely said, "It was a bit of all right."

One of the British captains with whom I developed a mutual attraction was named Johnny Clark. US officers, recognizing the differences on British pronunciation, called him Johnny *Clerk*. He responded good naturedly with the story of the dialogue between a U.S. and a British general. Said the American, "Where did you British learn to pronounce that word *shedule?*" Said the British general, "In Shool."

The memories of CBI tumble in almost as irrationally as everything appeared to happen to me then. I moved on from Agra to Allahabad, where the university was located and where Nehru was a prisoner at the time. The air was full of him and talk about Gandhi. I was troubled by the thinking of both of them, but not as convinced as many. It seemed to me then, as it does now, that too much pacifistic effort is directed at the most peaceful nations, and not enough at the militant ones. It seemed to me inevitable that such pacifistic efforts tended to be self-destructive; that war always involved at least two contenders; and that if pacifism was to mean anything it had to be applied to both sides equally, and perhaps even more so in the totalitarian nations.

I had promised myself, if I came out of the war alive, I would write a book, and if it were published, I would give all of the royalties to the Air Force to be used for the aid of the wounded and the dependants of those killed in action.

I wrote *Highways in the Sky*, during the first year of peace. Two publishers were interested—Houghton Mifflin, and Barnes and Noble. I contracted with the latter for two reasons. They had published my dissertation, *Origins*. Houghton wanted some changes in my manuscript that I could not accept. *Highways in the Sky* appeared in 1947 under the Barnes and Noble imprint, in two editions. The "Cadre Edition" was embellished with a frontispiece gold and red, and numbered, presumably for the first 500 who were willing to pay the extra price. It was oversubscribed, mostly by AACS men. The other edition sold out and was soon out of print. I have been unable to locate a copy for the many AACS men who have written to me.

Above all, the royalties must have been considerable, as the Army Air Force Aid Society rewarded me with a life membership, and a card I still carry proudly in my wallet.

July 1945. We had already celebrated VE day. The war in Europe had been won. We were well on our way toward VJ, but Hiroshima and the A-bomb were still to come. I was working away at making history pay with our Intelligence Analysis. My nine GI Ph. D.'s were reading unit histories and abstracting significances on 8 by 5 cards according to the plan I had outlined to the General. There was a deep sense of accomplishment as we were told our operation at CONAS had introduced a new element into intelligence at the world headquarters of AACS in Asheville, North Carolina.

The Intelligence Analysis involvement kept stirring up an idea for using military innovations in AV, in history, in education now coming to a peacetime armed forces correspondence and extension program; in scientific and technical research for the advancement of mankind. All through these stirrings, the mystic quiet that had impelled me to choose librarianship was playing some kind of role, so elusive I could not formulate it. Why, I asked myself, should not all nations maintain armed forces? Not to carry on war with each other, but to exchange ideas with the end of truly bringing about Wendell Wilkie's "One World?"

Discount it, if you will; or charge it to my impractical romanticism. But for some reason or other, a series of peace time challenges came right up to meet me. I had been discharged at Fort McPherson in Atlanta. Given the choice, I asked to remain in the AACS reserve. There were three levels of reserve, ranging from comparatively inactive to very active. I chose the most active, what was then called a MOB (mobilization assignment.) My terminal leave ended in June as I began my 1946 association with *Collier's Encyclopedia*. But my first reserve duty did not come until September 1947, at the beginning of my full time residence on the Florida State campus. I spent two weeks in Washington reorienting myself in AACS developments.

In that academic year, however, the first of my major civilian involvements with the armed forces began. President Campbell had been approached by the Air Force to offer an educational program to military personnel on neighboring bases like Eglin and Tyndall in Florida; but especially in Alabama, at Maxwell and Craig, where the Air University was opening up. Dr. Campbell called several faculty members who were in the reserve to advise him. There began, through Florida State University, I believe for the first time, "Operation Bootstrap" under which GI's could work toward a college degree on the base, doing the finishing term on the campus, assigned to temporary duty. About the same time, also, we gained two of the three ROTC's we sought—Army and Air Force; but not Navy, as we had hoped. There was a climate of receptivity to these fine programs, before the rather unreasonable later protests.

With Florida State University's approval, I began an association with the AID of Air University, advising on curriculum, on media and library use; lecturing to classes; and eight times being the choice as commencement speaker at graduations. When the AID was moved to Maxwell, near Montgomery, where the Air University HQ was located, I moved with it. There was, also, the great library, to be named for my boyhood hero, General Billy Mitchell. My involvement followed shortly.

There was then a board of visitors for the Air University. A civilian, Dr. Kenneth Williams, who later became president of the innovative Florida Atlantic University, was then Air University dean. Largely through his initiative, an Air University Library Board was activated.

Its seven members included a university president, two distinguished professors, and four librarians, from seven U.S. institutions of higher education. I was asked to serve as chairman of this board. My librarian colleagues on the board were Robert Bingham Downs of the University of Illinois, Jack Dalton, then of the University of Virginia, and Maurice Tauber, Columbia University.

The Board met four times a year at the beginning of our seven-year appointment. We were treated as VIPs and lodged at quarters on the base reserved for very important persons. Almost from the first we were confronted with a critical personnel study.

As the years went by the meetings became events to look forward to. Two Air Force aircraft were assigned to pick up the members and bring them to Maxwell. One of these VIP transports flew to New York, first, to pick up Maurice Tauber; then to Charlottesville for Jack Dalton; to Louisville for President Philip Davidson: to Athens, Georgia, for Merle Curtis, etc. Since Tallahassee was the only stop south of Montgomery, a second plane came to pick me up. On one occasion, Jack Dalton was in Tallahassee, before the meeting, and he and my wife and I drove the 200 miles between the Alabama and Florida capital cities.

As plans for the new four million dollar Billy Mitchell library for Air University progressed, the Board felt an outstanding librarian should be appointed as director. Several names were offered to General Barker for consideration. In the mean time, because of my civilian efforts at Maxwell, both with the Library Advisory Board and with the AID, it seemed desirable to transfer my reserve assignment from AACS to Air University. Hardly had this been effected than General Barker invited me to the Officer's Club for refreshments. We talked about the library informally, and in the course of the conversation he said, "That's an impressive list of candidates you presented for the position of director." And then, it appeared to me, he was just being complimentary when he observed, "Why in the hell should we get a civilian. I've got a top librarian in the Reserve. I'll just order him back to active duty." I was pleased about the compliment, but that was all I thought it was, and forgot about it.

Because of other commitments in Alabama I did not return to campus until a week later. As I went through the stack of mail that had accumulated I noted a large, unopened brown envelope from the War Department. I opened it unsuspectingly, because I received many such envelopes in connection with my various military commitments. But this one was shockingly different. It began

Major Louis Shores, 0916719
WP ACTIVE DUTY MAXWELL AFB RUAT CG AIR UNIVERSITY

Immediately I called President Campbell and he asked me to bring the papers. He was indignant. There was no war emergency and he felt, rightly, this was unfair to Florida. He began his protest through our Congressman.

But in the meantime, I was a reserve officer, subject to Air Force orders. I proceeded to Maxwell as directed, reported to the adjutant, from where I was sent to take my physical examination. In less than two hours I had cleared all the preliminaries and the Colonel in the adjutant's office, whom I knew, said, "Congratulations, Louis, you're back on active duty." And then he added, "It's a helluva trick. I got the Trial Judge Advocate to consider your appeal, immediately." The Trial Judge Advocate was a Colonel I had known, also. His decision was fair and prompt. "It is not in the National interest to remove a needed educator from civilian life at a time when there is no national emergency."

I saw General Barker, and he was understanding. He had to try, he said. And now he asked me to reduce the list of recommendations to three. He inclined toward Dr. Jerrold Orne, at that time director of Washington University in St. Louis. I was enthusiastic about his choice and the Air University moved rapidly. I had known Jerry at ALA and at various meetings. His doctorate in Romance languages and literatures appealed to me as especially important for the library mission increasingly involved in international researches. Jerry's brilliant mind, I believed, could cut across much of the military red tape that had handicapped his predecessors.

One humorous incident occurred in the handling of his papers. Somewhere along the line a typist had omitted the world "languages" from Jerry's specialization, so that it read "Dr. Orne is a Specialist in *Romance*." General Barker confronted me with this. "What can we do with a specialist in Romance at Maxwell Air Force Base?" Just then we both glanced out the window where at some distance a GI and his girl were locked in embrace. He grinned, and said, "Touché."

I finished my seven years as chairman of the Air University Library Advisory Board during Jerry's competent administration. I saw the library as the quiet force that would convert the armies, navies, and air forces into ideological forces for promoting tolerance, world understanding, and literacy, through an advanced type of public library service, as one of the three great military branches of world armed forces. The second branch I considered a super special librarianship to advance knowledge through research and investigations that would result in scientific and humanistic discoveries. The third branch would undertake the kind of library education we had so imperfectly realized in civilian life. My personal military involvement had related to all three branches: for example, *public librarianship*, in all of the base libraries where I had helped with reading programs for GIs; *special librarianship*, in Army Redstone, Navy East Coast Laboratories, and Air Force Air University; *library education*, in Air University's AID. There had been innumerable other Armed Forces impacts and involvements arising from reserve duty, from civilian consultantships, from invitations to address the Armed Forces library meetings, and especially from my commitment at Florida State to give special attention to Armed Forces librarian placement and continuing professional education.

The latter resulted in one of the greatest challenges of my library career. At ALA, Loutrell Cavin, director of the Air Force Strategic Air Command's libraries, located all over the world, asked for an appointment. Accompanied by military personnel she unfolded an approved plan for a world-wide refresher education program for the library personnel, to be offered by an ALA accredited library school. The course would last one week. The Air Force would fly its librarians in from bases all over the world. The curriculum was to be developed jointly by the School and by SAC. And then came the biggest compliment of all: "We would like Florida State University to be that school because you have been so concerned with Armed Forces education and placement; but above all because Florida State has been most innovative in Audiovisual librarianship, in extension education, in comparative librarianship and in a number of other areas that relate to our world-wide mission."

I responded with excited gratitude, I recall, but I cautioned this would have to receive University approval, and above all, approval by the Library School faculty.

As I had anticipated, my Faculty, though it meant an extra burden for them, on top of their already heavy class load, responded enthusiastically. President Strozier excitedly applauded, and assigned fiscal and other administrative resources.

Quiet World / Odysseys

Loutrell Cavin came and helped us to pre-plan. She and my assistant dean, Bob Clapp, hit it off and worked long and hard on the necessary details. Georgia, as Loutrell was nicknamed because of her Georgia accent, proved to be delightful company, as well as tremendously competent. Hers was a man-size job. There were SAC establishments as far away as Australia, Japan, Africa, Spain, and equally distant points. Georgia visited them frequently on Air Force transports and combat aircraft. She directed not only the book selection, acquisition, preparations, and dissemination programs with keen professional insight to the military requirements, but accomplished a personnel and public relations task beyond any we knew in civilian librarianship.

For example, we agreed that I should visit certain SAC bases for better understanding of Base library problems, as well as the research needs. An Air Force C54 picked us up in Tallahassee, and according to orders, flew to the Orlando Base, first. As Georgia stepped off the plane, her striking beautiful blond hair, her tall feminine figure stopped military traffic. Officers greeted her with a friendly, "Hi, Georgia." GI's who didn't know her stopped in their tracks and wolf-whistled. Georgia returned the greetings, equally, with her lovely soft "Hi y'all." There was no question of her charm or quiet assurance. It was the same at the several other bases we visited, and at all of them, the library staffs, especially, seemed to look forward to her coming.

We returned to Tallahassee, and she and my wife, who had become very fond of her, and I went out to dinner. During the course of the conversation, we liked to hear her refer to "Omeehaw" as this Southern girl told how she saw the midwest. I asked her when she had been in her native Georgia last. She said, "Lord, not in ages." I plotted. As the girls became absorbed in an animated discussion on the back seat about the minimum essentials for a girl's wardrobe on a world trip (important to my wife because she was to begin accompanying me on some of my foreign missions) I drove out Thomasville Road past the corner that leads to our Betton Hills home. From that point it is exactly 17 miles to the Georgia line.

The girls paid no attention to me or my direction, as girls will do when they converse about their most absorbing subjects like clothes, or menus, or men! and Georgia and Gerry took all three in turn. In 15 minutes drive I arrived at the big sign on the highway, WELCOME TO GEORGIA. I stopped; but the girls kept talking, unaware of the mere male driving, or of where we were. It was still broad daylight. Suddenly Georgia looked up and exclaimed, "Lord. Welcome to Georgia!" Reverently she stepped out in her nylon stocking. (Both girls had kicked off their shoes.) I had told Georgia several times how close our home was to the Georgia line, but as she said, "I kept telling myself I was in Florida, a million miles from my Southland."

The preliminaries were completed. My faculty and I had rehearsed the procedure innumerable times. We had made out our syllabi, calendar, daily schedule, and stencils in a style to do credit to the most exacting military specifications. We had considered this necessary since the Pentagon was sending ten field grade officers to *critique* the week's program.

About 24 hours before our October 20, 1959 "D-Day" the first Air Force C-54 set down in the Tallahassee Municipal Airport. The SAC librarians who had arrived from as far away as Australia deplaned to a grand welcome from newspaper reporters, camera men, University, City, and State Officials. Soltas (as our Library School was known) made the news, not only locally, but in the leading newspapers of Florida and other Southeastern states. For the next twelve hours, our Tallahassee control tower was busy landing Air Force aircraft, until the approximately 100 personnel involved in the first world-wide refresher course for Armed Forces librarians had arrived.

We began the program on time. Proudly, I watched each of my Faculty perform their assignments. Perhaps immodestly I have claimed the greatest teachers ever assembled in an ALA accredited library school. Agnes Gregory presented her inspiring unit on children's literature to an obviously converted lecture hall of Armed Forces librarians. Sara Srygley followed with more about school librarianship, in her inimatable style that captivated even the most sophisticated. Bob Clapp enthralled with his change of pace from solid selection and acquisition information to the provocative humor that especially brought giggles from feminine librarians. Otis McBride and Mary Alice Hunt, as well as the AV staff, gave SAC the refresher in graphics, equipment operation and maintenance that had been one of the reasons for choosing FSU. One after another the Faculty performed inspiringly. I closed with a "philosophical" essay, as prescribed by the military. It was titled "Return to Reading," containing a synthesis of my beliefs about quiet as a prelude to creativity; about the Generic Book as an answer to Maurice Duhamel's fear that the printed page was in danger of being replaced; and my concern with American neglect of meditation, already critical because of the growing accent on physical action. Unknown to me a field worker from the Southern Baptist Convention was present, and I was invited subsequently to present this paper to his colleagues in North Carolina.

The hard work of the day was complemented by dinners and picnics at night, trips to neighboring Wakulla Springs, and to the snow-white sand beaches of the Gulf of Mexico, for those incomparable sea food specialties that have made Florida world famous—red snapper and hush puppies; Apalachicoala oysters and shrimps; flounder; and (in my opinion) the superior, tender sweet Florida lobster. After the dinner, the librarians, especially from New England and the Great Lakes, enjoyed wading and swimming in the Gulf so late in the fall.

The University buses brought us back singing the songs so popular in both civilian and military life.

The reckoning arrived Friday afternoon. Our faculty assembled on the platform of the lecture hall. So did the Brass from the Pentagon, resplendant in their decorated uniforms. We trembled, I confess. The ranking Colonel began. It was an accolade of tributes to the faculty as a whole, and to each of us individually. The conclusion was a series of recommendations for future conferences, and suggestions that proved helpful to us in our classes.

Perhaps this chapter has overlooked other significances in my military missions for librianship. I am convinced that my association with the military since that first day on active duty in August 1942 has decisively shaped my philosophy of librarianship. I believe our profession owes a debt to the Armed Forces librarian we have not yet begun to acknowledge. Specifically, I believe we must enter the door these dedicated colleagues have opened to us to introduce the library quiet into noisy war. Let us show the military that victories can be won over intolerance, poverty, disease, illiteracy, delinquency, addiction, ugliness, and other evils, with libraries that will bring world peace.

6. Fulbright Year

I was excitingly informed my application for a Fulbright fellowship to study comparatively British Library Reference Services had been granted. My work was with our most loyal World War II ally, Britain. At my request I had been assigned to the Library Association with headquarters in the old Chaucer House, adjacent to the University of London campus. Included were provisions for travel to libraries in the United Kingdom. Two kinds of fellowships had been offered: teaching or research. Mine was the second, with opportunity for the first.

From April through August we prepared for our transatlantic voyage, by reading up on Britain and on the Fulbright exchange. There was much to do at home. Gerry walked on air in anticipation of her first trip abroad. We sub-leased our little cottage which we rented to two lady faculty members. My leave at the University was easily arranged with the President because my selection as a Fulbrighter was recognized. In the Library School my good faculty loyally promised to carry on in my absence. The summer session sped despite our impatience to take off.

The first sight of the SS *America's* smokestacks aroused all my love of the sea and brought back memories of the Southern Cross over the Pacific. Even the docks stirred memories of Lake Erie and my boyhood duty on the SS *State of Ohio* as she plied Lake Erie. Gerry's excitement was little greater than my own. We held hands and displayed the tears in our eyes without apology. The SS *America* was sliding down the dock and into the Hudson. We saw the tugboat disengage itself as it completed its maneuvering in the middle of the river, turning our huge 33,000 ton bulk loose to shift for itself. On the Manhattan side we distinguished the landmarks through our still tearful eyes: the Chrysler and Empire State buildings; the Brooklyn bridge in the distance; and then far ahead, the Statue of Liberty. Soon we passed it and were out in the lower harbor speeding toward the open sea. Sentimentally we clasped hands tighter. We could read in our eyes a loneliness that was beginning to penetrate our excitement—a realization that we were being separated from our home, and all we knew and loved, by the broad blue Atlantic.

Since we had no assigned housing in London, we were put up for three nights at Dartmouth House, headquarters of the English Speaking

Union. All of my readings in English literature trooped through my mind. The London chimney tops kept reminding me of Dickens and Scrooge. There were still the graces of England in 1951, uncontaminated by the Beatle surrender to American showbiz. My Anglophilism was gratified by little things. People queued for buses, for turns at the green grocer, for admissions to various events, without outside enforcement. The self-discipline of the English was like a religious experience for me. On the street corners, pennies were piled up on newspapers, in the absence of the newsboy, and no one thought of stealing either a paper or the money. At the theatre, much less expensive than Broadway, and better, there were expensive opera glasses to be rented for sixpence. The manager of one theatre told me he had never lost one. People replaced them when they were through. On the streets, walking or driving, there was an extra show of courtesy not seen, certainly in New York, or our larger cities.

But even more alluring were the long walks, with Santos Casani, who knew the city, and with Mr. Harris of Stechert, who showed us more of the city than the average American tourist ever sees. I recall Cheshire Cheese, and sitting in Samuel Johnson's chair. We went to Greenwich, and stood on zero longitude, and speculated what American enterprise would do with concessions. There would undoubtedly be peddled "Longitude Hot Dogs," and "Zero Eskimo Pies."

But my favorite excursion was to take the red double decker bus to Piccadilly, walk to the Cunard ticket office, and continue on Regent street leading to the stairs, which I descended to the Mall lower street level. If I turned right it led to Buckingham Palace. More often I turned left to Trafalgar Square, where Lord Nelson, high up on his column, looks out to sea. From there I proceeded on Whitehall past the Changing of the Guards, pausing for a few minutes to observe those erect sentries with their tall hats; then to Westminster Abbey, looking up at Big Ben as I walked. Then along the Thames embankment, enthralled and meditative about the history of a nation so great that, despite its own belittlement and depression about declining might, had proved the most lasting civilization in the history of the world.

The pub's symbolized the colorfully cheerful mood of London. Often, with the Casanis—Santy and Joan—we would go on a pub crawl, to famous ones liked the Prospect of Whitby. Mostly they had compound names, like Horse and Carriage, or Knight and Knave, and so my wife converted our neighborhood pub, The Busy Bee to the Busy and Bee. When haute cuisiniers lift their noses at London cuisine they don't know the London Pub. In 1951, a wholesome lunch, three course, could be paid for with *two and six* (thirty-five cents). An elegant dinner at the Gloucester, also in our neighborhood, was available for *three and six* (about fifty cents.) Not the least delightful part of eating at a pub was what the Germans call *gemutlichkeit*. Contrary to what I had thought *pub* meant, it was a community center. Mamma and papa brought the children, and every one sat down and talked. The bar part was in another room, where *bitter* was mostly drunk. Americans, at first referred to this as "warm beer." But it isn't warm in England, ever, and therefore the beers and ales are cool.

London life and libraries in 1951-52 was a full course in Comparative Librarianship. After some search we discovered a flat at 20 York Street, off the famous Baker Street, in the Sherlock Holmes neighborhood. Around the corner was the Marylebone public library branch, where we became registered borrowers from the first day. Fulbrighters lived like residents of the host country. Britain was still on rationing: one egg a week per person and two strips of bacon, for example. It used to wrench our heart when we were invited by our friends to share their ration. Since we, too, were on the ration, the cans (British "tins") we had brought gave us an opportunity to reciprocate. One day in November the postman rang our door bell to deposit a strange package. It was postmarked Knoxville, Tennessee. Bill Jesse, director of the University of Tennessee Library, had sent us an 18-pound Tennessee country ham. I will not take sides in a comparison with Virginia or Kentucky country ham. I will only say that in the fall of 1951, in food-rationed London, Tennessee Country Ham was the best. We knew at once what we wanted to do. As members of the English Speaking Union, we arranged to have the ham, and chicken, which was not rationed, and certain other delicacies cut of our cans, catered at Dartmouth House for 18 couples in Britain who had been very close to us.

I walked, nearly as frequently as I rode the red double decker bus, to Chaucer House, headquarters of the Library Association of the United Kingdom, my Fulbright assignment. At that time Chaucer House was an old, red brick, four story building. It adjoined the National Central Library and the main campus of University College of the University of London, which housed the School of Librarianship, in an old three-story structure, across the way from Chaucer House.

Romanticist that I am, I soon became attached to the grace and charm of Chaucer House, and the people who staffed LA headquarters. Percy Welsford was the Executive Secretary, then. As is the custom, he was a professional secretary, not a librarian. A mutual sympathy soon developed not only between us, but between our wives, and we enjoyed the pleasure of their company at a number of professional and social affairs. Above all, I looked forward to his presiding at the daily lunch in Chaucer House. He always performed as a gracious and fatherly host, not only to the LA staff, but to the librarians who came to pay their respects from all over the world.

Of the LA staff members, two were very close to us. Henrik Jones, the librarian, to whom I went about my assignment, must be placed at the very top of library literature bibliographers. Above all, Henrik personified the Quiet Spirit of librarianship. Bernard Palmer, the Education Officer for LA, was the other very close Chaucer House friend. He used to greet me each morning I reported to work at Chaucer House with his movie version of American gangster distortion of the King's English: "Take a powder. Scram. Let me look at your violin case." All of it was attempted in what he considered the excruciating American nasal voice quality. When Bernard arrived at the lunch table he was frequently accompanied by Jack Wells, architect of the *British National Bibliography*. Later, these two were to co-author the little volume on classification philosophy, which I consider another evidence of how much more deeply our British Colleagues have considered the epistemological question of how to order our knowledge.

On several occasions I visited, with Bernard, Jack's British National Bibliography headquarters near the British Museum. In my opinion, the BNB treatment of Dewey Decimal Classification is more sensitive frequently than the decisions represented on Library of Congress cards. At Chaucer House lunches, I gained new classification perspectives from Bernard and Jack. To cite one specific, for which I will not hold Palmer and Wells responsible, should they want to disown any responsibility, I changed my position on close classification. At Columbia I had come to understand that the larger the library the closer the classification. In London this new dimension entered my classification horizon: the larger the library, the broader the classification of the physical book. Reserve close classification for bibliography. This logic appealed to me: once the physical book is closely classified it is committed to favoring one discipline over another. This is contrary to librarianship's traditional impartiality toward all disciplines, but bibliographies can be closely classified to favor the discipline for which they are being compiled.

But the master of classification to Bernard and Jack was the great librarian from India—S.R. Ranganathan. The name had meant very much to me after I had met him through *The Five Laws*, at Columbia. During my CBI War days, I had hoped the army would place me on temporary duty in Madras so that I might meet Ranganathan. But the Army had other ideas for my time. When he arrived, we lunched at Chaucer House. What a memorable polylogue! I was struck by his strange combination of western and eastern dress. There was the sheet, the jacket, garters to hold his socks up. But one forgot about that when his animated talk began. Perhaps that invisible bond between us began then. I told him how I had hoped to see him in India during my army service. Despite the fact that Ranganathan had been a mathematician before he became a librarian, I found him less the scientist than the poet. Perhaps I shifted the conversation into my mystical concern about the *gurus* of India who could levitate, and who had such other strange powers as clairvoyance, precognition, and psychometry. Ranganathan did not try to call me back to comparative library science, our first subject. Indeed, he readily accepted my invitation to have supper in our flat.

When I reported to my wife who was coming to dinner, she rushed across the street to ask the Casanis what you feed an abstemious vegetarian. Joan, in her devilish way, said, "Gerry, go to Heal." After one startled moment, Gerry recovered and laughed. "Of course, Heal's specializes in vegetarian food." She remembered the place because it was the same stop on the red double decker bus as for Chaucer House. At Heal's she was introduced to *Nut Cutlet*, a delicacy that looked like meat and was just as rich in proteins.

Ranganathan arrived in our York Street flat promptly at six. He seemed to enjoy the nut cutlet. After dinner we sat in the living room and talked while my wife put things away. I, perhaps, was responsible for steering our conversation back to the occult. When I indicated my difficulty in sitting lotos leaf fashion, he obliged me by demonstrating on the carpet. I sat down beside him in my favorite position, legs crossed. Even without my Yoga instruction, which I had begun in London, I had discovered this restful sitting position. When I sit this way, especially in front of a fireplace, meditation comes on, and I suppose I am doing, in the contemporary cliche, "my thing." I sat this way as a boy of six;

I sit this way tonight when I am way past sixty. And what are these meditations? Mostly impractical dreams. There has always been a bit of revolt in these fantasies against "telling it like it is" in this temporal world, when I extrasense an ethereal universe of "once upon a time" and "they lived happily ever after." Perhaps Ranganathan extrasensed my mood. He entered into it with me and shared some occult experiences in India. My wife found us on the floor when she entered.

Inevitably, we turned to comparative librarianship. It got me started on the trialogue idea—the comparatives that might follow if one nation had been influenced by two nations, almost equally, and therefore were in a position to compare those two nations objectively, as a third party, instead of as a member of either, as was so often the case in comparative education or comparative librarianship. Indian librarianship was almost in that position. Not quite, because U.S. influence was just beginning in India, while British colonial influence is centuries old. But once the Fulbright and Mundt exchanges, and the other government grants had been brought to bear, U.S. librarianship began almost geometrically to replace British impacts. Ranganathan made some comparisons that night, especially in classification. It was apparent that he felt both Britain and the U.S. were still primitive in their "enumerative" classifications. Some years later he was to expand that in his lectures to my Florida State University students and in our Tallahassee home. My comparative librarianship was galloping daily in Britain, almost from the first few days in September.

My Fulbright mission was general and specific. Broadly, I was doing my bit for Comparative Librarianship, and a new crusade was irrepressibly welling up in my evangelistic soul. I saw, all at once, that libraries and librarianship could be the gateway to a new world understanding; to a peace on earth that politics and politicians could never accomplish because of traditional commitments in international diplomacy to *vital interests*, to *balance of power* and to *revanche*, (to borrow from Michael Demiashkevich's book *Shackled Diplomacy*). By beginning with libraries—the record of civilization—and with librarianship—the most tolerant of all interpreters of that record—the door might be opened to a more nearly "equal footing" communication among peoples and nations.

On a prototype scale I proposed to compare libraries and library philosophies in two nations with a common heritage and language. Some areas that particularly attracted me were public librarianship, where I began my career; school librarianship, because I have had a sentimental hunch that this type would lead all of the others to a realization of our high educational role; classification, because of its implications for that branch of philosophy we call epistemology; special librarianship, especially in its innovating relationship with Documentation, the forerunner of Information Science; academic librarianship, because it served independent study with a dimension in Britain that we had not yet approached in the U.S. and because the British university represented the birthplace of the Carlylian Library-College. But above all, my Fulbright had been awarded on the basis of a proposal to study British Reference comparatively.

British public librarianship immediately excited me. The 28 or 29 separate borough libraries of London impressed me with their advanced concept of cooperation. Even in 1951 they had mutually agreed on book selection specializations. Their liberal borrowing policies reenforced this specialization agreement. A registered borrower in any London Borough public library could borrow books not only in any other borough public library in London, but in any public library in the United Kingdom. Perhaps a little of this is coming into U.S. public library service in the 1970s.

Designation of the Chief Public Librarian as the Information Officer of a British city, borough, or town appeared to me then to be a concept beyond us in the U.S. The idea had come out of the 1940 blitz of Britain by the Luftwaffe. Frequently after a devastating bombing, families would become separated. The British government directed citizens to report to the Public Library headed by the Chief Information Officer to locate lost loved ones, or to obtain any other information. This official designation of the library as the community information center carried over after the war. It led to Britain's unique "Confidential Reference Service" described later.

There were other innovative excitements in my visits to public libraries, not only in London, but in Manchester, where unusual book selection had resulted in collections of literature any U.S. university would be proud to claim; in Leeds, where there were advanced examples of service to industry, as well as in Liverpool, Birmingham, Sheffield, Glasgow, and other cities which filled my notebook. If anything, the rural library service was even more trail blazing. I rode the bookmobile in Lancashire and York counties. The Mobile (Mobyle) service, they called it, and it reenforced the claim that no citizen of the United Kingdom had to walk as far as a mile for free public library service. Furthermore, the extension reference was something to conjure with. The bookmobile took all sorts of questions to the regional center, and brought answers back: on how to paint a chicken coop or care for animals, or cook a delicacy, or evaluate issues in the next election. Above all, I found the embryo for my idea of initiating as well as waiting for reference questions to be asked. I pondered the political and philosophical hazards. Planting the "right" questions in peoples' minds could approach brain washing. But permitting a national mind to lapse into inertia with no significant questions at all might make a people especially vulnerable to demagogic dictatorship. I thought British public librarianship was following the English democratic tradition: making sure that all sides of issues were thrust forcibly into the attention of an informed citizenship.

My concern about school librarianship was encouraged by the other Fulbrighter in librarianship to the U.K. that year, Mary Helen Mahar. Understanding Britain's elementary education posed a variation on the school librarianship theme, in which I searched for the independent study motif, so essential to both my Medium School and Library-College concepts. As for academic librarianship, I observed closely in the libraries of the University of London, first. From there to Oxford and Cambridge, I recall reflecting at Cambridge's library on how typical was their book count of the British modesty on all quantitative measures as contrasted to our American desire to be "bigger and better." When we have a set of 100 volumes of *Blackwoods*, for example, that goes into our reckoning of the size of our collection as 100 accessions. In the British university library, the entire set is *one* accession. But principally, I found reenforcement for my Library-College learning mode. At Oxford and Cambridge, at Edinburgh and Glasgow, and at other universities I discovered with delight that students did not speak, as we do in the U.S., of being enrolled in a class in French, or Economics, or Chemistry. In the British university it was always "He is *reading*, French; she is *reading* economics; they are *reading*, in chemistry, or philosophy, or even mathematics." And that is, of course, what we do in Library-College. We read in the *generic* book, which includes viewing and listening as well, and touching, smellin, tasting, and even extrasensing.

My special Librarianship involvement was extraordinary and

anticipatory. In Britain, I quickly found myself absorbed by ASLIB, and by the splinter of scientist—led Documentalists, of whom a leader was the chemist, Dr. Urquhart.

I restrained my evangelism in Britain, trying very hard to observe and listen, to compare approaches, on both sides of the Atlantic, to common professional problems. What excited me as a U.S. librarian was the extent to which the Urquhart group had anticipated by at least a decade our American urge to establish information networks—local, regional, state, national. In 1951, U.K. industrial and government libraries were already collectively indexing, abstracting, analyzing the scientific and technological literature, currently, not only in the English language, but in foreign languages, with special attention to the Russian. As I recall some of the cards and forms shown me there was a striking similarity to our KWIC and KWOC indexing, to SDI, to the concept of interest profiles, and to a systems approach. I discovered a keen attention to the U.S. abstracting services.

Stirred by the Urquhart group, I began to explore into fringes of our professional literature that somehow had escaped me both at Columbia and at Chicago. I discovered and began to study what I consider the classic of the whole Information Science movement, if not the Scripture —S.C. Bradford's *Documentation*. It opened a new horizon to the discipline on which I think our profession is based.

In all of the four library types, it can be seen I found exciting comparatives with our professional principle and practice. It was so tempting to follow every lure that led me off the main purpose of my Fulbright year—a comparative study of Reference—that I found myself again and again dragging my thoughts away from diversions to my dominating objective. But before I settle down to the Reference mission I must give some attention to the professional aspect which absorbed more of my life even than Reference, namely Library Education.

I early was attracted to the University of London School of Librarianship, located across the way from Chaucer House. I enrolled in lectures, visited others, observed in some, contributed to a few, first in the University of London, at the time the only professional school whose graduates were chartered upon graduation without examinations, as ALA, the preliminary to full FLA (Fellow in the Library Association). All other schools could only prepare their graduates for the Library Association professional examinations. Subsequently I was invited to lecture in many of the other schools—London Polytechnic, Manchester, Leeds, Liverpool, Glasgow, and others.

My associations with the faculty of the London school, however, became sentimentally close, probably because London residence permitted me to spend more time there than at the other schools. But also because I felt personally attracted to individual faculty members. Mary Piggott, in particular, meant so much to my wife and to me that I am afraid I cannot quite communicate in words those intangibles that exist beyond sensory experiences. Let me personally establish a comparative. Harriet Dorothea MacPherson had been my Columbia teacher and idol in cataloging and classification, because of her philosophical perspective. Mary was the first after her to challenge my thinking in both classification and bibliographic description. I was entranced by her London lectures, her gracious and kindly dialogues with students that were forever compelling the novitiates to explore excitedly.

I pondered over the contrast in Education for Librarianship as illustrated by our two professional associations. Of this I wrote for *Library Trends*. At the time I could not be other than a little troubled over the British accent on chartering the *individual*, and the American emphasis on accrediting the *school*. There were other differences, of course, but they all seem to emerge from the fundamental approach to professional qualification. I see the advantages and disadvantages of both ways and still favor the combination, if not the medicine and law tradition of separate license examination by each state, at least a comprehensive examination establishing the right to practice, jointly administered by the school and a federal or state agency.

My Fulbright was for the comparative study of Reference. I was aroused, from the start, by British approaches to service, measure, and materials. I have already paid tribute to rural Reference by way of the Mobile extension. This seemed to move ahead of us in *initiating* inquiry, rather than waiting for questions to be asked. I saw in British Reference a kind of prodding and provoking of citizens to be better informed—the foundation for building a stronger national mind.

I have further indicated my admiration for the British innovation of *confidential* Reference, which emerged from the London blitz. What I saw in Luton, Leeds and in other places, where an advanced confidential service was being nurtured was a small private room off the main Reference, frequently with direct street access, directed by a staff member who was a cross between two professionals—librarian and social worker. Citizens entered the private Reference door to consult on intimate questions. I recall the case of the mother of an unmarried pregnant daughter, when the "puritanethic" still shaped our mores. Not knowing where to turn for help, advice, or financial aid, the woman went to the Reference librarian, who not only provided a directory of agencies and individuals, but made preliminary contacts. Then there was the man with venereal disease, ashamed to go directly to a doctor or hospital. Another case involved a widow and her family facing eviction by a landlord. Fundamentally, the librarian served as liaison, revealing sources for help, and often providing intermediary services. The cases were treated confidentially in the highest medical and legal ethic. Even in my special capacity as a Fulbright Fellow the confidences I saw were cleared first with the inquirers involved.

I have also indicated the impact that Dr. Urquhart's Documentalists had made on my research reference outlook. Perhaps because of this early relation with an untraditional Information approach I began much earlier what I have referred to as my "modulation" from Basic Reference to Information Science. Even before Gerald Jahoda arrived to give us at Florida State the new look of Information Science, we had begun to orient our beginning Reference students in the University computer center, punching key words for retrieval. British innovations in 1951 unquestionably revolutionized my Reference thinking.

In November of 1951, I attended my first regional library association meeting, at Hove. I was entranced by the graciousness of the procedure; the organizational variations on our American vocabulary and committee activities. I had never before met a unit labelled "Working Party." This seemed so much more promising than "committee" although librarians in the U.K. have both. At the first general session of the regional meeting the two Fulbrighters were introduced. Each of us described our mission. When my turn came I must have bubbled over with excitement.

In less than three months of my U.K. Fulbright I had discovered so many library innovations that I could not contain my enthusiasm. These I conveyed comparatively, indicating where I thought British librarianship was ahead and where I thought I favored U.S. approaches. Among other things, I indicated that ALA's *SBB* and its committee concept were ahead of any Reference book reviewing or evaluation I had yet discovered in Britain. (I would maintain this even in the face of the

SBB criticism which has developed in *RQ* as I write this chapter.) But I also waxed enthusiastic over the confidential Reference, the Mobile service, the variations on the measure of reference as represented by the concept to multiply number of questions answered by the time required to answer each question.

When we returned from Hove I received an invitation from Percy Welsford to be present at the meeting of the Library Association Council. On the wall of my study is a framed photo of the Council that I treasure. There were approximately 50 members, only two of whom were women, which was quite representative, since in Britain, then, about 90% of all librarians were men. On the front row are seated, among others, the U.K. secretary of the Carnegie Corporation, Percy Welsford, Lionel McColvin, and the Honorary President, who under LA policy, was a distinguished non-librarian, every other year. That year the Honorary President was none other than Queen Elizabeth II's husband, Prince Philip, Duke of Edinburgh. My wife loves to show off the picture to my Florida State students with her words "among the boys." It so happens, I am seated in that picture on the front row, in the third chair from the Duke of Edinburgh's right.

I shall never forget the occasion. When the handsome Prince arrived in his chauffered Rolls-Royce, in front of Chaucer House, that early afternoon for the Council meeting, the University of London students lined the street across the way to welcome him. As he stepped out, tall, manly, and then quite young, the transformation on the faces, especially of the co-eds was photo-worthy. In chorus the students college-yelled, "Hip, Hip; Hip, Hip." He talked with me briefly and charmingly at the tea, afterwards, which Chaucer House had put on elaborately for the occasion. His interest in the United States generally, and in American librarianship particularly, was more than casual conversation making. He expressed an admiration for what the United States had done to extend, through its public library concept, education to all of the people.

After the Prince left, Percy Welsford invited me into his office for a grave conference. By the look on his serious face and the formal way in which he began to talk I feared I had been guilty of some breach of etiquette. I was electrified to exhilaration and moved to tears when he began, "You know the Library Association has a tradition in its annual conference of devoting a general session to what is called the Annual Lecture. We invite a distinguished speaker for this occasion. Always before he has come from outside the library profession. The Council has voted unanimously to invite you to deliver the Annual Lecture at the Bournemouth convention May 1952."

All through the exhilarating U.K. autumn the continent had lured. Again and again we were tempted to week-end in Paris, but I resisted. Two long vacations are in the British academic year—Christmas and Easter—a month each. I had planned the year so as to remain in Britain for the two big tasks I had set for myself. The first was the Fulbright study of Reference in U.K.; the second was a long overdue revision of *Basic Reference Books,* for ALA. Days I spent visiting, conferring, observing in libraries all over England and Wales, but not Scotland and Ireland, until after the Christmas holiday. Nights I worked away on my notes and wrote Basic Reference. I was pushing myself too hard, but refused to recognize it. Again and again the CBI fevers brought on the chills and spells of other-worldliness I simply could not describe even to myself, leave alone to the good Viennese doctor on whose panel we had been accepted.

When time came for the continental month at Christmas, I was much more fatigued than I would admit. We packed, and the anticipation kept my mind off my fatigue. We left the station, and the rhythm of the English train began; for me, *k-tivketock, k-ticketock*; for Gerry, *Tallahassee, Tallahassee*. The English countryside, neat and trim, looked for ever like a water color painting in pastel shades. I loved England more than ever as I contemplated a month's absence.

We arrived at Dover. Customs and immigration again. This time there was no Fulbright group to aid us. We were on our own. But it was fast and simple and soon we were on the channel boat. Hardly had we left dock then the little ship began to rock and roll. Fortunately, the crossing does not take too long. Even as the French coast came into sight, Gerry began to pick up psychological strength. My first sights on the Calais docks were two huge signs, one advertising *Compagnie Transatlatique,* the other *Wagons-Lits*. I had had a little French in high school and college and so I had some advantage over my wife who had taken only Spanish as her modern language. The train was different; the cars more the size of those in the U.S. and as a result the rhythm over the track ties forced me to find a new "beat." But Gerry still made *Tallahassee* out of the tock-tock, as we arrived in the Gare St Lazare.

Once settled we began our rubbernecking. We had already defied the sophisticates and begun our sightseeing with the overview provided by tourist bus. It enabled us to make our selections for concentrated attention in the following days. The Bibliotheque Nationale was number one, of course. I noted with pleasure that the Reference collection already had a set of *Collier's Encyclopedia,* and the catalog revealed an entry for *Basic Reference Books.* Sightseeing during the next few days included the usual stellar attractions—the Louvre, l'Opera, Notre Dame cathedral, Montmartre, and, of course, the famed Avenue des Champs Elysees, tree-lined and extraordinarily wide. Paris was a beautiful city to me from the start, but somehow I admired it with reservations. It never has, in my 14 visits to it, been able to approach my heart the way London does. I have tried to analyze it, and I can summarize my analysis by saying Paris is less *quiet,* than London, that is soulfully quiet.

Perhaps another forceful contrast is in what I titled a piece for the *London Observer.* "The Taste of Two Cities." I will disgust *haute cuisiniers* by admitting that Paris cooking has always been not only disappointing to me, but dangerously indigestible. I became so violently ill on our last day in Paris, this first visit, that we had to call a doctor to our hotel. Most distressing to me were the Paris sauces, usually of a sickly green color, that spoiled good *bifteck,* or fish, or even *poulet.* The heavy reliance on wine caused burning sensations in my stomach. I could never have made it but for the lucky discovery of Vichy water. In Paris, to order a meal without wine is to invite excommunication by the waiter. But Vichy water is acceptable, even with some compassion for the diner, the waiter assumes, must be suffering from a stomach ailment.

Despite the discomfort most French cooking in Paris restaurants seemed to cause me, I continued to be fascinated by the city, and a little startled by what appeared to be immodesties. Semi-exposed street urinals for males, on the streets, had been sufficiently celebrated on Broadway by the play *La Plume de Ma Tante.* But I had not expected that in the large public latrine for men, located near L'Opera and Thomas Cook, a woman attendant would pass behind the men while performing, collecting the one franc due for the privilege.

I have steadily inclined to the belief that the universe is the result of a struggle between chaos and order. Primitive Nature represents Chaos, and is the meaning of devil, Satan, Beelzebub. God is Order, contending constantly with the savagery and ugliness of a force so clumsy that it can be compared best with the "bull in the china shop."

What is beautiful about the human body is what the Spirit of God in the artist, the poet, the musician sees and communicates beautifully. When the artist celebrates the natural functions, when he insists on four-letter word honesty, when he attempts to justify his effort, if not his lucrative income, by declaring "this is life" he, in my opinion, takes the easy way out. He lets the easy chaos of primitive nature dominate the more difficult Order of God. It is why I believe "Once upon a time" and "They lived happily ever after" is more nearly the essence of art than "telling it like it is."

I do not agree with the French justification for exposed natural functions. It represents capitulation to the chaos of primitive nature, I do agree with the British modesty on these matters, at least before the advent of The Beatles. So, out of comparative librarianship, in France and in England, or out of the life that surrounds librarianship, came a re-enforcement of my speculations about the ultimates.

We left Paris by midnight train for Lausaane, Innsbruck, and the Alps. In the next few days we went into the mountains, rode the funicular, had hot tea on an outdoor veranda, from which we could watch the skiers. I was not sure then, even as I am not now, that I should ever care too much for this sport. I don't know just exactly why. There is no logic, probably, to my preferences for the various sports. I have always liked to walk, to swim, to play baseball. If I had been big enough, I believe I would have enjoyed playing football, my favorite spectator sport. I could enjoy sitting in a boat fishing, for the quiet and meditation, especially if I caught *no* fish. Indeed, I have admitted to those who know me, "If the fish won't bother me, I won't bother them." I simply could not bear to look into the eyes of a fish, gasping for breath, it seemed to me, as I pulled it in over the side of the boat. That is why I have been vehemently opposed to hunting. Indeed, it has troubled me that one of my close pacifist friends, who opposed killing in Vietnam, primarily of the North Vietnamese and Viet Cong by U.S. troops, still enjoys taking animal life with a gun. Still, my own inconsistency is apparent in my reluctance about skiing.

In the city of Innsbruck we toured the points of interest our guide books had alerted us to and visited the USIA library. The American librarian on duty talked with me at great length about the mission. I probed for the "equal footing" element, so important in my definition.

I believe she agreed with me that there was a danger in our intellectual warfare stance. We were set on overcoming, first of all, the residue of Hitler's previous Nazi totalitarianism. But we were more concerned with the current "Iron Curtain" threat, the tunneling Soviet communism, that was not so readily recognized as "aggression" not only by the nations brandishing "go home" and "ugly American," but more seriously, by the neo-liberal in the U.S., who increasingly seemed to me to have "courage" to expose only U.S. wrongs; never the wrongs of the other side.

The time came to leave Innsbruck and continue on our continental itinerary. Our destination was Firenze, and its art treasures. Perhaps the awe of my college history and literature classes combined with the strenuous sightseeing that drove us relentlessly not to miss anything contributed to an overwhelming fatigue. I conjured with the poetry of Dante and Petrarch at night. During the day we went from Uffizzi to Pitti Palace, across the Arno and back, viewing masterpieces, and art name-dropping in the juiciest American tourist fashion.

But I simply had to steal some hours from the art treasures for visits to two libraries. The first was the national library, in which I progressed poorly because of language difficulty. But in the USIA I had my eyes opened, not by the selection of materials as much as by the dynamics of the library mission there. To this day I recall the Italian shoemaker who had been reading up on American methods of shoe manufacture. His English was halting but understandable, and he seemed alert to responses. In a small nutshell, he had been communistically inclined. His conversation seemed to say, if they make shoes like that, have such wonderful facilities for their workers, how can America be as bad the communists say? (So this was how the USIA worked, I asked myself? And I told myself this is sensitive American librarianship. Don't knock the enemy that way, apparently, the enemy was denouncing the U.S. Instead, show the beautiful America; identify the good, and the solutions.)

And then to Rome. We had marked it as the epitome of our Italian itinerary, and it was. From the moment of our arrival we concluded we liked Rome better than Paris. Unaccountably the food suited our taste much more. I found myself enjoying wine in Rome the way I had been unable to in Paris. The pasta and the antipasta seduced me. They made soup, minestrone, and other kinds, too, to appeal to my great weakness. As others measure their dinner by the entree, usually by the quality of the steak, so I vote for or against the restaurant on the basis of their soup. I can eat soup at all three meals, and in between, and if nothing else is offered, I can be satisfied, provided the soup is good. Perhaps we were lucky. We had good soup everywhere we went in Rome, and the sightseeing was not as fatiguing.

So we began with the musts, after our rubberneck overviews of the city. We had placed St. Peter and the Vatican Library at the very top of our list, and there we went the second day. The panoramic view from the dome of the basilica in the Vatican framed a picture in my memory. In the Sistine Chapel we looked up at the Michelangelo paintings of scenes from the Old Testament, lying on our backs on a bench. Then there was the fabulous chamber containing his famous paintings of "The Last Judgement."

But my hunger was for the rare collection of manuscripts and books in the Vatican Library. The spirit of William Warner Bishop, I am sure, hovered over me as I examined not only such rarities as one of the early translations of the Old Testament (*codex Vaticanus*), but the evidences of his classification consultantship. Dr. Bishop had always to me been a professional name to worship. It was significant to me that he had advised Dewey over Library of Congress for the Vatican Library.

From Rome, with love in our hearts, we hurried away to the Rivieras—Italian, French, and Spanish. The guides pointed with pride to the oranges on trees that looked scraggly and pitiful to a couple of Floridians. We were not ugly Americans, though. We celebrated how good it was to be back in a home-like climate.

The Mediterranean holiday was a delightful close to our continental month. Tears welled in our eyes as we began to hear the distinctive *katicka-tock, katicka-tock,* of the British train. Still the same landscape painting, water color and pastel, of England. *Katicka-tock,* and soon the outskirts of the great city began to loom ahead. With each mile we felt the thrill of London surging through our arteries. We arrived. There was the black cab. We loaded in with our baggage and instead of having to make our direction known in broken French, German, Italian, or Spanish, we chuckled as the cabbie asked in crispy cockney, "Where to, Guvnor?"

We were at 20 York Street, and it was so good to be home again in London.

Between the Christmas and Easter holidays, I worked harder than ever. There were still very many libraries to visit in pursuit of my comparative Reference study. The British Information Service asked me to undertake a lecture tour in Scotland that would last ten days. I had to prepare, very carefully, my Annual Lecture to be delivered to the Library Association in Bournemouth in May. I was determined to devote some time each day to the new edition *of Basic Reference*. I could see that my wife was more concerned than ever with what she had begun to call my "work syndrome."

I began my library visits in Bristol. The public library added some new dimensions to my developing philosophy for Reference departments of promoting inquiry, instead of passively waiting for people to ask questions, sometimes insignificant to the individual as well as to society. There was something wrong about a Reference department that would not encourage inquiry. There could be no danger of brain washing under the British and American position of providing sources on all sides of issues. Bristol, and afterward Cardiff in Wales, thrust me along the path of promoting free inquiry.

Then I went back into the midlands. Henrik Jones had cleared the way for me at Manchester, at Liverpool, at Birmingham where the deputy librarian corrected my Alabama pronunciation of that city, (and ever since has put at the top of his letters to me, "NOT HAM"), to Leeds, Sheffield, York, Matlock, and to the two large county library services of Yorkshire and Lancashire. I was impressed all over again with the Mobyle service, the initiatory Reference, as I began to call it in my redeveloping definition of Reference as the *promotion of inquiry*. Each of the large city public and special libraries filled my notebooks with ideas. Manchester was undertaking a readers' guidance that accented a kind of intellectual responsibility for strengthening the local and national mind in a way I had never known at home. Because it was a kind of pulse feeling it is difficult to describe tangibly, except to say that the public library was continuously pushing citizens in dramatic ways to understand all sides of issues, to reform evils positively instead of forever excoriating scapegoats, to think rather than to march, to create prototype improvements.

At Leeds and Sheffield, the public libraries' relationships to the steel industry, and to the workers in it was extraordinary, both from the research and the popular approaches. At Leeds I saw the beginnings of the "retrieval" movement in some pre-computerized indexing of journals and scientific reports. For the workers, there was a sensitive range of reader guidances from vocational through recreational, social, and spiritual interest profiles. In those two cities especially the public librarian was living up to his responsibility as officially designated Public Information Officer by committing himself with earnestness to seeing that every man, woman, and child was the best informed citizen in the world.

In Manchester, Birmingham, Leeds, and other places that had them, I visited the so-called "red brick universities" and lectured where there were library schools. In these universities I saw a reenforcement for my belief in universal higher education, my fervent commitment to *college for all*, and my rejection of the "elite" position for a restricted definition of the term "liberal." In the library schools of Britain I found myself most frequently asked to lecture on three subjects: Reference, Book Selection, U.S. positions, particularly race relations, the views implied in a Southern accent. On the first, I began sharing my changing definition of Reference, crediting British librarianship with stimulating my thinking, but not holding it responsible for my heterodoxy. The dialogues that followed my lectures helped me to test my theories, and especially the hazard of brainwashing if the library undertook to initiate inquiries, or to "plant" questions in citizens' minds. In book selection we had some lively exchanges, especially on the "threat" of conformity which might be pressured by U.S. accents on "aids." It raised the question in my mind for the first time. Could our standard lists develop into a kind of procrustean bed? Could the institutional desire to be "accredited," to be ranked in the statistical upper half, force conformity to a kind of totalitarianism more subtle than Nazi Germany had ever been able to accomplish? I fought back, and some of the students and faculty were on my side.

The third subject was the one that the students enjoyed the most. I was flattered that they took their kid gloves off and went at me as the personification of race prejudice. I delayed acquainting them with my involvement in libraries for Blacks, and when I finally told them I was gratified to hear them say that they considered me a liberal, right from the start, and that that was why they tore into me so frankly. Over all they agreed with my One Race evangelism; my insistence that despite the injustices of the past, not only to the Blacks, and the Yellows, and the Reds, by the whites; by Christians to Jews; by Catholics to Protestants and Protestants to Catholics, reconciliation was much more important than vindictiveness. England could be very tolerant toward the Black as long as there were few Blacks. Let Blacks come to England in numbers and begin competing with whites for jobs and see what would happen. (Within one year after my last lecture at Polytechnic in London riots broke out in that neighborhood when immigration from Africa increased. I described Southeast United States as fairly as I could, displaying a large map I had brought with me. The segregation I described I denounced. But I matched it with descriptions of segregation in my North; and with comparables in India, and in other parts of the world. But I also described the regional graciousness of the South, its support of Britain in World War II when so much of the U.S. was still isolationist, the growing biracial movement, and apology among the thinking Southern white men and women. British student reaction was both exciting and comforting to me. They seemed to have comparatively more compassion than our student activists, more understanding that all of man is imperfect.

From the Red Brick Universities I returned to Oxford and Cambridge. Both inspired me on every visit. Despite my inclination to celebrate the curriculum they represented, my admiration for their organization and for their learning mode dominated my visits. The cluster college as an antidote to the growing impersonal education on our U.S. multiversity campuses came into my thinking from my Cambridge and Oxford visits. My Library-College organization concept was born during the academic year 1951/52 in England. Even more important was the documentation of the Carlyle idea in the mode of "reading" rather than enrolling in course subjects. At Cambridge and Oxford, especially, I saw the power of independent study in learning, of its essentiality to the student.

In February I began my 10-day lecture tour in Scotland for the British Information Service. It was an arrangement between Fulbright and the U.K. under which certain Fulbright Fellows were provided with additional travel money and compensation in return for prepared lectures on life in the United States. My subject was The Southeastern United States. I was determined to brave the challenges of labor and student liberals on the vulnerable question of race relations. I would denounce tolerance of segregation as vehemently as the most radical; but I would try to turn attention to positives, to how can we put integration into peoples' hearts instead of just on paper, by law, by compulsion. My first big test came in Glasgow, a radical miners' stronghold. The questions began on an ominously Marxist note. They were directed to the plight of the Glasgow laborer at six pounds a week. I had praised Churchill in my lecture, citing his half-American parentage. They respectfully demurred: "A great war leader, but he will never understand the working man's poverty." My lecture at the University of Glasgow was restricted to American librarianship. Again, comparatives in classification, in book selection, in Reference, dominated their questions; followed by queries about opportunities for library employment in the U.S., and comparative salaries. The lectures that followed in and around Edinburgh were less controversial. More questions were directed to cultural problems in America, relating to the arts, literature and the theatre. In one small Scottish village, a blind old gentleman asked simply and with childish sincerity, "We hear that gold grows on some trees in America. Is this so?"

I responded, "Yes, it is true in Florida. In the central part of our state you can see the gold growing on our orange trees." From the questions that followed about Florida's fabulous oranges I could tell the people liked my reponse to the little old blind man, and I allowed a little of my American braggadocio to come to the surface. I bragged about the statistics I had seen somewhere that Florida produced nearly 90% of all citrus in the U.S. and over 50% of all the citrus in the world.

The ten days, delightfully stimulating despite the numbing cold, at times, had a sad moment. On February 6, 1952 King George VI died in his sleep in Sandringham, England. I was scheduled to address a Rotary Club meeting not far from Edinburgh. I decided to keep my noonday commitment. There was a solemnity to the occasion that yet could not match an unaccountable despair I felt. I would have preferred not to speak at all. My heart was not in it, but I feared any undue sympathy expressed by an American might be doubted. I know I made a very perfunctory talk on Southeast United States, and these many years later I want to apologize to those good men who heard me out.

Perhaps two librarians from abroad will be illustrative of the comparative librarianship impact Chaucer House provided as a sort of mecca for world librarianship. One of these was Ranganathan who shook much of my classification perspective. As if to recall me to the other side, the Librarian of Congress, Luther Evans, came to Chaucer House. Percy Welsford entertained him sumptuously, and he asked Douglas Bryan and me, as two U.S. men librarians, to assist. After the Chaucer House reception, Douglas Bryant and I took Luther Evans to

20 York Street for a bit of additional refreshment, since there was still a considerable wait before Evans' plane took off for the U.S. Out of that long afternoon dialogue grew the idea for *Challenges to Librarianship,* published after my return to the U.S., a symposium to which Luther Evans contributed the essay "Challenge of Censorship."

The structure was to invite eight leaders in the library media field to spend a week in dialogue with students and faculty on "challenges," and to deliver one formal lecture to the university as a whole. The eight included Dan Lacy, then head of USIA, on "International Understanding," Fremont Rider, innovator, and inventor of Microcard, on the challenge of "Microphotography"; Charles Harvey Brown on the "Science" confrontation for a previously humanistically inclined profession; Edgar Dale, on "Audiovisual Media" to erase further "nonbook" divisiveness; Frances Henne to elevate "School" in the considerations of the other three library types; Louis Round Wilson, with some Chicago challenges to "Education for Librarianship"; Wayne Shirley on American library heritage and "ugliness"; and Luther Evans, to explode some leftist as well as rightist smugness about "censorship." The whole symposium idea was born in that afternoon with Luther Evans on 20 York Street, London. Verner Clapp, generously reviewing *Challenges to Librarianship* in the *Library Quarterly* (1954 p. 260-61) later said:

> Louis Shores is unfair to library journals. In this volume . . . he has taken the cream from a whole series of potential special issues . . . for every one of the essays condenses what is ordinarily found in a symposium and frequently exceeds in content the findings of an institute . . . returning in 1952 from a Fulbright year . . . brought back a fresh sense of the importance of librarianship . . . in a world in which a large proportion of mankind is still unfranchised of the good things in life, a world torn by a struggle for the minds of men . . . from his sense of the importance of library work stemmed this series of lectures. . . .

This sense resulted from my first full year of comparative librarianship in Europe and in the British Isles. That something had happened to me was confirmed when after my return from the Fulbright year Louis Round Wilson told my wife, "Louis has matured; he has an amazing world perspective now."

Travel enhanced this perspective, as we spent our Easter holiday on the Continent. It would be a somewhat longer sea voyage to The Hook of Holland. But our trip was not to be all holiday. At the request of the Italian government I was to lecture to three seminars, each one week in length, in Florence, Rome and Naples. Fulbright, Italy had arranged it with Fulbright France and Fulbright England. The Fulbrighter in France was old friend Leon Carnovsky; in Italy it was Anne Marinelli.

Our plans called for brief holidays in the Netherlands, Belgium, and Paris, where we would rendezvous with Leon, and then proceed to Florence for the first of the seminars.

On the Dutch train, solid, and more like U.S. trains, the *tickatock* was replaced by the French *tock-tock-tock*. The countryside confirmed what I had learned early in school geography. There was water everywhere, and land that seemed to be struggling to come to the surface. But the country side was so neatly cultivated, and everything looked as clean as I had been taught. We were in Amsterdam before we expected, and began to look out on armadas of bicycles. Everyone seemed to be pedaling, or parking a bicycle. We took our rubberneck in the afternoon, got our overview of the many museums, from Rembrandt House to the world famous Rijks. We looked at the large Royal Palace located on the Dam, the large square in the center of the city. The charm of the canals in the residential district, the information from the guide that the city was located on some 90 islands, supported the description of Amsterdam as the Venice of the north.

After two full days and nights in Amsterdam, where we enjoyed the cheese and fruit that went with every wholesomely delicious meal, we reboarded the train for Brussels, then to Paris and on to our real destination, Florence. The seminars I was going to conduct would include many students who spoke little or no English, and my Italian was limited to what a traveller necessarily picks up. Fortunately, Anne Marinelli secured for us a young Italian woman as interpreter and translator, who was just perfect, because she had recently married a GI who had returned to the U.S. She was waiting orders to follow him. She knew English very well, and especially the American idiom. Let me call her, here, Lucia, for the heroine of the great Italian novel, by Alessandro Manzoni (1785-1873), *I Promessi Sposi (The Betrothed)*.

To begin with Lucia translated into Italian my basic lectures on *Reference, The Education of an American Librarian*, and the *U.S. National*

Union Catalogue, the subject specified by them. Copies of my lectures were distributed to the seminar students in either English or Italian, as the individual student preferred. The pattern we followed was for me to read the English version while the students followed on the version they had selected. Informal interruption was encouraged. If the question was in English, I responded directly in English to those who understood. Lucia immediately translated both the question and the answer for the Italian students who knew no English. When the question was asked in Italian, Lucia translated in English to me, in which language I answered, and then she translated my answer in Italian. You can see that Lucia was earning her pay. From the dialogues that followed I could sense the sensitivity with which she was acting as my interpreter.

The seminars proved to be front line comparative librarianship. Excited comparisons among Italian, French, British and U.S. librarianships ensued. At least once or twice during each seminar all three U.S. lecturers were placed on the platform at the same time for excited free-for-alls.

There were political overtones, too. "Non-violent" violence against Americans was swelling. In the spring of 1952 Trieste was the cause of riots in Rome. One Wednesday of the Rome seminar week, violence erupted all along the route to my class. The wild-eyed demonstrators gathered in the streets with rocks and rifles, attacking anything American from the embassy to pedestrians who looked like they might be from the U.S.A. We had been advised not to walk, but to proceed by taxi from our hotel to the National Library where the seminars were being held.

As we approached the National library we saw fires in the distance and heard shots and an explosion. Italian Carabinieri (military police) in green uniforms were lined up along several streets through which our taxi driver drove cautiously, obviously taking a circuitous route to the National Library. Despite frantic maneuvering we were soon confronted by a wildly shouting disorganized mob that brought our cab to a sudden halt. Gerry and I were thrown to the floor of the cab by the sudden stop. The cab doors were opened and we were shouted at: "Go home, American pigs." Italian police came storming up and the wild ones tossed handbills into our cab. The driver struggled and maneuvered the cab free to a side street.

As we entered our seminar room several of the students surrounded us with deep concern. Lucia came forward with a wet cloth she used on my forehead. Unknown to me, I was bleeding. My wife's nylon hose had been torn and her leg was bruised. I suffered more from the suffering of my students than from any of the minor physical hurts that had been inflicted on us. They represented to me the thinking youth, the compassionate youth, more deeply concerned with reform of society than the demonstrating youth, usually dominated by leaders whose chronology reminds them regretfully they are no longer physically young.

We escaped personal injury throughout the ugly days that followed, both in Rome and in Naples, headquarters of the third seminar. Throughout it all Lucia was touchingly attached to us. On the night before the last seminar lecture I warned Lucia, at dinner, that I had a particularly difficult page of translation for her as my close. I worried her by employing Demi's favorite reference to "nuances." It will require your fine intelligence and skill in translation, I had tormented her. "Because of the nuances," I persisted, " a very sensitive translation will be required." To make it worse, I said I had not yet written it and would have to hand it to her just before the lecture, for spontaneous translation. She accepted the challenge, but told me later she worried about it all night. I was ashamed of myself, later.

The next day after I had finished the formal lecture on *Reference* and parried all of the questions and the dialogue, I handed Lucia the page to translate spontaneously, out loud, for the class. I thanked the class, expressed my deep appreciation for stimulating me to reexamine much of the principle and practice of American librarianship—what comparative librarianship is meant to do, basically—and then devoted a whole page to Lucia. "If these seminars have been at all successful a very large part of the success is due to our interpreter—a brilliant young woman, with an extraordinary mind, and rare feminine charm and beauty, etc. etc. . . ."

Lucia had not been prepared. She began translating, blushed, stopped embarrassed, and then pleaded, "No Signor—I can't go on praising myself. . . ." The students began to applaud, stamp their feet on the floor, and shout demands that she continue. There was no way out. Cruelly she had to read every word of praise about herself. And then the students presented her with a gift, hugged her, and would not let her go. With tears in her eyes, Lucia could find no words to thank all of us for the undeniable affection we all had for her.

The two months remaining pointed to Bournemouth. I worked and worked on my paper. Anita Hostetter at ALA headquarters helped me trace the history of the two associations' relations since 1876 and 1877, the respective founding dates. I wrote and rewrote the introduction in which I aimed to accomplish two purposes: (1) express my gratitude to the Library Association and to Fulbright for this wonderful opportunity to study comparative librarianship, and (2) to recap the several joint efforts of the two English-speaking library associations in their respective conferences and in such common enterprises as the cataloging code, and the Poole Index to periodicals. The main part of the "Lecture" was to be devoted to my mission—the study of comparative reference—out of which my philosophy of information was developing.

The big day arrived. We had planned to make the trip with Frank Francis. But on that day his son arrived from school to spend his spring vacation at home. I asked, with a prayer in my heart, if the young man could accompany us as our guests for the three-day conference. Parents and son were delighted, and we rode the train together from London to Bournemouth, and saw much of each other throughout the three days.

The Annual Lecture was scheduled for an afternoon general session. It was published in Library Association proceedings in its entirety, reprinted in several anthologies, and almost in its entirety in the Library *Journal*. I redefined Reference as *the promotion of free inquiry*, challenging both orthodox Reference and heterodox Documentation (just before it emerged as Information Science) to move from passive retrieval to active synthesis of the information most significant to mankind. In the area of Comparative Librarianship I acknowledged, not generally, as a guest might thank a host for hospitality, but specifically, six areas of librarianship in which I considered British dimensions superior to their counterparts in the United States. I did this fully aware of the fact that this admission would find its way across the Atlantic. Anticipating this, I began working on a paper or two which I might present through professional outlets in America.

I believe my essay was well received. Hard as I had worked on it I was still unsatisfied. Both in content and form I had not achieved that idea, that Platonic idea vested deep inside of each of us, I am mystically convinced. Why could I not realize my hope, I kept torturing myself before and after that Annual Lecture? Why could I not live up to that signal honor the Library Association had paid me by inviting me to be not only the first American, but the first librarian to deliver the Annual Lecture? Perhaps this essay was not as imperfect as I blamed myself. But then why, since I considered this one of my most philosophical tries of many efforts to write about the theory of information did librarians continue to insist there was no Reference philosophy?

Shortly after we returned from Bournemouth, a brilliant, crowning affair was held to honor the Fulbrighters. A magnificent reception and dinner at University College was capped by Anthony Eden's address for the occasion. The affair was formal, giving the ladies an opportunity to display their London style acquisitions, and the gentlemen their British variation on the dinner jacket.

From then until June I visited libraries and spoke at library schools more ardently than ever. I went back to the midlands, to Manchester and Leeds, to Preston and Derby. My final library school lecture was at Loughborough. And then the rounds of remorseful goodbyes began.

In the early morning at the railway station, Henrik Jones joined the Casanis, Mary Piggott and Ron Staveley to see us off. It was a touching farewell. It was all I could do to hide tears that kept trickling down my cheek despite every artifice to appear to be brushing an insect off or scratching an itch. We kissed and clasped hands. London had been home to us for nearly a year because of these good friends and many others. Do you wonder why I love England?

Our train *tickatocked* us to Liverpool, the Britannic's port of origin, ten days before our ship. Therefore, we ferried to Belfast. There was still some comparative librarianship to do. Our host was librarian Graneek of the University of Belfast, and his charming wife, who were to host us many years later in Australia. I made copious notes on library ways at both the University and in the public library. Although I heard of tensions I saw no violence in Belfast during our brief stay.

We said farewell to the charming Graneeks and proceeded by train across the border of Eire into Dublin. We had already visited several libraries and had arrived at Trinity to pay librarian's homage to the Book of Kells. All of my library school notes, and many references since to the illuminated manuscript of the Four Gospels, the work of the 7th or 8th century scribes in Columba's Monastery in Kells, Ireland, trooped through my memory. As we stood entranced before the glassed case exhibitions of some of those decorated initials, a young Irishman begged our pardon. "You are Doctor and Mrs. Shores, the American librarian? Would you grant me an interview for the *Irish Free Press*? As you know, this paper is Eamon di Valera's."

We went to a room which the library had provided. I had no idea that my philosophy on comparative librarianship and its potential for world understanding would appeal to a journalist. To my amazement it made front page next day, and my wife's observations were included in a rather lengthy article. At the conclusion of our interview, the young man said "You have provided me with a good big story, for which I shall be paid handsomely. May I do anything for you while you are in Dublin?"

I took advantage of the offer, spontaneously. "That pub to which James Joyce went often, could you take us there?"

"I'll do more than take you there. Will you be my guest for a bit of his favorite Irish whiskey?" We accepted. And when we arrived he insisted that I must sit in the chair that was James Joyce's very own. So we sat with our host and sipped James Joyce's favorite whiskey, and my thoughts went back to the heated dissents about the place of *Ulysses* in which Martin Ross and I indulged so often.

From Dublin we proceeded to Cork, by train, noting such romantic names, en route, as Kilkenny and Tipperary. The countryside was, indeed, very green and lovely. We were in Cork only briefly, for lunch, and a quick sightsee by taxi. A shuttle-like train picked us up about mid-afternoon and bounced us along to idyllic Cobh, where we had anchored on the America, last September.

Our hotel was almost exclusively for passengers awaiting their transatlantic liners. The next morning, all of us who had booked passage on the *Britannic* were picked up in a bus and driven to the dock. There we boarded a Cunard cutter and sailed out into the harbor. The open ocean framed by the verdant Irish hills looked like a landscape hung in an art gallery. For some reason, the Cunard representative attached himself to us for conversation and guide-like description of Cobh and the reason transatlantic liners anchored outside its harbor. It seems Cobh became Cork's harbor in the late 18th century as a supply base for the American and French revolutions. Suddenly, our guide broke off his history discourse with an exclamation and a pointing forefinger: "Thar she blows, with the bit in'er teeth. It was the *Britannic*, quickly and majestically parting the water before her with a white spray. She looked as beautiful as he declared, and all of the passengers admired with *ahs* and *aws*. When the *Britannic* had anchored we drew up alongside her, and she threw out her lines, to draw us to her. We all went to the tender topdeck, which barely reached to the lowest deck of the liner. And then we entered the huge city that was the *Britannic*.

The voyage was idyllic. A calm sea, beautifully sunny days, and romantic starlit nights sped us toward America. How awesome that word sounded to us, after a year's absence. I felt again the anticipation I had felt after that famous *Uncle Sugar Able* message had been received in the CBI war theatre. We over-ate from the tempting Cunard menu with its unlimited variety and quantity. In the morning we walked briskly around the deck, read, and I wrote, a little. But mostly I looked out at the sea and let it lull me into that library quiet that is a prelude to meditation, to asking the unanswered *Why* questions; the meaning of men and the universe, and what was God's purpose in so much imperfection. Or was He also struggling to bring some Order into a chaos into which He had been thrust? This is what the sea did to me always: confronted me with Ernest Haeckel's "riddle of the universe."

We supplemented the Fulbright allowance for passage from our personal funds to pay for first class. It was worth every dollar. Elegant evenings enabled Gerry to dress formally for dinner and dance with the new wardrobe she had acquired shopping in London, Paris and other European cities. We danced every night after dinner, and on board ship dancing was pleasant, especially because the ship's orchestra favored soft, melodic music, and many waltzes. Above all, we could stroll out on the deck, look out at an awesomely still dark sea, and up at a hauntingly restful star-filled sky. Nor did we dress the last night at sea. Every one had begun to pack for the long-awaited sight of America. Late that last night we saw the light from Montauk Point Lighthouse, on the extreme tip of Long Island. Naively, we thrilled, as we clasped hands.

The next morning was bustle and straining eyes for the first view of the skyline. When some one saw it a shout spread along the deck. Soon U.S. immigration and customs came up along side, boarded, and the process began in the cabin. We presented our papers and passports, filled in forms for customs. Then we returned to our posts on decks, watching the Statue of Liberty and the tallest skyscrapers increasingly distinguishing their individualities.

It was nearly a decade before I returned to Great Britain and visited London again. But in the interim, the fruits of my Fulbright year were put to professional use. I had made a report at Bournemouth, in June 1952. My acknowledgments of British library triumphs as I had observed them and as they had revolutionized my professional thinking had to be repeated when I returned home. I felt honor-bound to say as much to my American colleagues as I had conceded to our colleagues in England. This, it seemed to me, was the essence of Comparative Librarianship.

On an equal footing, I must describe what I had found superior in British librarianship, and especially those elements that had forced me to rethink positions we had assumed in the United States.

A series of opportunities developed. First, Luther Evans invited me to address the Library of Congress staff association at an elegant luncheon. I devoted myself to British Reference and Information innovations—those early forerunners of the Information Science movement to follow. I referred also to the public library dimensions of accessibility and cooperation through the regionals and National Central Library, to the city librarian as public information officer; and to the *mobyle* services. I could not avoid referring to the British commitment to Dewey and UDC classification, but I tried to do this as graciously as possible, without directly stating British librarianship's apparent rejection of Library of Congress classification.

To the American Library Association convention, that summer, I made my full report, at a general session, and before the Reference librarians. There was considerable dialogue, and some marked reluctance to acknowledge British superiority in the six areas I enumerated. Strongest dissent was expressed in the classification area, especially by librarians who had recently adopted or were in the process of adopting LC. I enjoyed most the dialogue opportunity offered by the ALA for Robert Collison to indicate "If I Were An American Librarian" and for me to respond "If I Were A British Librarian." The two essays were published in the *ALA Bulletin*. I consider Bob Collison one of the more original, provocative and sparkling minds in our profession. It was a real accomplishment for Comparative Librarianship when UCLA added him to its faculty, as it was when Clem Harrison joined, first, the Illinois faculty, and then Pittsburgh, and finally Dalhousie in Canada.

For the next eight years I principled and practiced Comparative Librarianship, chiefly at home, in Organization Librarian; in writing and publishing and editing; and above all, in library education. I returned to the second year of my term as president on the nine-state Southeastern Library Association, and from my presidential address on, an international tone, with a British accent was evident. My immediately following presidency of the Florida Library Association emulated the Comparative accent, not only with librarianship abroad, but among the four library types, in a first-ever, certainly for our state association, of intermingling problems. At the general session, a representative leader of each type undertook to compare with the other three types on solutions to professional problems. This was followed by cross-dialoging at sectional meetings. It excited me to hear school librarians making suggestions to Special Librarians, and vice versa; to listen to public and academic librarians undertaking to erect bridges between local colleges and the city library. This, too, was a dimension of Comparative Librarianship that must not be blinded out by the glamour of libraries abroad.

But above all, Comparative Librarianship entered the life blood of our education for librarianship at Florida State. Perhaps the most dramatic how was our world wide refresher institute for the Strategic Air Command. Much more fundamental was the day to day approach with our increasing number of students from Latin America, from Asia, Africa, Europe and even Australia. We had some extraordinary students from Thailand, especially after Ruth Rockwood of our faculty returned from her Fulbright year there. But the students from Taiwan, India, Pakistan, Japan, Egypt, and elsewhere in Asia were equally stimulating. Then came a group from Central and South America. All of them became affectionately devoted to the School, I believe, because of our "equal footing" approach to Comparative Librarianship.

Several of my most deep thinking students from Taiwan and Japan have reminded me again and again of my rather evangelistic appeals to them. "You are here to study American library methods, of course. But please challenge everything we do and teach. Ask yourselves, always, what do they do better in American libraries than we do in ours? But also, help U.S. librarianship by asking What do we do better in our country than they do in the U.S.? You do somethings better, I know. I have always learned new and better ways when I have gone abroad. That proves you do something better than we do in the U.S."

Perhaps our dramatic triumphs for Comparative Librarianship in the School were published in the volume *Challenges to Librarianship*. The symposium evidenced comparatives at home and abroad, especially in the attention to intellectual warfare, and in the format comparative of audiovisual media and microforms; of the two cultures; and of school to the other three library types.

I remained fairly close to home until the end of the decade, except for some holiday travel. And then at the close of my year and a half leave to complete the major revision of *Collier's Encyclopedia*, I was rewarded with an assignment to Britain. For the company, my major purpose was to study, comparatively, British encyclopedia production and distribution. I would do more, I vowed, for Comparative Librarianship between the two English-speaking Nations.

At my request, sea, rather than air travel, was authorized. The *Britannic*, our favorite ship, had already been decommissoned. I looked over the Cunard sailings for early June and decided the two-class *Sylvania* was most nearly comparable. For the return, I selected the *Queen Elizabeth* because I thought my wife would enjoy this magnificent ship. The company's generosity was touching. When I arrived at my desk the next morning my secretary handed me a big brown envelope containing the round trip tickets for both my wife and me. The accommodations were beyond our means. The Chairman of the Board soon convinced me that we would be representing the company.

Despite the anticipation of our return to the England we loved so much, there was sadness in our eyes as we looked at each other. It is not without pain to leave home. I write this and sense such sentiment is almost unacceptable in our day. Despite the claims of some activists and their defenders that they are less materialistic than the establishment against which they protest, I find the essence of my dissent with both in their very lack of sentimentality. Neither side appears to have the courage to dream it like it should be instead of forever insisting on "telling it like it is." I find nothing like the jubilation in a rock festival that I find in a transatlantic sailing.

I was enjoying the sea. Day and night I looked out and gained comfort about life's riddles. Out there among those little waves were the answers, if I could but read them, to what is the meaning of life, of death, of man and his struggle for survival. The sea did that for me. It pulled me out of this temporal world and back to where we all came from. For perspective on anything there was nothing like an ocean.

We arrived at Euston station. Santy and Joan were waiting for us. He had his monocle on, and was leaning on his cane. Joan kissed us, in turn. Santy said his familiar "keeshes" and hugged us both. It had been eight years since we had seen each other. But we had never stopped writing. All of us were looking hard to discover what age had done. The women began talking about weight. Joan was noticeably heavier. She said, "I could easily slim back to normal in a fortnight. The problem is finding the fortnight." How much that sounded like Joan, and her wonderful sense of humor, about her wooden limb, and about life in general.

We proceeded by cab to the hotel room we had arranged for. And then Santy went to work on finding us permanent quarters. He found a beautiful flat for us, on Ennismore Place, near the Prince's Gate and Kensington Gardens. We moved in on Sunday morning. Joan and Santy helped us carry things in, and then they departed for an appointment. As we began unpacking we took time to admire the surroundings. About midmorning, that Sunday, we noted that the back flat was also being moved into, by a tall, elderly gentleman. My wife remarked immediately: "He looks like Aldous Huxley." I busied myself unpacking, mostly books, including a set of *Collier's Encyclopedia* that the Company had sent ahead for me. Then there was a knock at our door. The tall gentleman who was to be our neighbor said apologetically, "I am sorry to disturb you. My portable typewriter appears to have been damaged in transit. Would you know anything about the mechanism?"

I volunteered that my wife had taught typing and knew quite a bit about typewriters. We accompanied him to his flat and my wife worked on his typewriter. It was beyond repair. In the process of manipulating it she looked up at him and asked, directly "Are you Aldous Huxley."

"Yes, madame."

I was as excited as she. We had read *Brave New World*, together. Later, we had puzzled over *Point Counterpoint* and *Eyeless in Gaza*. He told us, quickly, that he had business in London for about four weeks; after that he would meet his wife in Switzerland, and together they would proceed to an international conference in Nice. We learned of the devastating destruction of his library in the Los Angeles fire, some time back; that he was working on a new novel; and that the lack of a typewriter would prevent him from writing that day. Immediately, I offered my portable. Old as it is, I will not part with it, as much because part of *The Island* was typed on it by Aldous Huxley, as because some of my own evangelisms were wrung out on its keys. Before we left, my wife and I invited him to breakfast the next morning. He accepted, and said he had a twelve o'clock luncheon in Piccadilly.

Although he came to breakfast at eight in the morning, he jumped up late for his luncheon engagement. The reason for the four-hour conversation came out of *Collier's Encyclopedia*. He noticed the set on our shelves, and I asked him if he would like to read what Purdue's English professor Harold Watts had written. Modestly, Huxley said "not now." But I persisted: "He refers to your mystic interests, and suggests you have been involved in study of extrasensory perception."

"As a mater of fact," he commented," the international conference I mentioned I was going to in Nice is on psychics. Then followed an excited exchange of incidents that could be described as supernatural. They involved telepathy, clairvoyance, precognition. I related some of my war happenings that underlined for me that I had not been born into this world to shift for myself. I recall I said to Aldous Huxley that I did not see how any of us could live in the face of the hazards that confront us daily, without some supernatural help. During the next four weeks we saw quite a bit of our famous neighbor.

On several occasions we rode the red double decker bus to Piccadilly Circus together. We noted with concern that Huxley's vision was failing, even more that we had believed. He had difficulty seeing the bottom step of the bus, and we tried, as inauspiciously as possible, to guide him. We had read about his refusal to wear glasses; his commitment to eye exercises. Indeed, the London newspapers had been full of feature stories about the Surrey boy who had come home—Aldous Huxley.

In the course of our many conversations, breakfasts, and excursions into the city, we found out about his experiments with various mushrooms, and with drugs that anticipated the rage over LSD that came somewhat later. One day we told him we had been invited by Christine Foyle to one of her literary luncheons at which brother Julian Huxley was the speaker. Although he had high regard for the famous scientist who was his brother, I discovered in some of his observations considerable doubt about science's method as an approach to reality.

From Aldous Huxley I gained encouragement and incentive to pursue a bibliographic undertaking I had long contemplated; to search the literature of the occult, of science fiction, of world religions and philosophy, for some overlooked clues to the riddle of the universe. Particularly, I wanted to discover some out-of-the-way theories about the meaning of death; the possibility that somewhere, sometime in the history of earth someone had discovered some miracle means to health, to beginnings and ends of this world, to the possibility of transmigration of human souls and even bodies to other planets, after death. Perhaps somewhere in obscure verse a poet had in a flash opened the way to some new understanding of the meaning of existence. At least, you can see what was the subject that engaged us in such animated conversation with Aldous Huxley for four weeks in the summer of 1961.

When the four weeks were over, he headed for reunion with his wife in Switzerland. We drove off in our rented Hillman for a holiday in the

Midlands. We had chosen a resort at Matlock Bath. Nearby was the city of Matlock, itself; some 15 miles south, the cities of Derby and Nottingham. Manchester and Liverpool were hardly 50 miles northwest. We were surrounded by history, and we did, indeed put in solid afternoons sightseeing at places like Chatsworth House, country estate of the dukes of Devonshire, with its spectacular cascades and fountains, often compared to Versailles.

At Matlock Bath we secured a spacious room looking out on the pool, in the rather old fashioned English hotel. Once we tried to swim, but despite their effort to heat the water the outside air was paralyzingly cold for us. We marvelled at the sturdy English youngsters cavorting in the water almost all day long.

The holiday at Matlock provided me with some hours each day to go over my notes on the past four weeks of the second London visit. Mostly they were concerned with comparative encyclopedias. I had begun a systematic study of British encyclopedia production and distribution, as much for myself as for the company. In turn, I had visited the editorial offices of the major publishers. It was quite apparent that some developments had been comparable on both sides of the Atlantic. Distribution in Britain as in the U.S. was largely by subscription, that is door to door sale, although more sets were sold through the trade over there than here. They had adopted the same installment buying tactics, which they called "hire-purchase" or "never-never buying."

Editorially, our biggest difference was on the matter of encyclopedia revision. We in the U.S. had committed ourselves to "continous revision" a term that had been defined jointly by librarians and editors as constituting from 5 percent to 20 percent text revision each year, as distinguished from "periodic" revision which represented a "refolioing" and complete overhaul of the text and illustrations, perhaps every decade or so. British editors did not approve of the "continuous" concept, and favored the periodic revision. I suspect part of this was due to their smaller sales and the consequent lack of resources to revise continuously and put out a new printing each year.

There were some challenging exchanges about arrangement and indexing, especially, with that distinguished editor of *Chambers's*, with whom I had lunch. We exchanged mutual admirations of Lavinia Dudley, another great lady editor in chief, and her creative work with *Encyclopedia Americana*. Then we proceeded to a philosophical consideration of the short versus long article—what size chunks of knowledge deserved separate article treatment in encylopedias. Which led to classified versus alphabetic indexing. She understood better than some of my editorial colleagues in the States the relationship between each kind of indexing and article size. Consequently, *Chambers's* has had my admiration all of these years because it offers both classified and alphabetic indexes.

There were many other conferences and visits to editorial offices. Perhaps the one that deserves special mention here is the one with John Armitage, London editor of the *Britannica*. My long association with Walter Yust, Jack Dodge, and John Rowe, in the Chicago headquarters, opened the door to the London office. We engaged in a long comparative encyclopedia conversation, first, and then moved to comparative education, British versus American, from elementary through secondary and higher. John Armitage had written a little book, *Our Children's Education*. (Pall Mall Press, 1960, 96 pages, hard covers), a copy of which he kindly autographed for me. Using the device of letter writing to an American friend who is mystified by the British school system, he succeeds better than any writer I know in unravelling the mystery of the so-called "Eleven-Plus" examination which decided irrevocably the future of the child. Despite his generosity toward American education, I doubt that we have yet bridged the gap between so-called "liberal" and so-called "vocational" education. Indeed, even in our specialized professional and lay educations for libraries, we have some irrevocable barriers, at times, that were responsible for my heart breaking articulation crusade, as I shall indicate in the library education chapter.

As I recapitulated these first four weeks of our return to Britain I marvelled at how much we had accomplished. Besides my comparatives in encyclopedics, which might be considered a part of comparative librarianship, I had been able to continue my Fulbright mission of comparative reference. Before leaving the U.S. I had accepted the chairmanship of an ALA committee to study the "measure" of Reference—to develop some standards for evaluating Reference service in various types of libraries. Concurrently, and independently, the British Library Association had activated a counterpart. Dr. A.J. Walford, editor of the *Guide to Reference Materials* had been named chairman, and at his invitation, I attended their Saturday session in Chaucer House. It was an exciting meeting because their trends of thought were so much like what we had gone through in our American committee.

For example, they, like us, had separated the tangible measures of materials from the intangibles of service. But whereas we had persisted in our determination to measure the inquiries qualitatively, but without satisfaction, they shifted their attention to quantitative standards for stock, personnel, quarters, finance, etc., on the assumption that these might provide an index to Reference quality. They had already published their pamphlet on *Reference Book Stock*. The dialogues in which I had engaged with Dr. Walford and committee member had proved to be comparative librarianship at its best.

7. Mission Extraordinary

Seventy-six extraordinary days in the fall of 1964 challenged my developing theory of Comparative Librarianship. A long distance phone call from New York started it. Ever since I had begun designing *Collier's Encyclopedia* in 1946, one of my most compelling incentives had been to produce a summary of the knowledge most significant to mankind that was truly international in scope and treatment. I had urged this on the publishers from the start. But I was not unaware of the economic necessity to favor the nation of imprint. All encyclopedias tended to be national. We had been able to give more attention to other nations than most encyclopedias in the English language. But as long as our sales were almost exclusively in the U.S. and Canada, we were bound to allot more space and resources to the interests of the consumers in these two nations.

Steadily, *CE* sales spread all over the world. By 1964, the publishers felt there were at least nine nations to which we should give more coverage, because of increasing sales. The telephone call suggested that I might visit these nations to have the coverage for them reviewed, and perhaps to add some editorial advisers. Needless to say, I was thrilled at the opportunity. The nine nations to be visited were (1) United Kingdom, (2) Denmark, (3) Germany, (4) France, (5) Italy, (6) South Africa, (7) Australia, (8) Philippines, and (9) Japan. The Publisher decided to mark the occasions of the visit to each country with a presentation of the original manuscripts of all the articles in the Encyclopedia pertaining to that country, for their national archives. The manuscripts were handsomely bound in hand-tooled leather, with an illuminated manuscript title page, silk end papers, and gracious dedication. Each presentation was to be made at a modest ceremony that would express cordial relations between each nation and the United States. The mission had the blessings of the U.S. State Department.

For my own part, I was most anxious to prove a good will ambassador; to enlist at least one librarian adviser from each nation; and, perhaps, to contribute to Comparative Librarianship by exchanging with librarians abroad. The kickoff was to be at the United Nations' Dag Hammerskjold Library, where I was to present the first of the bound manuscript volumes of the articles relating to the UN. I called on the new director, who had just taken office. Lev Vladimirov was the first UN library director to come from a so-called "Iron Curtain" country. He was director of the University of Wilna in Lithuania. I had written to him in advance inviting him and Mrs. Vladimirov to have dinner with us in our hotel. I had known or met all of the heads of the UN library from the very beginning, because the first head was my Columbia classmate from Denmark—Sigurd Hartz Rasmussen.

We had dinner at our hotel, several nights before the scheduled UN luncheon. It was a charming evening. Mrs. Vladimirov's English is perfect and elegant. Her husband's is adequate and gracious. While the ladies discussed comparative home making, Lev Vladimirov and I plunged into comparative librarianship, enthusiastically. I learned that the University of Wilna had well over two million accessions; that it was located only 800 kilometres from Moscow; that he went in to that city at least once a month. How much we librarians spoke a universal language was amusingly illustrated when in almost the exact American library words he observed, "I wish Kruschev were more library-minded." After dinner we strolled up Fifth Avenue, the ladies stopping to look at styles in the windows of such stores as B. Altman, Arnold Constable, Lord and Taylor. The husbands conversed absorbedly in comparative library classifications. Again a preference for Dewey was expressed by a librarian from abroad. For reasons quite logical, librarians abroad find Library of Congress classification cumbersome and awkward, if not completely inadequate because of the over-accent on U.S. history.

The UN luncheon was a reflection of the host's graciousness. Librarians and publishers of the New York area had come from as far away as New Haven and Philadelphia. I appreciated so much the presence of John Ottemiller of Yale, Bill Dix of Princeton, and so many from the metropolitan libraries.

The next day we began our world flight. London again, still my sentimentally favorite city of the world, and all that the city had meant in our life was just ahead. We were descending, and my heart was thumping, not over the descent, because flying like sailing has never caused me any discomfort; but because I knew the Casanis would be waiting for us there. We had asked Sir Frank Francis and Lady Kitty to have lunch with us before they departed for Rome and the international librarians conference, and they looked as young as always. Every one ordered from the lunch menu. I had to be last so that I might ask the waiter for something special.

"I know it is past breakfast time. Would you forgive me if I asked for a pair of kippers?" The waiter's eyes sparkled with appreciation. "Right-oh."

In London, I began the two serious aspects of my mission. For the publisher my purpose was to recruit additional library advisers for our international board. I admired Dr. A. J. Walford, in the Ministry of Defense, whose monumental *Guide to Reference Materials,* compiled by a group of distinguished librarians and scholars in other disciplines, under his direction, had done so much to establish the literature of Reference. Again and again my students at Florida State had profited from comparing the annotations in Walford with the U.S. *Guide to Reference Books,* started by Kroger, continued by Mudge, and Constance Winchell. Dr. Walford accepted our invitation.

It was now necessary to arrange for the deposit of the handsomely bound volume of manuscripts of the articles in *Collier's Encyclopedia* relating to the United Kingdom. After explorations through our Embassy's cultural relations department, it was decided to deposit this volume in the library of the House of Lords. With these two company missions fulfilled I turned to my personal quest in Comparative Librarianship.

The mystique persisted. History will record that the year 1964 marked the beginning of a crescendo in noise and violence. The Vietnam conflict was accelerating; Red China detonated its first nuclear bomb. On our side of the Iron Curtain, physical communication took the form of demonstrations, marches, picketings, sit-ins, bombings and bomb scares.

Quiet World / Odysseys

Everywhere noise and violence appeared to dominate, and intellectuals who at one time might be cited as liberals were justifying demonstrations as necessary to accomplish reform. Still unconvinced that truth and beauty could result from these noisy efforts, and certain that men's noblest creations had resulted in tranquility, I determined to discover whether there was still some quiet, deep thought in the world. My only hope to find it was in the libraries of the nine nations I was scheduled to visit.

The London days were over too soon and we were aboard a flight for our next stop—Copenhagen. On the bus from the airport to the Royal Hotel, we sat beside a Swedish father and his little boy. Both spoke English with almost no accent. I asked him, half-seriously, "Do you have difficulty switching to Danish?" He responded in the same light vein, "Oh, no. Danish is just a corrupt Swedish." Our hotel window looked out over the Tivoli Gardens which was in its last week before closing for the winter.

As was our custom we overviewed the city by Rubberneck. The guide had the profession's usual stock of humor. He pointed out, for example, that the embassies of the U.S. and the USSR were separated by a graveyard. There was much merriment over the mermaid statue which had gained world-wide publicity over losing her head and being otherwise ravished by some "nonviolent" youth. The city sights were lovely and relaxing and I caught some of the liberal spirit I had gleaned from some of my Danish classmates in graduate school at Columbia and Chicago.

I struggled philosophically again over the conflict about sex. So many of my liberated friends in the U.S. had cited Denmark's "sensible" attitude toward pornography and extramarital relations. There was not time to verify the universality of permissiveness in the Copenhagen mores. The newstands had their share of salaciousness, but it did not seem to me that it was more extreme than the displays in Paris, or New York, or even in smaller cities like Tallahassee. I had been told by one or two of the male graduate students from Denmark that when a girl accepted an invitation to eat it meant also to sleep. Again and again I had asked myself, as far back as puberty, and perhaps before, should not man be as free as the animals? And then I would counter-inquire, what had impelled man toward puritanism, to disciplining himself in a way the animals apparently did not. I had found one could not pursue this philosophical trend too far, either because that aspect of sex would produce no best sellers, or because suspicion of abnormality might arise. Copenhagen, for some reason, compelled more introspection. I discovered no evidence of greater or less "liberality" on sex in Copenhagen.

My principal interest soon dominated when we made our first visit to the Royal Library. I had hoped to meet and talk with librarian Kierkegaard, but he was in Rome. Nevertheless, he had made most thoughtful provision for my visit. We were welcomed by his staff and Deputy. The tiers of stacks with the cracks between the marble and the steel, enabling one to peer many floors below, intrigued my wife, and then frightened her when her high heel got caught. She was fascinated when, instead of the usual mid-morning coffee, there was a delicate glass of sherry. We talked comparative librarianship with members of the staff, and were delighted to learn that the Royal Library wanted the volume of manuscripts relating to Denmark.

The next day I met with Axel Andersen of the faculty of the Royal Library School. We had lunch at Tivoli Gardens first; a delicious one, because Danish cuisine suits my gustatory biases. Their soups are quite superior to my partiality for that part of any meal. I never tasted a filet mignon more delicately cooked. The Royal Library School was a revelation in comparative library education. As late as 1964, no U.S. school of librarianship had as yet a separate building. But the Danish school had its own four-story structure, much more modern and better equipped than the London school's old, separate building, which had reminded me somewhat of the Columbia East Hall in which I had earned my BS in LS. Their curriculum, too, revealed an advanced attention to audiovisuals, as well as to paleography, at the other end. Professor Andersen accepted the invitation to join our international library advisory board, and so the mission in two of the nine nations had gone well.

Macmillan's West Germany *Collier's* manager, Tag Pedersen, was at the Frankfurt airport to greet us as we stepped off our plane. Once settled, luggage unpacked, I performed my first duty—taping for broadcast, on the Hesse radio station, the nature of my good-will mission. The radio announcer had brought his wife, who spoke a bit better English than her husband. After the taping, the five of us went down to dinner and a humorous, relaxed evening. German food delights us always and the beer is excellent.

Quiet World / Odysseys

After dinner my wife tried to explain to the accommodating German waiter that she liked to have a thermos of coffee in her room, and would he please rinse the bottle with hot water first. The waiter didn't understand. Every one tried to translate into mixed English-German. To clinch the confusion the radio announcer's wife shouted in German, "Rinse *without* water." The poor waiter's bewilderment was expressed "In God's name, how without water."

The manuscript volume ceremony the next day was simple and with a sincere touch of affection. Perhaps in a small way we had contributed to understanding between our nations. I discovered also librarianship's Berlin Wall. West German librarians had stopped meeting with East German librarians because the latter took every opportunity to propagandize. I was told, however, that when Russian librarians participated they were much more circumspect and stuck to professional dialogue. I became aware of the two great bibliographies—*Deutsches Bibliographie* for West Germany and *Deutsches Bucherverzeichnis* for East Germany.

The public library visit startled me. Looking back I recognize an embryo "open university" in their 1960s efforts to provide adult education for all of the people through guided independent study. At the university library I gained through library education and library architecture comparatives. They had anticipated our later paraprofessional recognition by activating a junior college education that prepared for these positions. Instead of capitulating to the modular trend that had begun to dominate U.S. library building, the West Germans had compromised in their new university library by constructing fixed stacks and modular reading space. They also introduced me to a flooring made in Paris that seemed to combine the economy and suitability of all U.S. floorings.

Paris was next. On the first full day I fulfilled my two major items of business for the company. First came the Bibliotheque Nationale. The director was in Rome and I sought out M. Marcel Thomas, director of the Manuscript Division. As we entered the main reading room I noted with satisfaction that the very striking black, red and gold bindings of our 24-volume encyclopedia stood out on the shelves. M. Thomas and I settled down to a tour of the great library. He is a tremendous scholar, with a command of English so elegant that it was inspiring to dialog with him on many subjects. In the course of the day's conversations he accepted the bound volume of manuscripts relating to France for inclusion in the Bibliotheque Nationale. When, later, he also accepted my invitation to join the Encyclopedia's International Advisory Board I was overjoyed.

Paris had been kind to us on this visit. We left with nostalgia, arriving in Rome mid-Saturday afternoon September 19. Collier manager Jay was at the air terminal to meet us. The Mediterranean Hotel, at which he had booked us, was comfortable European, with old fashioned rooms that were clean and convenient. Dining was gracious, and at the very first dinner I experienced again my decided preference for Roman over Parisian cuisine. After dinner we visited the railroad exhibition at the station nearby, showing the evolution of locomotives and passenger car accommodations.

The treat came at midnight, when Jay decided to hire a horse and carriage for a tour of the city. It was one of those soft, romantic nights—starlit sky and pleasantly warm weather. In the many lovely parks, lovers were embracing on benches. Over the lava-paved Appian Way the horse's hoof beats tripped out an accompaniment to the dialogue in Italian Jay was carrying on with the driver, mostly arguing over price and direction. We stopped near the Trevi Fountain and got out for another nostalgic look. Everywhere history awed us: the ruins of the Forum Romanum and Colosseum; the Spanish steps banked by shrubbery and flowers rising from Piazza di Spagna to Trinita di Monti; the Church of the Trinity built in 1495 by Charles VIII of France. It was just four in the morning when we finally pulled up in front of the Mediterraneo. The carriage overview had surpassed our usual rubberneck beginning.

Sunday was a good day to rest, to rent a typewriter for typing up my report for the publisher. And then on Monday the main business began. Accompanied by Jay we went to the U.S. Embassy and met our very cultured and articulate cultural affairs attache. He had already arranged for the presentation of the bound volume of manuscripts to the National Library. He introduced us to the USIA librarian, Jane Fairweather, jolly and quick at repartee with Jay, whom she had met previously. I discovered another unexpected association with Jane. She had served in the Army Air Force with my general—Ivan Farman. We talked about him with enthusiasm; we both loved him. She quoted my dedication in *Highways in the Sky*: "To the most underrated general of World War II." She looked at me with that twinkle in her eye: "How true. I used to listen to the top brass, decorated with oodles of salad say absolutely nothing, pontifically in stentorian voices that came from big mouths at least six feet high. Then Ivan would get up, all five feet six of him, and in a few well chosen words sketch the whole operation so clearly that there was nothing for the big boys to do but say, 'Proceed, Ivan.' "

In Reference Literature the four great bibliographic names were, then, Constance Winchell in the U.S., A. J. Walford in the UK, Louise-Noelle Malclès in France, and Olga Pinto in Italy. I had been unable to see Malclès in Paris, despite the effort in my behalf of both the Ecole and Marcel Thomas, because she was not in the city. But Dr. Pinto graciously accepted an invitation to have dinner with us in our hotel. Jane Fairweather and Jay joined us. It was a delightful evening. The Mediterraneo set a sumptuous table for us and the conversation was unrestrainedly jolly, thanks to Jane's continuous probing into Jay's "business engagement" at eleven that night. Under her persistent, suggestive allusions to Italian men's business engagements with women not their wives, Jay finally broke down and admitted he had met her—the business engagement—while sitting in the park doing what many Italian men and women do—looking around for prospects of the opposite sex.

When the jollity was over, Dr. Pinto and I settled down to talk Reference. Jane joined us in a separate conversation over after-dinner coffee, while Jay and my wife strolled around the lobby looking at displays. Dr. Pinto's English is impeccable; her knowledge of the literature of Reference wide and profound. I was captivated by her charm and graciousness, her kindly Christian consideration for people. I consider her one of the great librarians I have known. I was overjoyed when she accepted my invitation to join the Encyclopedia's International Advisory Board.

The Rome part of the world mission had been gratifyingly successful. Ahead was the most intriguing part of the entire around-the-globe assignment—Africa, Australia, and Asia. We were booked for an all night and forenoon flight which would take us to Athens, for a brief stop, and then on to Nairobi, Kenya. From there we were scheduled to proceed to Salisbury, Rhodesia, where I was committed to address an all-Africa meeting of university librarians at the University of Rhodesia and Nyasaland. After that we would fly to Johannesburg, for a brief stop, and then on to Cape Town, where the South African Library Association was holding its annual convention. The itinerary called for continuous air travel from midnight in Rome to midnight in Cape Town. I had just turned sixty and I wondered whether both of us had the physical health, despite our mental excitement over the challenges ahead.

Approaching Johannesburg, tired as Gerry and I were from an all night flight from Rome, and the effort in the Salisbury visit, anticipation continued to buoy up whatever developing fatigue this old couple was experiencing. In our exhilaration over this adventurous flight we had no idea of the surprising episode that awaited us in South Africa.

From the start I was attracted to South African people. The few I spoke with on the flight from Salisbury were warm and solicitous that we from America find their country as wonderful as South Africans believed it to be. Rene Immelman began reenforcing my reading and conversation about the only independent African state, until Rhodesian independence, to be governed by a white minority. In these first hours of flight I could not quite reconcile the friendly musical *dankee* the beautiful South African stewardesses repeated so charmingly with complex segregations so tragically described in Alan Paton's great novel *Cry the Beloved Country*. Because of my early Fisk commitments, I thought of Paton's words—what if when the whites finally want to make amends for injustices, the Blacks are no longer willing to forgive. Sadly I had begun to fear that many of our militant Blacks in the U.S. had arrived at this unforgiving stage. What would it be like in South Africa? Immelman was one of those South Africans deeply concerned. He reviewed what I had read about the makeup of the population. Of the 16 million people, only three million, or less than one fifth, were white; yet they ruled the country. Of the "non-white" remaining 13 million, 11 million were Black, the indigenous African population called Bantu in South Africa. There were also about 1.5 million "Colored," a term officially used by the Government to differentiate those of mixed ancestry descended from the Hottentots, Bushmen, and descendents of Dutch East Indies and African coastal slaves. Then there were about a half million Asians, including immigrants from India and China who were treated as "non-European," the term used on signs to segregate accommodations for "non-Whites." An exception was made of the Japanese, who because of their commerce and industry were important to South African foreign trade were rated "European." How artificial and cruel these separations of humans seemed, especially underlined by the South African complex.

Rene understood my feelings. But he sensed, also, that maturing influence Charles Spurgeon Johnson and others had exerted in my Fisk days; that my inclination was for reconciliation and against revenge. He amplified further, "Nor are the whites together. We are strictly bilingual; every South African speaks English and Afrikaans with equal nativity. One of my parents is Afrikaans and one English." I knew from my readings that the English were only 40 percent of the whites; that Verwoerd, the head of the government, and *apartheid*, the official government policy of segregation and discrimination against nonwhites, were Afrikaans. Indeed, much of the English minority opposed *apartheid*.

It was all sensitively complex to a foreigner, and I was determined, especially as an American, to avoid any comment. But events forced me, unwillingly, into the controversy now involving the world, as the South African Union withdrew from the British Commonwealth and faced United Nations and world censure.

Unsuspectingly, I began to be thrust into the tension, at the Johannesburg stopover. Herb Heidkamp, whose headquarters for Collier sales was in Johannesburg, had arranged for the local paper to interview me. I tried to be especially circumspect with the reporter, praising the South African warmth and hospitality I had already experienced. Perhaps I should have been more sensitive to what he was driving at; but as I look back I am glad I was not. He asked me about *Collier's Encyclopedia*, and its editorial policy on controversial issues. I told him how hard we tried to be objective, our use of advisory boards, notably our activation of a Faiths Advisory Board. I did sense that somehow I was not giving him the "show" which I believe plays too large a part in determining newsworthiness in our mass media in the U.S. Even if I had been tempted to introduce a bit of drama for American media, I was determined not to touch on any subject related to *apartheid*.

After the interview, Herb Heidkamp treated us to supper in the terminal. I thought Rene was worried about the interview, but if he was he did not let on. There was just time to finish dessert before the announcement of our continuing flight to Cape Town. We boarded a somewhat larger aircraft, and took off in the twilight. September in the southern hemisphere, is, of course, more like our March in weather. We were flying south, into the most temperate zone in all Africa, to the fabulous Cape of Good Hope, where the Atlantic and Indian oceans meet. I was full of travel anticipation.

Rene and I continued our conversation, dividing it between two subjects—*apartheid* and Comparative Librarianship. He answered directly my question about equal library service, the crusade I had begun in 1928 at Fisk. "They may come into the reading room, but they must sit at tables marked for "non-Europeans." My wife dared "we are non-Europeans. We are Americans." Rene grinned, and observed, "I guess you know what we mean when we designated the Japanese 'Europeans.' They may drink at the same water fountains as whites."

At our Cape Town hotel there were the usual gatherings of librarians engaging in post-meeting conviviality. I could have been at any ALA meeting in the States. Humans were humans, and librarians were even more characteristically the same. As I registered at the hotel desk two arms embraced me from behind with an affectionate exclamation "Lou." I turned around and recognized him instantly though I had not seen him since June 1928, and this was September 1964. It was Marais, Columbia Library School classmate from South Africa. He was director of the library at the University of Stellenbosch. We picked up as if Columbia graduation were just the day before yesterday. More South African librarians came up to be introduced and we agreed to join a group for lunch the next day. But we were now so weary that we excused ourselves for a night of sleep.

At the general session next morning I was introduced for my brief talk. As soon as the meeting began I was struck by the extraordinary bilinguality of the discussion. A speaker would begin in English, and in the middle of his remarks change to Afrikaans, switching back and forth between the two languages several times. Rene Immelman did exactly the same thing in his remarks, but after lapsing into Afrikaans he would look in my direction, be reminded that I was not bilingual, and repeat the Afrikaans part in English for my benefit, and for the few other visitors who knew only English. I remarked later to Rene, "I can see this American is cramping your style." I spoke my prepared talk in English, of course, or at least American.

There was the usual milling around in the lobby of the Rotunda after the general session, and then my wife joined us for lunch. Jolly conversation gave no hint of the lightning about to strike. We finished our dessert, talked with several librarians who crowded around us to ask questions about America, and then went up to our room to refresh and relax a bit before the afternoon meetings. There was a knock on our door and Herb Heidkamp entered with another man, whom he introduced as from the Collier Cape Town office.

Herb said with a rather grave tone, "The Cape Town *Times* reporter is waiting to interview you." The two men exchanged glances nervously. Herb said, "About what you said to the Johannesburg reporter, I believe, will be all right." The men hesitated a little, and then said, "But you better know that something has happened." I looked at them completely bewildered. The Cape Town man broke it open. "For some time, the Minister of Information has been wanting us to have the article on South Africa in the encyclopedia completely rewritten, as well as several other sections relating to people and events in this country. The coming of the Editor in Chief has triggered a demonstration. Look at today's editions of the Johannesburg papers." He handed me one newspaper in English, and one in Afrikaans. The English paper reported circumspectly and with British restraint that the Verwoerd government accused *Collier's Encyclopedia* of publishing an unfair and inaccurate article on South Africa, demanded withdrawal of the article and an apology. The Afrikaans paper was obviously more virulent, and when their story was translated to me it was apparent there was a threat to suppress the *Encyclopedia* in South Africa, and to force the publisher to refund purchase price to all South African subscribers.

I went out to meet the Cape Town reporter. Since Cape Town is more English and Johannesburg more Afrikaans, I began to sense that the reporter did not side with the government. Nevertheless, I confined myself to the purpose of my mission: goodwill and presentation of the original manuscripts for the nation's archives; the enlisting of South African scholars to contribute to the Encyclopedia; and my interest in libraries. The Cape Town story the next day was friendly although it referred to the stir in the Afrikaans press.

During the ten days that followed in Cape Town we were entertained courteously and graciously. Rene Immelman, his charming wife and beautiful daughter, Lelong, called on us and we had dinner together at the hotel, Herb and his daugher, whom he called Skooter, joined us. Then came the memorable drive south along the Atlantic beach. Of the many landscapes all over the world that I have seen, none is more picturesque. The semicircle formed by Devil's Peak, Table Mountain, and Lion's Head provides a sort of oval frame for the legislative capital city of the Republic of South Africa. At one point, Rene stopped the car to show us beds of the famous South African rock lobsters.

My heart was pumping excitedly as road signs and the Immelmans' conversation pointed to the geography books' fabled Cape of Good Hope. My wife strained for a glimpse of the Indian Ocean, which she had never seen, but about which she had heard so much from my World War II experience on board the *Penelope Barker*. We pulled up at a refreshment stop at False Bay, south of the Cape, where Rene could point with his finger and say, "There. The Atlantic Ocean ends here, and the Indian Ocean begins there." My wife left the car, ran over to the far point on the beach, and asked Rene, "Is this the Indian Ocean?" When he replied in the affirmative, she removed her shoes and waded out into the water without removing her nylon stockings. Long afterward, I used to tell our friends, "and the Indian Ocean hasn't been the same since." After this effort we all had tea and scones.

In the next few days the Encyclopedia crisis mounted. We tried to fulfill our commitments, to enjoy the lovely city of Cape Town. In succession I made talks to the South African representatives of *Collier's*; to an assembly of library school instructors held in Rene's home; and to a gathering of Information Scientists concerned with comparative British and U.S. stirrings in the computerized approach to information handling. In between, we toured beautiful Cape Town by day and night. It was rapidly becoming one of my favorite cities. I was naming them in order to my friends: first, London, of course; second, San Francisco; thirdly, Cape Town; and at the moment Cape Town was crowding the other two out of my affection. I remember one last walk down Cape Town's lovely Adderley Street before the storm broke. Despite the mounting tension over the Encyclopedia I noted for the last time how Adderley was prolonged by a wide boulevard named Harrengracht on the foreshores. At the other end was Government Avenue, closed to traffic. Somehow I was reminded of my Piccadilly walks to the Thames in London. But there was no such crisis in my Fulbright days as there was now.

As the Government's pressures increased to modify our article or have the Encyclopedia barred in South Africa, the Macmillan New York office decided to step into the picture. My good friend Bill Halsey who had succeeded me as editorial director and been promoted to senior vice president was despatched to help us.

We left Cape Town for Johannesburg where Herb Heidkamp and I were to meet Bill upon his arrival. En route we scheduled a day in Durban, the third largest city. How intensely the Afrikaans had been stirred was illustrated when two men confronted me threateningly as we were about to board the plane. For several days newspapers had been displaying my picture on the front page with indignant demands for apology. The two repeated that demand with a request for refund on their set. Heidkamp tried to reassure them that we were studying the South Africa article and that a refund would be given if desired.

At Elizabethtown, en route to Durban, there was a half hour layover where I held a meeting with the local Collier sales staff. Their concern over the potential censorship was unmistakable. Heidkamp and I outlined a defense and reported on plans.

Our arrival at Durban airport was marked by a second confrontation, even more vigorous. But this time we were aided by the librarian of University College who had come to meet us. In no uncertain terms, as one South African to another, he told the confronters he was ashamed of their lack of hospitality toward a visitor from so far away.

It was a delightful day in Durban. Librarian Oeschger invited us to his home for lunch where Gerry remained with his wife to rest, talk, and shop while the men went to the University. Comparative Librarianship flourished all afternoon as Oeschger and I compared U.S. and UK (where he had been library educated) librarianship with illustrations as we walked about his library. With pleasure I noted how many of our Macmillan imprints were in his new acquisitions. There were two sets of the Encyclopedia in his Reference room. Because University College serves Durban's large Indian population much of the book selection reminded me of my days in India.

Later that afternoon we visited the publisher's Durban office. Concern over the confrontation was evident. I addressed the staff and helped apply our present strategy to their local situation. Then Gerry joined us for supper. We were all intrigued by "monkey steak" on the menu, and enjoyed it when we learned we were eating not monkey meat, but good beef.

We arrived in Johannesburg late that night. There was a reserved suite for us in the Waldorf Hotel where we slept soundly after a rather strenuous, long day. In the morning things began happening. Bill Halsey arrived and immediately we went into a council of war. It appeared the press was clamoring for an interview.

About mid morning we met representatives of the South African press in an assembly room provided by the hotel. No different from U.S. newspapermen, they pushed hard to get Bill Halsey and me into some kind of corner. *Apartheid,* separation of Blacks and whites, was integral. I kept thinking back to Alan Paton's great novel centered right there in Johannesburg. We were as conciliatory as we could be while maintaining our ground that we could not maintain objectivity and endorse *Apartheid.* The Afrikaans press reported the interview less than sympathetically; the English press backed us.

That afternoon and the next day I concentrated on Comparative Librarianship despite the blazing headlines in the Afrikaans press. There were cartoons of the Collier editor-in-chief tearing pages out of the encyclopedia and throwing them in the waste basket. But the South African librarians I met with consoled me and apologized for the lack of hospitality.

In succession I addressed and met with the Transvaal Library Association in the Johannesburg Public Library; with academic librarians in the Teachers College and in the University of Wit. At the Public Library I discussed U.S. Reference. After the meeting, which was well attended, I examined Reference records and compared our approaches to measuring services.

At the Teachers College I addressed an overflow assembly of students and faculty on the Southeastern United States. There were several questions that sought to compare segregations in South Africa and the south of the United States. The principal defense seemed to be that since the Blacks outnumbered the whites five to one, the Dutch and the English who had brought modernity to the Union would be unable to develop the country.

At the University of Wit (Witwatersrand, a hilly region of the Transvaal called the Rand) I conferred with director about the plans for their new library building. It revealed knowledge of U.S. modular trends and some European continental dimensions recalling the advantages of fixed stacks. There were comparatives at other points too—book selection, when a society is committed to a postition like *apartheid*; bilinguality.

On Friday, we drove to Pretoria for the showdown. We had been invited by the Minister of Information to meet with a member of Parliament and a committee of Pretoria Professors who had been most critical in the press of our treatment of South Africa in the encyclopedia article. When we arrived in the other South Africa capital—Cape Town for the English and Pretoria for the Afrikaans—I separated from Bill Halsey for a bit of comparative librarianship in the University of South Africa. I had an appointment with the library director who received me most cordially.

Bill and the Collier man picked me up about half an hour before our committee appointment. This gave us a few minutes to stroll over the spacious campus of the University of Pretoria, which had then some 11,000 students, and faculties in most of the major academic disciplines as well as in the professions. We admired the modern buildings, but there was no doubt of the worried look we all exposed. Ten minutes before three, we entered the academic building we had been asked to report to. The room, which was one for a seminar class, had a square table in the center and a blackboard on the wall. The five faculty members were already assembled and presided over by a Professor of Theology, who had been quoted by the press as being most critical of our main article. Right behind us came the Member of Parliament, who looked very stern, and acknowledged our presence quite formally. We sat down at the table where they indicated, so that we faced all six of them sitting on the opposite side.

The Chairman briefly introduced the purpose of the meeting as a review of the treatment of the Republic of South Africa by *Collier's Encyclopedia*. Turning with deference to the Member of Parliament, the Chairman asked him to summarize. Angrily, the MP accused us of falsifying and maligning the good name of his country, and demanded recall of all sets, correction of the article to comply with government specifications, and a published apology for misrepresentations.

When it came our turn Bill and I described our commitment to truth and objectivity, the employment of advisory boards of scholars and authorities to review work done by contributors; our policy of continuous revision and annual printings; and our desire to correct any errors of fact or opinion that had unintentionally crept into our work. To this end, we proposed to appoint a committee of scholars, one of whom should be selected by this committee, meeting with us, to review all material in the *Encyclopedia* relating to the Republic of South Africa.

We had hardly finished our proposal when the MP arose angrily and shouted, pounding on the table for emphasis, "That is unsatisfactory. We will move to bar the sale of *Collier's Encyclopedia* in the South African Republic, and compel you to refund all money to purchasers." With that he walked out of the room. We remained seated with the professors, some of whom had arisen. The brief scattered dialogue that followed was inconclusive. All but the chairmen excused themselves for classes or appointments. At the theology professor's suggestion we adjourned to the coffee shop for refreshments. Much more graciously, the Chairman explored with us possible compromises, and candidates for our review committee.

It was a tense period in the life of the Republic. I appreciated the crises the nation was facing, both at home, where the non-whites had an overwhelming numerical majority, and abroad, where the members of the United Nations were censuring South Africa rather vindictively. Our Encyclopedia was only a minor concern. Within a few months the *Encyclopedia Americana* was confronted with a comparable situation, as Lowell Martin indicated in a long distance call to me. But a review committee was established. We corrected certain errors in fact, and perhaps helped realize our editorial objective of giving both sides in controversial issues. At any rate, we were gratified when it was possible to revise the material in such a way as to satisfy the good South African people, and yet protect intellectual freedom. *Collier's Encyclopedia* was commended later by the South African leaders.

Qantas took us Down Under from Johannesburg with two island refueling stops—on Mauritius, 1400 miles from the African mainland, and Cocos, about 1200 miles from the announcement, "We are approaching the western coast of Australia [pronounced Austrylia in our ears] and we will be landing at Perth in about 20 minutes." Perth. My memory raced back to 1942 and the Penelope Barker. Would I recognize the city?

It began with a tour, starting with the King's Way panoramic view. I searched in vain for familiar sights, but the city seemed so much more modern that I could not make the picture of then blend with now. Perth is the city in Australia I should choose to live in. Its Mediterranean climate, its proximity to the sea, about 12 miles from Fremantle, and cultural life which blends a certain rural wholesomeness with the cultural sophistication of the University of Western Australia appeal to my life rhythms.

The strikes for comparative librarianship were highpointed at the State Library and at the University. The former introduced me to the pattern of state librarianship in at least three of the states of Australia where library service is centralized. All local public library service emanates from the State Library under a contract which specifies local and state mutual responsibilities. I had never before experienced such direction of state-wide public library service from the state capital. It appealed to me as I saw it in the Australian states of Western Australia, South Australia, and Tasmania. In each case—at Perth, Adelaide, and Hobart, respectively—the state librarian had that innovative spirit so essential to experimenting with new dimensions. There was a brief meeting with the staff at which we exchanged comparatives on all aspects of librarianship, ranging from philosophy to extension.

Here was born the idea of triangular comparison. Not as much as Canada but enough to introduce the idea, Australia was showing the impact of the two great English-speaking librarianships. The British influence was greater, due to emigration of such creative librarians as Sharr in Western Australia and Wray in Tasmania; Graneek in Canberra; and others. U.S. influences had been less resident, more represented by exchanges through foundation and government grants, and short periods of service by American librarians in subordinate positions.

The other high point was the visit to the University of Western Australia. The campus reminded me of several I had visited in California. Librarian Jolly, to whom I was attracted from the start, revealed some advanced architectural concepts in his new building, which had much open air exposure in the Florida and California styles. I met with the staff and with several faculty members to have a feel of the literate freedom of Australian academia before flying to Adelaide.

About that beautiful city itself: what dominates my memory is the broad ribbon of parks which separates, with the Torrens River, the business district from the North Adelaide residential section. The city was named for the wife of King William IV, who has the main street named for him. The stately boulevard of North Terrace flanks the art gallery and the public library.

To the latter and to the State Library I went for further orientation in central state library service. Among the professional eye openers was a publishing enterprise in the state library that resulted in many significant bound books relating to the history, geography, sociology, economics, and culture of South Australia. The architect of this publishing enterprise was the state librarian, Hedley Brideson, whose hospitality and consideration were unsurpassed. For many months after, he generously sent me copies of their fine volumes. Because our own publication budget was cut I was unable, embarrassingly, to reciprocate.

In advance, I had been invited to address three branches of the Australian Library Association. The first of these was the South Australia Branch in Adelaide. Before a large audience of librarians and townspeople I spoke of my "Around the World" mission, and of some library comparatives I had noted in the various places en route. It was a gratifying evening because Australian librarians seemed to confirm my faith in the Quiet Force.

Then to Melbourne. The first day was a busy one. Art Palmer, and the local Collier manager, Peter Block, arranged a series of appearances for me with the press. One of the interviews trapped me as an unsuspecting participant. Unknown to me a censorship case had developed locally around several "frank" novels. With my six years of ALA Intellectual Freedom defending still strong in my literary positions, I said I had always considered Australia an advanced and liberal nation, and that I would be surprised and disappointed if censorship occurred. When the story appeared the next day the "if" was omitted in quoting me. The story left the impression that I was disappointed in Australia, and that I criticized the lack of intellectual freedom. I was badly disturbed by this distortion of my response to what had apparently been a loaded question aimed to support a protesting group.

Just before, I learned subsequently, there had been a demonstration at the University of Melbourne. I approached my visit to the university library diffidently. What I saw was the familiar sight of a building that had been outgrown by a rapidly expanding multiversity. Numbers were beginning to create the same problems of impersonality that were causing campus unrest in the U.S.

The next morning we left for Hobart, Tasmania. Art Palmer had insisted we maintain our expensive suite even though we would be spending that night at a Hobart hotel. When my wife remonstrated about the double hotel bill he replied with words we have quoted often to some of our more penurious friends, "It's only money."

We were met by librarian Wray, himself, and by some staff members. We knew each other from my UK days and reunion talk began almost immediately. Wray confronted me with the news that a young lady was most anxious to see me, and that there was a barbecue picnic waiting for us out in the country some 50 miles away, as soon as we had checked in at our Hobart hotel. The smallest of the states in the Australian Commonwealth, Tasmania had always intrigued me from my geography study, and from the fact that we had to sail south of it in 1942 on the Penelope Barker to avoid Japanese submarine activity. Besides, I wanted to see the two fabulous and almost extinct creatures, the Tasmanian devil and the Tasmanian wolf. We hoped also to see a kangaroo running wild, as all my wife had been able to see so far is one in a zoo.

After a relaxing drive we reached a camp high on a cliff overlooking the Tasman Sea. The young lady came to greet us by throwing her arms around my wife and me in turn. It was Norma Rodriguez, one of my Florida State University students who had served as one of our co-ops on the Miami Public Library staff while attending library school. She greeted me with "Remember, you used to tell us that once we got our master's in librarianship we could get a job anywhere in the world. To prove it you suggested we blindfold ourselves, come into your office, put a finger on the globe, and the chances are there would be a library opportunity there. Well, I did just that, and my finger rested on Tasmania. I wrote a letter and Mr. Wray responded. It took me three weeks by boat to get here. I love it."

To move directly to Wray's top innovation, in my opinion: I had always heard in my public library work that schools teach reading, libraries provide the books. Librarian Wray dared to say the library will teach reading, also, in our way, and in friendly competition with the schools, and with reading clinics. So the Tasmanian State Library taught reading to illiterate adults, to pre-school children, to school and college students who were slow readers or who were having reading difficulties. "Why not?" Wray had asked. "The better people can read the more library business we will have. There is nothing wrong in friendly competition with the schools in which we compare our methods of teaching reading, learn from each others successes and failures." I know some U.S. public librarians who would be horrified at the thought of libraries teaching reading, of "spreading ourselves too thin." Not Wray. And his extension Reference was something to write home about. It had some of the counter-passivity elements which my Reference philosophy was developing. He did not wait for people to ask questions before answering them. He planted questions they should be asking, and then followed carefully the English liberal tradition of offering impartially answers from all sides on controversial issues.

We visited the University of Tasmania, its modern campus and library;

I was interviewed by a newspaper, and had Sunday lunch with a group of librarians before we returned to Melbourne. Both of us were so tired that we had to decline Peter Block's kind provision for supper at their home. We saw the Melbourne newspaper's sensational distortion of my interview, and I was disturbed at the implication I had been critical of Australia on intellectual freedom.

The next afternoon we flew to Canberra, after an instructive morning with the State Librarian of Victoria, where I was comforted by a view of the other aspect of state librarianship: archives. It seemed pertinent that of all the Australian states perhaps Victoria should give more emphasis to archives than to extension. This is probably not necessarily so, but it seemed to fit my sense of appropriate locations.

I discovered at the Australian National University the first campus with separate new buildings for undergraduate and research libraries. Everything about both libraries suggested tomorrow. Then we proceeded to the National Library, met Harold White, now Sir Harold, the national librarian, a friend of both Quincy Mumford, Librarian of Congress, and Sir Frank Francis, Director of the British Museum. We toured the Australian National Library with Harold as our guide. Later, we were guests for cocktails at Harold's home, where the ladies carried on with comparative homemaking, while the men reviewed the plan for presentation of the bound volume of manuscripts for the Australian archives. The presentation was to be made in the office of the President of Parliament, who would accept in person.

That night I made one of my major addresses—to the Capitol Territory Branch of the Australian Library Association. We had dinner, first, with the Graneeks, and we reminisced about Belfast and our meetings during my Fulbright year. Then we proceeded to the lecture hall for my talk. Accenting what I considered some major challenges for U.S. librarianship, I cited the trend to independent study in schools and colleges as confronting libraries with a new role, less ancillary to the classroom than before. For the public library, I saw a new opportunity to convert the growing unrest and physical communication into positive thinking and action for reform. There was no question but that research in special libraries might be revolutionized by the evolving Information Science that was harnessing the computer to cope with the cascade of new facts. There was much dialogue and comparison of Australian and American approaches.

The next day, Sir Allan MacAllister, President of the Upper House of

Parliament accepted the bound volume of Collier manuscripts in a gracious ceremony. I made my brief presentation talk, and Sir Allan accepted with thanks, while Harold White stood by and directed the press to vantage points for interview and photographing.

Shortly afterwards we left for our last Australian point of call—Sydney. Comparative librarianship began in earnest when we met John Metcalfe. I had heard a great deal about him and we were immediately attracted to each other. He reminded me of Charley Brown in the U.S. who had been a sort of professional godfather. Metcalfe has a brilliant mind, is very outspoken, and Australian librarians have learned to wait for his critical evaluation. His little book on the revised Decimal Classification reflected his deep thought on the position of DC, and pointed out that librarians could not complain about updating if they refused to accept the changes involved in readjusting a classification scheme to the changing relationships among disciplines.

I visited the University of New South Wales first. It had the only accredited graduate school of librarianship in Australia then, and I addressed the faculty and students in assembly. After I had finished my lecture on aspects of U.S. librarianship I asked the students if they would sign their names on an overseas letter to be sent to my students at Florida State. They did, many of them adding greetings, and when I returned to my library school I found this letter had a prominent place on the bulletin board world map they had set up to follow my itinerary. From the beginning of my journey I had made it a "first" at each stop to send a picture post card to my students. They had arranged to post these cards and tie them with ribbons to the spot on the map from which they were mailed.

When we returned to the city, the newspapers were headlining an event we had not heard on radio or tv. Khrushchev had been removed from office. Almost simultaneously, the People's Republic of China exploded its first nuclear bomb. And in England, a general election brought the Labour Party to power by a paper-thin margin in an election that was marked by overt racism. Patrick Gordon-Walker, the Labour shadow Foreign Secretary, lost his seat in Smethwick to an opponent whose unofficial slogan was "Vote Labour for a Nigger Neighbour." I began thinking ahead about how I might talk on the role of libraries to promote both quiet and conciliation. I left the Palmers and my wife to visit the University of Sydney library with John Metcalfe as my guide; then to the New South Wales State Library. That evening we were guests of the officers of the New South Wales branch of the Australian Library Association for dinner preceding the address I was scheduled to make. It was the largest audience yet and my description of U.S. professional trends as I saw them elicited many questions and much dialogue, in which John Metcalfe made many incisive comparatives. He drove my wife and me to our hotel and we sat up past midnight, talking not only library but literature and life. He and my wife developed a conversation of their own about the place of women in modern society. The evening was a fitting capstone to our visit Down Under. We left with sentimental fondness for Australia, and especially for the friends we had learned to love.

The last phase of our round-the-world trip was, of course, the journey home. Stops were planned in the Philippines, Hong Kong, and Japan, before returning to the U.S. by way of Hawaii and San Francisco. I hoped both for further comparatives, and reflection on the experiences we had already had, but the all-night flight to Manila kept us firmly rooted in the present.

There was little sleep because of the turbulence. Our Electra was tossed about in the sky, frighteningly at times, as we flew north over the South China Sea. Indeed, the storm was so violent that no refreshments could be served. The absence of any coffee was almost as serious for my wife as the turbulence, which despite dramamine she had taken was threatening to give her a bad case of air sickness. She repeated her jibe at my book: "You know what you can do with your highways in the sky."

After a welcome rest following our arrival, I made the first of my major addresses, before a called meeting of the Philippine Library Association in the National Library. After a most generous introduction that featured Basic Reference and the Encyclopedia, I launched on the first version of my essay *The Quiet Force*, in which I undertook the thesis that in a loud, noisy decade like the Sixties, shouts could no longer be heard. Perhaps Quiet would, by contrast, attract. Libraries epitomized the quiet creative force which had resulted in man's noblest deeds and thoughts. I proceeded then to suggest a library solution to the world's major problems of war, delinquency, illiteracy, prejudice, mental illness, etc. My proposed solutions to these problems I elaborated in later addresses, finally summarized and published in the *Hawaii Library Association Journal*. The demonstrative applause that followed my address touched me.

The refreshments that followed in the library gave me an opportunity to talk with many librarians. I was particularly struck by the men's costumes which featured the barong, a white silk blouse trimmed with lace which was worn over the trousers, much like the Russian. The ladies' frocks were cool and colorful. Since we had just come from Australia there were a number of questions about that country, one or two of which circumspectly revolved around the color restriction. With the exception of the pygmy Negroes or Negritos, native Filipinos belong to the Malaysian branch of the Mongoloid race. Reflections of exposures to Spanish, American, Chinese and other presences distinguish the various groups of people who inhabit the Islands. Perhaps some have looked to the vast underdeveloped continent down under as a prospect for emigration from the rapidly overcrowding conditions. By 1964, the Philippines had three times as many people as Australia crowded into one thirtieth of the area of that vast continent. It was apparent why Australia looked with concern toward the hazard of invasions from the overpopulated Asian and oceanic countries to the north.

One of the high points of the world tour occurred the next day. In a touching formal ceremony in the office of the President of the University of the Philippines I presented the bound volume of manuscripts for the library archives. The university president was General Carlos P. Romulo. From my history study of World War II I recalled that the next day, October 20, would mark the 20th anniversary of the U.S. return to the Philippines. Romulo had been aide-de-camp to Douglas McArthur, and had landed at Leyte Gulf with the invasion forces. I included note of this anniversary in my presentation talk, and paid tribute to the General for his significant contribution to Philippine-U.S. relations.

After the ceremony we were guests, along with a distinguished delegation from Indonesia, headed by the Prime Minister. The General responded to my wife's contagious laugh, and indulged in repartee with her, to the amusement of the company at the table. Even the Indonesians, in their distinctive little caps, were soon rollicking over the light conversation. When the General said we are having our special fish, Lapu Lapu, my wife asked, "How do you spell it?"

Unhesitatingly, the General quipped, "Madame, if you can spell *lapu* once, you have only to spell it a second time." The roar of laughter that followed encouraged him to continue in this light vein. Later, when coffee was served, my wife recounted her first experience with Kenya coffee, at the conclusion of which she asked, rhetorically, looking at the General, "I wonder where I could get some more Kenya coffee?"

Just as promptly the General responded, "Why in Kenya, of course."

After lunch, which was really a state dinner, we were all taken into the University President's "Briefing Room." I was struck by the similarity of this room to the military briefing rooms I had experienced in the Pentagon and at CONAS during my World War II days. Romulo had apparently carried over much of his military background into university administration. I wondered if Eisenhower had done the same at Columbia, Mark Clark at the Citadel, and wherever else higher education had employed generals in administrative positions.

Library absorption has always overcome my physical fatigue. For nearly two months, now, I had been rising early, retiring after midnight, crowding all of the minutes in between with talking and conferring, with library visiting and social gatherings. Nature was about to revolt, in spite of the fact that we had a new top priority when we got to Hong Kong. As we left Tallahassee some of my students had asked my wife: "We know what your husband's mission is on this round the world trip; but what is yours?" She had replied promptly, "All my life I have wanted to buy a beaded sweater in Hong Kong." My students, especially the women, had been captivated by this top priority for a round the world trip. We could not let them down. Our eyes literally popped at the displays we encountered in fashionable and modest stores. We saw many we liked; but we both felt, somehow, that one beaded sweater in all of Hong Kong was destined for us. This sort of mysticism belongs especially in a place the name of which means *beautiful lagoon*. After shopping Kowloon stores, we returned to the Peninsular, and passed a shop in the corridor of the hotel that irresistibly drew us in. It was there. Black with white beads, it stopped my heart for a few seconds, I am sure. We looked at each other, her fingers caressingly lifting it as only a woman can lift a precious bit of feminine wearing apparel. The saleslady wrapped it for us, and we impatiently fled to our room on the fourth floor, to conduct our private fashion show. There was no doubt. It was perfect. I went back into the lobby to write and post the first card, as always, for my students. I saw it later on that map of the world they had put on the bulletin board to keep up with us. The card said *Hong Kong—October 22—7 PM—Mission Accomplished—One beaded sweater.*

The wonders of sightseeing had kept my mind off the fatigue which seemed to send pin prick aches up the whole length of my body from toe to head, somewhat like the delirium aches I had felt on my return from the CBI in World War II. We returned to the hotel for lunch, and lightning struck. Suddenly I dreamed I had descended into a go-go world. Traffic was racing madly: trains whizzed by each other; a driver was trying to control a bucking bronco in front of his carriage; the world was running mad and I caught a glimpse of an engineer whose hand was frozen on the throttle as he was having an apparent heart attack while his train was tearing along the track at 100 miles an hour. That world melted away and I was being carried by men out of the dining hall, into the elevator, and up to our hotel room on the fourth floor. There was a doctor at my bedside. I recall his name was Smith, and I chuckled because there was something comforting in the name of Smith in such a far away from home place as Hong Kong. I knew what he had wrapped around my arm. He looked very professional, and quite grave, for a few moments, and then removed the apparatus from his head, with a broad smile. "Your heart is perfect. A little rest and you should be OK. Here is my card. Call me if you aren't."

As in the Paris incident, the blackout was only less surprising than the speed with which I recovered. When a tailor came for the appointed fitting I went through it all, my wife's as well as mine, as if nothing had happened. Indeed, we went out shopping that afternoon, did a little more sightseeing, and spent a restful night. We had hoped to fly to Bangkok where Frances Spain was giving a Fulbright year to library education. Even if I had been able to convince my publisher to allow an extra two days before my Tokyo commitment, the health incident suggested I reduce travel. We left for Japan.

As we talked with Collier manager, Yoshimoto and Keio Professor Sawamoto in Tokyo, I reviewed my ten-day itinerary. If anything it was more crowded than those that had preceded in all of the other places. Comparative librarianship began the first day with a tour of the city that ended with a visit to the library of the International House of Japan, where a dinner was held for Japanese librarians. This was the beginning of a series of thoughtful and gracious attentions by the librarian, Miss Naomi Fukuda. I had met her very briefly at an ALA meeting when she was visiting the U.S. At the dinner I was asked to speak, and after expressing my affection for associations with students and librarians from Japan, over the years, specifically mentioning the student in

Louis Shores

Florida State University at the time, a librarian from Rishu University on leave, I launched into the thesis that persisted hauntingly throughout the world trip: In this noisy world a quiet voice like ours, in library work, should provide the contrast necessary to capture a different kind of attention—the attention of the more thoughtful and creative members of our various nations, to spearhead a world renaissance of tolerance, of peace, of innovative reform. I closed with that paraphrase of the International Workers of the World slogan, convinced that I had convinced them by my remarks that I was philosophically opposed to Marxism: "Librarians of the world unite; we have everything to gain for mankind."

The next day was highlighted by two top events. In the forenoon I presented the bound volume of manuscripts to the director of the National Diet Library, Tahao Suguzhi. For the ceremony, Collier manager Yoshimoto was a tremendous help. Not only did he act as interpreter, since the Chief Librarian spoke no English, but he had anticipated the ceremony with proper custom, writing gracious letters in advance and wrapping the volume in the cloth prescribed for all gifts. Immediately after, we proceeded by taxi to Keio University, where Dr. Sawamoto greeted us and took us to the library school director's office for a box lunch. My wife and I especially enjoyed the contents—the delicate fish and Japanese supplementaries. The lecture I gave subsequently was in a large school library class. As in the Italian seminars, my talk, in English, was translated by the interpreter at convenient stopping points. Afterward, Dr. Sawamoto and several colleagues dialogued with me on comparative library education, noting similarities in content, teaching method, and differences.

The next meeting was held in a high school gymnasium on the outskirts of Narita City. First we reported to the principal's office in the school building. Like everyone else, we removed our shoes on entering the building, and we were furnished with backless slippers, which I have always had trouble keeping on my feet as I walk. There were fish box lunches for all of us. We were introduced to the men present, in turn, and they made that bow which we had begun to admire so much in Japan. Then it was time to head for the meeting in the gymnasium building, several hundred yards away from the main high school structure. Halfway across the campus I turned to find a young Japanese gentleman running after me with my slippers in his hand. They had slipped off my feet unknowingly and I had continued my walk in my stockings.

Quiet World / Odysseys

When I arrived in the gym auditorium, I was immediately struck by the overwhelming majority of men. I had been told that most Japanese librarians, unlike those in the U.S., were men. My interpreter and I went to the front and left Yoshimoto and my wife sitting in the audience. I was touched all over again with the spirit of world librarianship. Except for the language, which I could not understand, I gathered from charts about problems of finance, buildings, and book stock, which were posted in English as well as in Japanese, that our professional concerns on both sides of the Pacific were just about the same. Faculty recognition for the school librarian was quite prominent, and I began comparing with our own professional troubles.

When I was called on for my part in the program I was introduced in both languages, and proceeded with my brief remarks according to the rhythm we had followed at Keio: I spoke a few words in English, halted and waited for my interpreter to translate. There were over 2,000 delegates in the audience, representing some 40,000 school librarians in Japan, in 1964.

Collier hosted an elegant banquet at the New Otani which, with our Tokyo Prince, represented the two new hotels built for the Tokyo Olympics. Distinguished Japanese librarians, the Embassy's Cultural Attache, the director of the USIS library, and Miss Fukuda, my favorite librarian from International House, were among those present. Again I made a brief talk. After dinner we adjourned to the Top of the New Otani to look out over the lights of the world's largest city, as our tower slowly rotated. A Japanese orchestra featured American music and at my wife's suggestion I requested one of her favorites—*Mack the knife*. She had been captivated by the *Three Penny Opera* from the first time we saw it in Greenwich Village, and this tune has always haunted her. The Japanese orchestra performed it with sensitivity, and my wife declared afterward their performance was second only to her favorite rendition—by Louis "Satchmo" Armstrong.

Comparative Librarianship is reenforced by attention to comparative culture, generally. My visits to the libraries meant much more because of my concern with comparative religion, for example, and the ways of Japanese life on the Ginza, where I compared Japanese cameras, tape recorders, and the most popular automobile—Toyapet (manufacturer of the U.S. import Toyota) with out counterparts. When I developed a cold I was able to purchase in a Japanese drug store on the Ginza a package of the U.S. Contac capsules. And so I conclude the Japanese visit with accounts of three library visits, in particular. The University of Tokyo library seemed to reflect the traditional best. Its collection was rich in Japanese archives, although I was not competent to appraise; yet there was a solid surrounding of even English language reference works.

We spent a delightful day at International Christian College with librarian Miss Tani Takahashi, who had attended our Collier party and invited us. A modern building and a well-organized library judged by even the highest U.S. standards convinced me that Japan provided the climate to select the best from other nations and then go on beyond them.

As a final observation in comparative librarianship, I visited our armed forces libraries at Kanto Base. One of my Peabody graduates was one of the librarians. There were Japanese staff members, too. School, public, and a type of special as well as academic librarianship were illustrated by the various community interests the library served. Much more significant for Comparative Librarianship was the Japanese influence on U.S. librarianship, not only in book selection, and in reference, both of which adjusted to the interests of the host nation, but in the adaptations to supplies and equipment manufactured in Japan, and even to such circulation devices as I had seen in Japanese libraries. This seemed to fulfill a cardinal principal in my theory of Comparative Librarianship—comparison must be on an *equal footing*.

All departures are sad, and we left Japan with regret, but in the knowledge that our next stop would be on American soil, in the land of Aloha. After a day's rest, swimming, and shopping, which added some Hawaiian touches to Gerry's wardrobe, we toured the Island of Oahu— 100 miles in an early morning to late night round of perhaps a dozen libraries of all types. Beginning in Marian McDermott's own Main Library of Hawaii I observed public library service at its modern best. Perhaps to begin with, the open air reading rooms gave me a sentimental feeling of being back home in Florida. I learned early, however, not to compare the two states too much. Despite so many similiarities between Hawaii and Florida each prefers to be considered unique.

Central processing by the State Library, not only for public but for school libraries, captivated me most of all. We went to the warehouse-like quarters where the acquisition, classification, cataloguing and other processes were going on, rather systematically, I thought, for an operation that had only begun. Inevitably, the critics had begun to find fault. My professional eyes danced at the sight of such central processing because I hoped it would release the professional librarian for his role of destiny.

We visited two branches before we left the city of Honolulu. En route, Marian pointed out the two landmarks, 25 miles apart—Koko Head on the east, Pearl Harbor on the west—that established the city limits. In between, she indicated Hawaii's most famous volcano—Diamond Head. Kalihi Valley Branch Library was first and I recall how inviting it looked; the fact that the children's room can be converted to an auditorium and that the projection opening is in the form of an open book. I loved that symbolism for my Generic Book theory.

Next we drove to Aiea Branch, a highly original hexagonal architecture designed by a disciple of Frank Lloyd Wright. I could not help comparing it with the famous architect's own effort at Florida Southern College in Lakeland, where the triangular motif sometimes causes functional difficulties when stack range ends and walls formed apexes that made shelving awkward. The disciple, it seemed to me, had come closer to library architecture realizations.

The remaining days and nights in Honolulu were a perfect blend of library visits in the day and recreation at night, mostly swimming, followed by dinner in the hotel with librarians, of whom Marian McDermott became our sentimental favorite. Most of one whole day was devoted to the University of Hawaii library and to the East-West Cultural Center. At the former we had hoped to renew associations with Ralph and Viola Shaw. But Ralph was on one of his periodic visits to the mainland, and Dr. Stroven hosted us most graciously. A gentleman and a scholar, I discovered that he had edited one of our Macmillan books on English literature of the Pacific. At the time the University's collection was approaching a half million volumes. It was undergoing LC reclassification, which especially seared my soul when he estimated the process would cost at least $500,000. All I could think of was the quantity and quality of library stock that could be acquired with that money, and to ask again, from my Fulbright UK indoctrination, would posterity understand? A new building was being planned to seat 5,000 for a university that had then 12,000 students. They had caught the automation bug like almost every one else in academic librarianship, but Dr. Stroven indicated that some of them questioned much of it. I comforted him by reporting a recent visit to a California library with a new building where the librarian told me confidentially, "It takes longer and costs more, but we are automated. It has increased our budget because the president likes to show us off to visitors now, and he never came to the library before."

The Hawaii week closed climactically with an address to a special dinner meeting of the Hawaiian Library Association. A well-attended hotel dinner, tastefully cuisined and decorated included the presentation of an orchid lei to my wife. There were refreshments in the Surf Room first; then more social conversation at the banquet tables. I had written my address which was subsequently published in *Hawaii Libraries*. I had planned my paper as a summary of my world trip, of my search for *The Quiet Force* in this noisy world.

We began our homeward flight Saturday November 7. Our jet reached San Francisco that night where Ed and Minnie Wight were waiting to greet us. After another of those delightful weekends in their Berkeley home, and some jaunts to key points in one of our favorite cities of the world, we resumed our flight to New York, first, for a brief report to the publishers.

We had travelled 42,000 miles, mostly by plane. Some 14 nations had been visited on all of the continents except one. Everywhere we had met good people, of whom the best had been librarians. Yet my wife and I thrilled over the loudspeaker announcement "We are approaching Tallahassee."

III Crusades

Introduction: *Evangelisms*

Among twenty crusades in quest of our professional destiny, five engaged me more deeply and for longer than the other fifteen. In chronological order, perhaps, they were for ONE RACE without prejudice toward minorities; BASIC REFERENCE in behalf of an informed national and world mind; ENCYCLOPEDIA (as the most promising implosion for the celebrated information explosion) LIBRARY-COLLEGE as the way to universal higher education; MEDIA UNITY as the key to learning; and LIBRARY HISTORY as insurance against sweeping away some eternal constants in the contemporary rage for change.

Although the crusade for One Race really first took on proportions in 1928 when I began my Fisk University librarianship, there had been unmistakable signs of concern for minorities of faith, color, and national origins in my earliest childhood. My playmates in Cleveland and Toledo included American Blacks and Chinese. Jews, Catholics, and Protestants of all denominations sent their children to the public schools I attended and strangely those segregated for their differences attracted me. In Cleveland and Toledo so many of my playmates were first generation Americans of Polish, Russian, Italian and Balkan parentage that I tended to side with them when children of American parentage shouted "Wop," "Hunkie," or any of the other derogatories.

Perhaps a psychoanalyst would attribute this to an "underdog" complex. It was certainly true in sports. I tended to favor the unfavored team or contestant. It had begun in my fairy tale and mythology reading. I came out for Hector over Achilles in classroom discussion of Greek mythology. When the Boston Braves in 1914 rose from last place to first and went on to win the world series I had my greatest satisfaction. And then in 1918 when much smaller Jack Dempsey knocked out the giant Jess Willard I believed my prayer for the underdog had helped.

When I arrived at Fisk in 1928 I knew at once that God had meant for me to use my new profession to help eliminate the discrimination that segregations in the South then symbolized. Fortunately, two Black colleagues, especially librarian Edward Christopher Williams of Howard University and sociologist Charles Spurgeon Johnson of Fisk taught me the superiority of concilation over confrontation.

The other four major crusades all contributed to the first. I was convinced that ignorance was the chief cause of prejudice—the obstacle to one race. To inform the people I began with Reference when I discovered the R books in libraries. Here were the facts with which to strengthen our national mind first, and the world mind ultimately.

Inevitably as I browsed among the Reference Books, so sadly neglected, it seemed to me, by my teachers and professors, and therefore by their students. I became convinced my mission was to evangelize for these good books. I began by teaching their use to my students as my teachers had never taught them to me. Then I wrote about them in *Scholastic* magazine, first, and later in professional and literary journals. Reference became the top attraction in both library practice and library education. The *Basic Reference* series of books climaxed this crusade.

It was inescapable that the "Queen of Reference Books" would attract. My early discovery of the encyclopedia helped me to good school grades. Soon I was teaching encyclopedias, reviewing them, contributing to and editing them. A major part of my professional life went into two, especially —*Compton's Pictured* in the 1930s, and into *Collier's* from 1946 to the present.

Dissatisfaction with my undergraduate education, of which neglect of the literature of Reference was no small part led to the prototyping of an ideal college. I found my inspiration in Thomas Carlyle and sketched an ideal higher education in a 1933 paper for the American Library Association, beginning the Library-College movement.

Part of the Library-College learning mode is independent study made possible only by the concept of the Generic Book, which I first suggested in a *Saturday Review* essay that Norman Cousins made his editorial for the first National Library Week. Out of the Generic Book concept developed the crusade for media unity—the so-called "shotgun marriage" of audiovisualists and librarians. This was the most painstaking of all the crusades because of the crossfire between the two groups.

Finally, of the five, there was Library History. My love of history had led me to search for constants in a growing climate of change. My master's thesis was in educational history. My doctoral dissertation was on the *Origins of the American College Library*. My crusade led to the establishment of the ALA American Library History Round Table and to the *Journal of Library History*.

That is not to say that the other 15 crusades were not major. Having devoted 36 years as head of two ALA accredited graduate schools in librarianship I would be inclined to call Library Education my super crusade, my overriding one. But this evangelism as well as several others are reserved for other parts of this book.

8. One Race

Fisk confronted me with the human injustices of *color* as never before. In Toledo, my adolescent home, several of my high school classmates were referred to as "colored" by the white majority. To be perfectly honest with myself I had to admit there was nothing like the tolerance up North that I had tried to boast about in my first few months in the South. Toledo had been an underground station for runaway slaves in pre-Civil War days. As U.S. cities went, this extremely northwest city in Ohio could be considered as liberal as any. Yet there had been incidents there which illustrated the white man's prejudices.

One I had suffered from most deeply concerned a student with whom I studied homework. He was my own age of fourteen, but much taller, and with a dark brown skin that covered what were referred to as "negroid" features. Working together as we did daily, an affection developed between us that seemed to disturb some of the more intolerant of the white boys. One day when we were working together on the school lawn, two bully types confronted me with "Hey, nigger lover." A fight followed in which I was badly hurt—more inside than by the bloody nose and swollen eye. My friend did rather better, inflicting more than he received. The two of us left with the jeers of the white boys gaining some support from the other whites who had gathered.

There were several comparable incidents in Toledo. For some reason I seemed to be drawn to children of minority groups—Jews, two Chinese and one Japanese students, and many others whose parents came from the Balkans. Without telepathy it is difficult to communicate what really goes on in peoples' hearts. I believe I have always been drawn to ,individuals for what they are. Skin, faith, national origin seem to have had little effect upon that mystical attraction I seemed to feel for certain individuals.

It was that way from my first day at Fisk in August 1928. I was instinctively drawn to some individuals; casually affected by others; ashamedly I admit, repelled or even repulsed by a few. Race, faith, national origin seemed to play little part in my inclinations. I began confiding and listening to confidences of certain faculty colleagues to whom I was irresistibly attracted.

One day, after an exciting cup of coffee with Dr. Charles Spargeon Johnson his words stirred something. "As a sociologist I cannot find an institution in our American society more tolerant than the library." I knew instantly that this was true. Quiet and tolerance were the two characteristics that had influenced me most for librarianship. Why not conciliate through the library, though my profession of librarianship. There were several major developments under way that were centered in the Fisk Library. I determined to exploit them for the cause of ONE RACE.

The library, itself, could be a source of pride. From the start I worked with the architect, Henry C. Hibbs, to introduce some new dimensions. At the time, Yale was pioneering its tower stack for Sterling Memorial Library. Both Hibbs and I saw some advantages to placing the stack vertically above the horizontal service areas. Working excitedly day and night we came across the idea of the gravity chute for delivering books from the stack to the loan desk, rapidly, and returning books more leisurely by elevator or lift. Fisk's gravity chute was one of the first.

Ground breaking day arrived, and the laying of the cornerstone ceremony, with memorabilia to be deposited for posterity, before that stone was concreted. Then came the days of watching the steel tower rise above the three service floors. As I recall the dimensions, the building extended some 150 feet skyward, and as it did I noted that all of us—faculty, students, and the surrounding Negro community raised their heads higher with pride. A great number of Nashville white citizens came to wish us well, and I glowed over the symbolic evidence of conciliation.

Confrontation emerged quickly. It was prompted by the militancy of Ernestine Rose, of the New York Public Library's Harlem branch. Several of the Southern white librarians objected strongly to what seemed like her rather vindictive positions at times. In the end I was forced to the onerous task of disengaging her from a prominent place on the dedication program. Painfully I realized that conciliation was not easy and that confrontation might well be the less courageous course.

Quiet World / Crusades

The big day of dedication arrived in the fall of 1930. Nearly 100 librarians came. I began my lifelong professional effort at conciliation. There were potential tensions in every meeting, private as well as public. Tolerant as librarians are inherently the climate of 1930 Nashville, and of the region, was not friendly to integrative efforts. Merely to have whites and Blacks eat together was unheard of. Nashvillians shook their heads in fear. One Virginia schoolman said to me quite sternly, "I'm sorry. As a Southerner I cannot eat with them. I am anxious to help them with their education." How to hide this prejudice from the others became a deep concern.

Despite moments of delicacy in helping whites and Blacks "cross the line" at various social points, the Conference went through to an inspiring final session. All of the papers read had been exclusively professional, treating such subjects as book selection, classification of Negro literature, fact finding for students and faculty, and library architecture. The testimonials at the end extolled the Conference as a landmark in both professional librarianship and in race relations. Adding up the pluses and minuses afterwards Dr. Charles Spurgeon Johnson agreed with me we had not come out in the red in our enterprise for One Race.

Four decades have followed the Fisk conference of 1930. I believe I have never faltered in my crusade for One Race—the human race. It has not been easy. Every evangelism—and there have been many these 40 years—has been fraught with sufferings. My efforts began in an American climate quite different from the one we know now. In 1930 there had been no Brown vs. Board of Education Supreme Court decision, no busing of children to achieve balance in school population, no urban confrontations like Watts in Los Angeles, nor campus unrests like those at Cornell and dozens of other predominantly white institutions of higher education. What the South had openly, and the North covertly, was brutal and socially approved segregation on the basis of skin coloration. The Negro in American society was clearly a second class citizen, tolerated with condescension "as long as he knew and observed his place."

There had been a story on the Fisk campus about the Burrus brothers, two young Negroes, too poor to be able to afford college. One day they heard a lecture on the Negro by a white academician. Vindictively, he had declared in the course of his lecture purporting to prove the inherent mental inferiority of the Black, "Show me a Negro who is capable of studying Greek or calculus." The story went that right after the lecture John Burrus said to brother Jim, "You take the Greek and I'll take the calculus," and off they went to Fisk. In four years they made fantastic grade averages and went on to white universities to amaze faculty and students in their major fields.

I sensed on the Fisk campus what my colleagues were attempting to do in their respective specialties—develop pride in the inherent talents of the Negro. The new Fisk Tower Library was a start, a symbolic pointing skyward not only in a new profession for the Negro but as a more effective way to unify the human race in its common quest for truth and beauty. From the Fisk Library began my personal crusade for the conciliation of differences between humans of different skin coloration, of strange, for the Anglo-Saxon, national origins, of differing faiths.

Upton Sinclair, my college favorite novelist, wrote a little known novel about a ship-wrecked young man who awakes on a remote South Sea island where telepathy is the only medium of communications among the inhabitants. He awakes to find a beautiful girl looking down on him and she blushes immediately when he transmits his first conscious thought.

If we had the talent to communicate telepathically, as I am mystically sure we shall some day, we would know for sure what is in the hearts of individuals. Today, despite the show of tolerance on our networks, there is considerable doubt that real integration is going on in the hearts of even the most demonstrative against discrimination. From the beginning of my Fisk days I was challenged to communicate honestly what I believed and felt on the Fisk campus and in white Nashville.

At first I was determined to confront some of my white colleagues abroad with the discriminations. Under Dr. Johnson's influence I restrained my outbursts. Most of the librarians were on our side to begin with. Besides I began to see the strength of Dr. Johnson's approach in bi-racial meetings. We could force the white man to correct his injustices to the Blacks; or we could help the white man want to do what was just. Nevertheless, I kept torturing myself: am I shirking by not marching militantly every moment, crying out against the indignities inherent in public segregations.

My involvement in writing about a new Negro library, first, and then about the Negro's achievements in journalism and published scholarship opened the road to reconciliation. Fellow librarians responded favorably to this orientation in selection of current Negro publications. I began comparative studies of Black and white reading interests, rather informally, almost from my first year at Fisk, primarily from the standpoint of selecting for the community in which I was rather than academic communities in general as I had been taught at Columbia.

Armed with a modicum of statistics I proceeded with my comparison of the reading interests of Negro and White students. I had begun with my illustrated article on the new library at Fisk for Eileen Ahearn's famous professional journal of that day, *Libraries*, in February 1929. That had been followed by an article on the first Negro Library Conference, which the rival *Library Journal* gladly accepted. I had communicated Negro Librarianship in the two major professional journals. Next I was determined to "sell" what I considered professionally "tops" —the *ALA Bulletin*. The editor took not one but both of my articles —the "Negro Press" in February 1932, and "Negro Magazines" in July.

Looking back over these four decades since I left Fisk I can count nearly a hundred confrontations in race relations and about as many efforts at conciliation. A few of them may be indicative. Tallahasse, more even than Nashville, was a Southern city when I arrived there in 1946. In the War Between the States, as the Civil War was called in the South, only one Confederate capital east of the Mississippi had never been taken by the Union troops. That capital was Tallahassee, which had made a valiant stand at the battle of Natural Bridge, six miles south of the city, and defeated on March 14, 1865, the Union army sent to liquidate the resistance. Tallahassee is proud of that victory, and in 1946 the city clearly demonstrated its commitment to the traditions of the Old South.

Florida State University was restricted to white students as was then the law in the Southern states. Across town is Florida A&M for Black students. Although the two campuses are now nearly integrated they were strictly segregated then. Almost from my first day in town I established cooperative arrangements with both the A&M library and its undergraduate department of library science. Miss Copeland, head of the department, and I conferred regularly and attempted to articulate our offerings for the day when holders of bachelor degrees could begin working for master degrees at Florida State.

At the earliest opportunity, when it looked like Tallahassee was progressing toward acceptance of the educated Black, at least, I invited Miss Copeland and Mr. Thomas, the librarian, to a conference on our campus. Again I was crushed by moving too rapidly. For lunch I scheduled another session in one of the privately owned restaurants, bordering the campus, that served faculty and students. We had hardly sat down when the stocky proprietor, in shirt sleeves and scarlet face confronted us menacingly. We withdrew and adjourned to a small campus snack bar. Not wishing to risk another embarrassment I asked an officer of the Board of Control whose office was near the snack bar, and was excited to hear, "Of course. It is illegal to practice segregation anywhere in the state universities." That was evidence we had progressed toward One Race.

In 1950, I became president of the Southeastern Library Association, an organization of librarians of the nine states in the South that were then most segregated. But librarians were not. In Florida we had tried to move even more rapidly. At the Tampa conference before 1950 we invited Negro librarians to attend the meetings. When an afternoon session ran into the dinner hour, the waiters began setting tables. Immediately, one Negro librarian, a very diffident lady from Jacksonville, got up from the table and sat by herself at a table in a corner. A Southern white male librarian followed her promptly, but inconspicuously and remained with her throughout. Slowly we integrationists were infiltrating. The test came at Southeastern.

The southeastern meeting was scheduled for the ultra conservative Atlanta Biltmore hotel. We had informed the management that Negroes had become members of the Association for the first time. They agreed to the meeting. But when we arrived ahead of the convention to hold our SELA Board meeting we were informed that Georgia law would not permit eating together. At an emergency Board meeting, director Ben Powell of Duke University made the motion that set the pattern for integrating in stages. We voted to remove all banquets and social meetings involving food from the official program. The hotel protested strenuously at this loss of revenue. But we were adamant.

I recall the challenge of the opening general session. As I mounted the platform I saw through the corner of my eye five Negro librarians disperse at the door and seat themselves in separated places, back, front and middle of the hall. It was obvious the first integrated meeting of librarians in the Southeastern region was being tested by the militants. Would Blacks and whites really be permitted to sit together?

Then out of the corner of the other eye I saw a half dozen White librarians hesitate at the door, recognize the challenge and disperse in the same way. Each librarian in turn walked to where a Negro librarian was sitting alone and sat down beside him or her. As if intuitively librarians began to disperse themselves to destroy once and for all the ugly segregations the South had enforced by law. That Southeastern convention of librarians was a trail blazer in many directions.

In Britain, some of us Fulbright fellows were asked by the British Information Service to undertake a series of lectures on our respective parts of the United States. I spoke about my Southeastern United States. Invariably in the question period that was part of these lectures, and in the Fulbright plan to stimulate cultural exchange among nations, I was asked about our "inhuman" treatment of the Blacks. Mostly, the questions were gentle and in the English tradition of "you are innocent until proved guilty."

One notable exception occurred in my lectures on Reference and Book Selection for the library school in London Polytechnic. Again and again in the question period students, not quite in the activist dimension of the Sixties, but as if anticipating that neo-"democratic" format, demanded that I apologize for the South's treatment of the Negro. I might have confronted them with the history of British colonialism, especially in Africa. But my commitment to conciliation as more communicative than confrontation moved me to challenge them to invite me back to devote a whole lecture to the Southeast United States.

Within two weeks I was back at Polytech, speaking to a packed assembly. With true British democracy, they heard me out, engaging in none of the histrionic interruptions of the next decade of American activists that appealed so much to network newscasters. When I had finished my presentation, with maps and illustrations of our Southeast region, a full hour was turned over to dialogue and questions.

My defense in the comparison of London's comparative tolerance with the South's apparent intolerance of the Blacks was based largely on economics and numbers. I concluded the dialogue with a prophetic assertion: "give London more Blacks than the city now has, at least as many in proportion to whites as some of the Southern U.S. cities, and the competition of cheap labor and see what happens."

Not many months after the end of my Fulbright year there was an influx of African Blacks from some of the British colonies. You may recall the riots that resulted in London. Blacks were taking over many jobs because they would work for less money. When I returned to London some time later one of the Polytech faculty members recalled my prophecy.

Confrontations and conciliations have continued to lacerate my mind and heart despite all of the outward signs of integration. Perhaps the former brought desegregations to our schools and colleges, more job opportunities for Blacks, better housing, greater representation in government, perhaps even an understanding that when two people are in love the color of their skin may actually be one of the intangible elements that draws a man and woman together. But I cannot help asking whether conciliation might not have gone deeper into peoples' souls and proved that we all really belong to one human race.

Let me close this chapter on One Race with two more experiences that began as confrontations and developed into conciliations. I relate them probably through sentimental rose-colored glasses, because I believe, fundamentally, that man is good. No matter how much this may affront some Christian theology, I cannot accept the position that "man is naturally bad." Indeed, this seems sacrilegious to me. Since God made man I cannot see how or why God would deliberately make man naturally bad, give him a free will which God, through his omniscience, knew in advance would choose wrong. I believe God in his infinite compassion suffers with man over his imperfections.

Intolerance is one of man's imperfections. And the spirit of vengeance which intolerance may provoke is another weakness. Perhaps the incident I now report will not be seen by the participants exactly in my perspective. One of my graduate students at Florida State University, during the Sixties, chose as the subject for her master's thesis (before the thesis for that degree became academically unfashionable) "The effect of the U.S. Supreme Court Decision upon the Treatment of the Negro in the Major American Encyclopedias." She was from Mississippi, perhaps a state as deeply steeped in the segregationist tradition as any. I was doubly gratified, as any teacher is when one of his students is captured by two of the professor's deepest concerns. One of these concerns was of course the Encyclopedia, my favorite teaching unit in Basic Reference, and one of my major professional crusades. The other concern, of course, is the subject of this chapter—the unifying of the human race.

A keen student, one of my kind of young people, she had probed quietly and deeply into the causes for the segregations in her state and the prejudices of the people she knew best. Among her startling findings was one that disclosed an article written on the Negro for the *Britannica* (which by that time had become an American property), before the

Supreme Court's 1954 decision, was quite objective. But the article written for *Collier's Encyclopedia* after the Court's decision and in a climate of mounting Black militance, was less than objective. Interestingly enough both articles were written by the same author, and surprisingly enough by the distinguished and scholarly historian Dr. John Hope Franklin, my wonderful student and debater of Fisk days.

As Editor-in-Chief of *Collier's* and during one of my extended leaves in New York, I invited John Hope to have lunch with me and my associate editorial director. In advance I had sent him a copy of that part of my Florida State student's thesis that pertained. John Hope Franklin opened our meeting by offering to rewrite the article for us. He conceded immediately that the Mississippi student was discriminatingly right. Dr. Franklin has not only a keen mind, but the spirit of conciliation which is the only future for the human race.

In 1967 I was invited to serve on the faculty of Johnson C. Smith University, primarily to work under and with the Library Director to develop a collection and service to match the new million dollar building made possible by a Duke foundation grant. Charlotte, North Carolina, where Johnson C. Smith is located, has a downtown bookstore with an extraordinary collection of paperbacks. We put together $1,000 from our two grants, and arranged with the bookstore to charge paperback purchases up to ten dollars to each student ID card presented. Then we met with the student literary club, who joined us in the plan and augmented it with a number of devices for involving students.

Briefly, we informed the students that they might shop for up to $10 worth of paperbacks and charge their purchases to their ID cards. "Choose anything you want. In your classes you read what your professor puts on the reserve list. Make up your own course. This is your curriculum, your profile of interests. These books are you, they are relevant to what concerns you most." And I added in my unforgivable way, "And don't bar any of those covers that picture girls with dresses that won't choke them. If sex is your top interest buy as much *mature audience* literature as you want."

We set up a rummage table in the browsing room where students were encouraged to exchange paperbacks. No records were kept. If the students wanted to keep their purchases or the purchases of others that was all right. Once a week we had coffee in the lounge where we bubbled over our finds.

Race was a key subject. Johnson C. Smith was beginning to integrate in 1967. The top high school track star in the state, who happened to be white, chose Johnson C. Smith for his college. There were quite a few white faculty members, too, and we talked confrontations and conciliations with kid gloves off.

Perhaps the whole One Race effort that year was climaxed by the performance of the theatre version of Alan Paton's great novel, *Cry the Beloved Country*. My wife and I had been tremendously moved by our reading of the book. It had been reenforced by our visit to South Africa, just before, and the days we spent in Johannesburg in connection with the intellectual freedom confrontation I had experienced relating to the encyclopedia I edited.

At Johnson C. Smith my wife and I went to the Chapel for the performance of the play with a group of faculty and students. The cast was a talented travelling company. All of the Black characters in the book were played by Blacks; and all of the white characters by whites. Ours were not the only tear-filled eyes in those touching moments when the Black father and the white father consoled each other about the loss of their respective sons.

That great passage in *Cry the Beloved Country* that has haunted me all through the militancies of the Sixties underlined every lesson Dr. Charles Spurgeon Johnson had taught me at Fisk many years before. Somewhere in the book Alan Paton has one of his heroes say something like this: "What if when the White Man is at long last remorseful for the wrongs he has done the Black man and asks to be forgiven the Black Man is no longer able to forgive him?"

I hoped this was not what was happening in the United States in the Sixties.

9. Basic Reference

The concept of Basic Reference was born in my Columbia Reference course, some time during the academic year 1927-28. But the Basic Reference idea was only part of a philosophy of Reference that had begun developing as early as my library commitment. Pierce Butler's words that librarians had no reference philosophy, repeated almost parrot-like thereafter by some sophisticates, had always seared my soul. I had protested to Professor Butler once during my GLS days in 1929-31. But I had not written much yet, then. It has been the repetition of this assertion since, and even recently, that has troubled me.

On the one hand so much criticism of my Reference writing has been that I am too theoretical, and not practical enough. But on the other hand, there have been those who have continued to declare there is little or no philosophy of reference. Which leads me to ask, how critically do we really read our own professional literature? Can we recognize philosophy when we read it? How widely do we read? Or do we suffer from what Eugene Garfield has called "bibliographic incest?" That is, we tend to cite the same comfortable references over and over again, in our library school stencils, and our "approval of motherhood" writings. Do we search for the out of the way heterodoxy on the chance that a real discovery may turn up serendipitously?

Immodest as it may read, I must insist that I have published thousands of words of Reference philosophy. It may be bad philosophy, and even worse Reference. But it is there in print. Philosophy can be found in the over 1200 pages of my *Basic Reference* volumes. There is philosophical redefinition of Reference in the Annual Lecture for the Library Association of the United Kingdom, read at the Bournemouth conference in 1952; published in their Proceedings; condensed by *Library Journal*; and reprinted several times. Three decades of Encyclopedism reveal Reference philosophy at various points: reviews, essays, prefaces, editorship designs and dimensions. Then there are such specific examples of writings that are almost entirely theory; "The Ideal Encyclopedia," for *Wilson Library Bulletin*, and also "The Future of Reference," for them, after a reading for the Reference Services Division; "The Measure of Reference," summing up some meditations for the RSD committee I chaired, published in the *Southeastern Librarian*. Something I did for *ALA Bulletin*, before it became *American Libraries*, philosophically approached the literature of reference and its reviewers.

Before I pick up the story of the Basic Reference crusade as it began at Columbia, let me state here a few of the contributions to the philosophy of Reference that I believe I have made over these four decades. In my study, as I type these words, I glance at the framed "Isadore Gilbert Mudge Citation in the year 1967 For Distinguished Contributions to Reference Librarianship." I treasure this recognition, not only because of the memory of a great teacher at Columbia, and sentiment about RSD, which I crusaded for, and which honored me on the occasion of its 10th anniversary dinner, but because the authors of the nearly 200 words of citations recognized my contribution to the philosophy of Reference. I could reproduce those words as evidence.

But I prefer to "precis write" six fundamental conclusions in my rebellious philosophy of Reference. At the start, the definitions of philosophy that appeal to me for the purpose of this precis include reflections on the ultimate nature of Reference, and a system of speculative beliefs about the information process. *Number one*: I redefined Reference as *the promotion of free inquiry*. That, debatably, moved Reference Librarianship over from the passive stance of awaiting the inquirer's query, only, to the active effort to stir inquiry, also. Such a Reference philosophy might just toughen the national mind enough to prefer mental dialogue over physical demonstration.

Two: there is a Literature of Reference as creative, informational, imaginative, provocative, literary, and authorative as the literature of the Essay, of Oratory, of Satire, of Miscellany (to take them in Dewey order), and possibly with some of the inspiration and imaginative elements of the literatures of Poetry, Drama, and Fiction. The Literature of Reference deserves to be studied *per se* as a literary form, not only in Library Education, but in the departments of Literature, and especially in survey courses of English, American, Comparative.

Three: Basic Reference as a concept emerged out of some frustrations in library practice and in library education. There were in 1927-28, already, an estimated over 10,000 reference titles. Since Alice Bertha Kroger's first compilation of the *Guide to Reference Books* in 1902, teachers in libraries and in library schools have overwhelmed tyros with all of the titles, not daring to omit mention of any of them for fear of being considered lax or ignorant. There must be a very small number of titles on which topnotch practitioners rely to answer 99.44 percent of all the questions asked in school, public, academic, and perhaps even in special libraries. On this hunch, I began laying my plans as early as the close of my Columbia library school year in 1928 to query Reference librarians and teachers.

Four: I attended my first ALA in 1928 right after I received my Columbia BS in LS degree. (A master's was not given for the first year of post graduate work then.) My greatest disappointment was finding no separate group meeting on my favorite division of librarianship: Reference. I resolved then that ALA must have a Division on the Information mission of libraries. When the ACRL was formed a Reference Section was born. I became a charter member and the Section's meetings became an ALA must. Some time later Public Librarians activated their own section somewhat in protest against the academic accent in the ACRL meetings, and because of the feuding spirit between the two library types after the Third Activities Committee there were rather bitter denunciations at times of public library dominance in ALA. I joined the Public Library Reference Section as well. And then began the long and sometimes painful effort to reconcile the leaderships in the two sections.

Five: Comparative Reference as part of Comparative Librarianship thrust itself into my consideration of ultimates in the library's information mission. As the ALA organization struggle unfolded I could not help comparing the Public approach to Reference with the Academic approach. From this comparison emerged the theory that both library types engaged in both *instructional* and *research* Reference and that there were different philosophical accents in these two kinds of reference. The former was concerned with interpretation, and the latter with discovery. In the first instance the goal was to communicate what man already knew; in the second to extend man's knowledge frontier.

Six:"The Fourth R" I called it in my Kentucky paper, as I inevitably carried the comparative process into the school library. School librarianship spurred me through something in their Reference approach that introduced new dimensions both into Reference and into elementary and secondary education. I believed I saw the embryo of a new learning mode. I saw that the Literature of Reference was the gateway to independence, the fundamental measure of quality education. With a mastery of basic school reference sources the student could educate himself under teacher guidance more effectively than through classroom group teaching.

These six concepts, in overview, are representative of my rebellious Reference philosophy. In concert I play them under the title Basic Reference, which I first introduced to the Reference literature with *Basic Reference Books*, in 1937. Of course, Reference should interpret the collection to the patron. But the destiny of this aspect of librarianship is nobler than interpretation. If I had to limit my substitution to one word it would be, rather, "inspiration." Similarly, the identification of three schools of Reference philosophy as "conservative" or "moderate" or "liberal" has the same effect on me as today's "establishment" or "protest" or even the vaguely identified "silent majority." In all cases the categorizations are too superficial. At its best, the conservative school could be seen as building independence in the patron by doing nothing for him that he could do for himself. There was a bit of liberalism in the moderate who was willing to help the inquirer to the point where he could help himself. As for the swinger liberal who would do anything for the patron, there was a real spirit of service present.

My disappointment centered on the passivity of all three schools. All were based on readiness to serve the inquirer when he felt a need for his inquiry. Perhaps there was a threat of censorship in any overt action to force the patron to make not only an inquiry, but to ask the right questions. Words being what they are, the implication is always there that this kind of Reference philosophy would, like Hitler, make sure the "wrong" questions were never asked. On the contrary. My definition of Reference as "the promotion of free inquiry" would underwrite the asking of all possible questions for a subject, and insure that every side would be represented in the answers. The ultimate choice would be made by the inquirer.

Under my definition of Reference we must assume a share of the blame for the form communication has taken today. We have not anticipated the causes for which citizens march, rather than think. We must promote rather than await inquiry about war, race, national origin, faith, poverty, pollution, addiction, contraception, or any of the other issues for which the activists engage in their neo-democratic action of nonviolences. Not that we haven't worked valiantly at our kind of library.

If Reference were to anticipate and initiate inquiry, as well as respond to it, we might contribute to moving communication off the streets and into the libraries. With what advantages and results? As I suggested in my 1968 election eve address to the Denver Metropolitan Library Association: orderly reform of our society; of our town and gown. How? By reviving colonial town meeting in our thousands of American libraries of all types.

Perhaps because I have been an English teacher I have seen reference books as a form of literature. Certain masterpieces intrigued me at once as even the discovery of the English and Russian novel; of Nicholas Rowe and Upton Sinclair; of the Restoration Period. Counterparts in the Literature of Reference were, almost from my high school days, the encyclopedia; the dictionary; the almanac. I was ready and willing to compare our Reference masterpieces with even the classics of poetry, drama, and fiction.

Beside the identification of a literature of Reference I was ready to place my classification of types as I developed it for *Basic Reference Books*, and refined it for *Basic Reference Sources*. Mudge had been tremendously helpful. But the edition I studied at Columbia identified only four general groups: (1) Periodicals, Essays, Debates, Dissertations; (2) Encyclopedias; (3) Dictionaries; (4) Bibliographies. The rest of the Guide was given over to special subjects.

In the *Basic Reference* series of books I provided separate chapters in the part devoted to general reference books to Handbooks, Manuals, Directories, Indexes, Biographical, Geographical sources, Yearbooks or Annuals, Audiovisual Sources. For each, I developed criteria, which I then used for critical reviews of titles and groups. Much as I inclined toward seeing Reference as literature, pragmatic pressures were exerted to relate these titles to Reference methodology.

My compromise tended to favor letting the literature rather than the reader initiate the method. Not entirely, of course, as the lists of questions asked in each type of library, appended to *Basic Reference Books* confirmed. Again and again, I would present my classes with lists of actual questions asked in representative libraries. But always I complemented these lists with questions stimulated by the great Reference literature. Perhaps this is because the philosophy of Reference believes in initiating as well as responding to inquiry.

Although Basic Reference as a philosophy was born at the top level of education for librarianship, the concept permeated and increased involvement in general library education. To begin with, discovery of the literature of Reference as something distinct from other literatures, as early as my high school days opened a new road to learning for me. As I revelled in the encyclopedia organization of knowledge I found myself becoming increasingly independent in my school and college study. I have already told the story of how studying magnetism in the encyclopedia made it possible for me not only to understand the subject, but to break out of the stifling classroom routine in which students were called on to recite the contents of an incomprehensible and sometimes erroneous physics textbook. And as I have also said before, the overview from encyclopedia study of economics helped me get an A from the young, beautiful teacher for whom I had an adolescent infatuation —and helped me discover that the essence of learning is what Count Keyserling has called "creative understanding." These two incidents are selected from many to reveal a growing realization of the unique educational power of the literature of Reference. Browsing in the open shelves of library Reference Rooms became an irresistible temptation thereafter. And out of all this came a belief that with the mastery of a few, basic reference books one could self-educate himself. Indeed, in process, is one of my next books—*College Educate Yourself*.

From this theory about general education it was easy to modulate a theory about Reference practice and Reference education. All through daily reference work, beginning in the University of Toledo and the New York Public libraries I kept mentally tallying which Reference Books most frequently answered inquiries. I began ranking them in a sort of order for self study. These titles I began examining as if under an X-Ray; tucking away in my memory unusual sequences and stray facts.

After I had adjusted to assuming administrative responsibilities in my first job as chief librarian—at Fisk University—I resumed my exploration of the idea of a basic list of reference books. From my Columbia notes, from my Toledo and New York reference experience, from my love of the literature of Reference, and from Mudge I selected 100 Reference titles that I would consider basic in any library. These I sorted by type, beginning with dictionaries, encyclopedias, annuals, biography, geography, serials and indexes, government publications, before turning to special subjects. It was fun. I had enjoyed making ranked lists before: the ten greatest novels I have ever read; my ten most favorite poems; etc. I used to argue about my selections with Martin Ross and some of the members of a dialoging group called the *Briar and Java*. In the same way, I now took my list of 100 best reference books to some of my colleagues across the city in Nashville, at Vanderbilt and Peabody; at the Public and State libraries; at Ward Belmont and David Lipscomb. Many revisions resulted.

But the list was refined and refined. I began keeping notebooks, 8½ by 5½ size, a basic reference title for each sheet. From the books themselves I began writing notes like an English teacher reviewing poetry, fiction, drama, essay. I developed a passion for reading prefaces to Reference books; nursed an idea, some day, to reproduce some of the quaint ones, like Brewer's in which he suggests a girl might clinch the knot with her boy friend by revealing a store of knowledge nuggets taken from his *Historic Notebook*. Brewer should have known his courting better than that. It is probably true that men don't like girls who either know or "no" too much. I stored all kinds of delicious quotes from the introductions to Basics; used them from time to time in my papers, classes, conversation. These exercises helped me strengthen my basic lists.

Finally, I set to work systematically to produce a textbook for the beginning Reference course in library schools. In the spring of 1935 I addressed letters for the second time to teachers of Reference in the accredited library schools, and to practicing librarians in the several types of libraries, now with the reenforcement of possible ALA publication of my book. Description of my procedure is described in Chapter 16 of the 1937 edition of *Basic Reference Books*. Briefly, I asked each teacher to "X" titles taught intensively; check titles mentioned in class; zero titles omitted. Using the same symbols I asked practitioners to indicate titles used most frequently in answering questions; used occasionally; almost never used. It was a quite new approach in 1936.

The first "Preliminary" edition of *Basic Reference Books* was published in March 1937 by the ALA. It began a publishing venture which continued until *Basic Reference Sources* went out of print early in 1970. What the total sales of this book were, ALA records will undoubtedly reveal. I recall that at one time long before the book went out of print, someone in the publishing department wrote to tell me that over a half million dollars of the books had been sold. Beyond the sales triumph my deepest gratitude went to ALA for the line in its news release on the occasion of my being honored with the Isadore Gilbert Mudge Citation at the 10th anniversary banquet of the RSD: "Dr. Louis Shores, whose *Basic Reference Sources* is the most widely used textbook of its kind. . . ."

If I were asked to review the 1200 plus, pages, I would concentrate on what I consider a rather extraordinary number of pages committed to the philosophy of Reference. I begin with the redefinitions of Reference, debatably dissenting with accent on assistance rather than on promotion, in the quest for information. Next follows the concept of Reference recording and the approach to practical bibliography in a scholarly world of multiple forms.

Classification of the Literature of Reference as it develops in *Basic Reference* is itself a venture into that branch of philosophy known as epistemology. The overview classification and identification of each type sets the stage. Among the type chapters, opening the approach to dictionary classification by vocabulary size had some elements of a first. English language history evolution in three stages from "hard word" through "respectability" to "scientific method" toward an absolute of unabridgement is philosophically speculated. Then come the sub-classes with more-than-previous association with school examples from pre-primary through 12th grade.

Not to write here still another edition of *Basic Reference*, I cite for consideration by my colleagues in search of Reference philosophy my three chapters on the encyclopedia; my treatments of audiovisual reference (for the first time, I believe), annuals, biographical and geographical sources (and especially in my chapter for *Instructional Materials,* Ronald, 1960), serials, indexes, handbooks, manuals. In the last, attention is paid to the cookbook literature, to home maintenance, health, etiquette, and some of the other practical arts, still beneath curriculum consideration by espousers of the restricted liberal arts. There are some new dimensions in the approach to subject and special reference.

Even before the first 1937 edition appeared I pondered how to keep the book up to date for the profession. I proposed to Mr. Halsey Wilson the possibility of a monthly review of reference books in the *Wilson Library Bulletin.* He and the editor, Stanley Kunitz, were immediately enthusiastic and thus began in 1938 *Current Reference Books,* which I edited until I went to war in August 1942. Still anxious to spread the recognition of Reference as a literature, I was instrumental in starting two more reviews. Because I wanted my colleagues in English teaching as well as in librarianship to become aware of the literature of Reference I persuaded the *Saturday Review* to let me roundup, annually, the new reference books. I edited this annual review for the first five years. Similarly, I convinced the *Library Journal* to initiate an annual checklist, which I also edited for the first five years, and which preceded the present RSD list.

The Basic Reference concept inevitably permeated my library use teaching, from elementary through graduate school. For the former, I prepared a text for *Scholastic,* as early as 1928. For the latter I introduced a required library search course for all graduate students in Florida State University, the famous (on that campus) "500 course" required of all graduate students, excepted those in library school, or exempted by examination. As a corollary, all master's theses and doctoral dissertations in the University must be approved for bibliographic sources and form. The content of "500" became the basis for the *Collier* article on Library Search which I wrote. Basic Reference is more, too, as a Reference philosophy and as Reference practice.

10. The Librarian as Encyclopedist

Before 1933 I considered the librarian's role in encyclopedias as exclusively that of a consumer. In libraries I had learned to use encyclopedias effectively as overview tools to earn better grades. As a Reference librarian, I increasingly depended upon the encyclopedia to start me off on the inquirer's quest. Library School oriented me to evaluation, and to comparatives among the major sets, English language and foreign. But all of this attention only helped me trace the line that separated the consumer librarian from the producer publisher.

After library school, another crusade possibility challenged me. Householders were appealing for help from their public libraries against unscrupulous door-to-door salesmen. Spurious sets, outdated and inaccurate were being sold to unsuspecting families at seductive installment bargains. The British aptly refer to this kind of business as "hire-purchase," or "never-never buying." The year 1928 was at least four decades before buying anything for cash had become almost indecent. Therefore, when the salesman offered an attractively bound set of books "free," for an endorsement by the householder, and only ten cents a week for an up-dating service, any consumer, almost, jumped at the opportunity.

Only later, when the householder looked at the contract he had signed, did he realize he had signed for ten years of service, totalling $52, and that in very fine print there were the words "not subject to cancellation." In desperation, people appealed to their public libraries for help. Libraries in turn brought the problem of spurious sales to their state professional associations and to the American Library Association. By 1928, one regional library association, the Pacific Northwest, had undertaken to develop some guidelines for encyclopedia selection.

In 1928, the ALA activated the Subscription Books Committee, and in January 1930, volume one, number one of *Subscription Books Bulletin* quarterly appeared. It was a courageous undertaking by the American Library Association. The jury of librarian-reviewers began to close their reviews with the words publishers soon learned to dread: NOT RECOMMENDED. In the analyses I made of some thirty years of SBB committee reviews, to arrive at some criteria for teaching encyclopedia evaluation, and for later designing and editing encyclopedias, I noted that about half of all of the encyclopedias reviewed were designated "not recommended" or "recommended with limitations". There was something refreshing in this new backbone of literary review.

Louis Shores

I took up the cudgel to help make encyclopedia publishers "honest" by reviewing new works and revisions of old sets for various outlets, from local newspapers to notable ones like Walt Whitman's *Brooklyn Daily Eagle*, Irita Van Doren's New York *Herald-Tribune Books*, *The New York Times Book Review*, and, eventually, for Norman Cousins' *Saturday Review*. I even reviewed encyclopedias for local radio stations, for some house organs, and for women's club meetings. By the summer of 1930, when I undertook to teach in an ALA accredited library school for the first time, at McGill in Montreal, I drew up my first list of criteria for evaluating an encyclopedia. It became a library school stencil, long before it formed the basis for Chapter Three in the 1937 edition of *Basic Reference Books*.

I was still on the consumer side of the line that was drawn taut between librarians and publishers as late as 1933. It was considered unprofessional, if not unethical, to associate with encyclopedia publishers. I understood that at one time members of the Subscription Books Committee were not permitted to accept a free lunch from a publisher's representative. The climate was such that even the reputable publishers were suspect. Citizens had been exploited by many upstarts who were concerned only with merchandising for profit. Perhaps the same motive that impels Ralph Nader today was stirring me to be a thorn in the flesh of the encyclopedia publisher.

As long as I remained on the consumer side of the line, exclusively, I tended to assume that all publishers, editors, and salesmen were committed to profit, above all, and to gaining as much economic advantage as possible by producing an inferior product. To some extent, this climate had been created by unscrupulousness in the ownership and distribution of the inferior sets. To an even greater extent, suspicion was bred by the reluctance of some publishers to submit their new works, or revisions, to the ALA for review. I shared, and reflected in my reviews, this distrust of the subscription book publisher, in general, and encyclopedia producers in particular.

In reference classes at Peabody, I began to make dramatic productions out of my encyclopedia unit. We analyzed sets comparatively; I devised all kinds of stencil problems that would subject the approved and the non-recommended sets to analyses such as even SBC could not undertake. With 30 to 40 students in my class, and sometimes as many as sixty in the summer session, we might investigate as many as a hundred different subject areas, and arrangement aspects, in the course of a four-quarter academic year.

In the summer of 1933, *Encyclopedia Britannica* announced it would release in the fall its new encyclopedia for young people. I wanted very much for my large class in summer session, mostly teachers, to have a look at the set before they went back to their respective schools to express an opinion on purchase. Besides that, I had a number of hawkish questions to ask. I had noted that *Britannica* had purchased an eight-volume children's set published in Cleveland, called *Weedon's,* and I wanted to know if the new *Britannica* set would be a revision of that, or an entirely new work. If the latter, would it be a simplified rewrite of some of the articles in *Encyclopedia Britannica.*

Among my top missions at the Montreal ALA that summer was to confer with a *Britannica* official, to whom I directed my questions. He assured me that *Weedon's* had been purchased to eliminate some competition in the "juvenile" field. *Britannica Junior,* he assured me, would be an entirely new work in 12 volumes, instead of *Weedon's* eight. I then asked him if he could ship me a pre-publication set before the middle of August so that my students might examine it before they returned to their jobs. I offered to do something I had never done before: purchase a set before seeing it, solely on the fine reputation *Britannica* had.

As soon as the set arrived, I locked myself in my office, late at night, after the library building was closed. After a quick overview of the twelve attractive volumes, which disturbed me almost at once, I placed the set of *Weedon's* I had previously acquired beside it. Without waiting, I wrote my review for the *Peabody Journal of Education* in which I pointed out that *BJ* and *Weedon's* were identical, with some minor exceptions, in content and form—the eight text volumes of *Weedon's* had been made ten thinner *BJ* volumes. Volume one, I suggested, was the Compton Fact-Index pattern, assembled in one volume instead of in the back of each volume; volume 12, I thought, resembled the *World Book* ready reference classified index. Taking the *D* volume as a sample comparative, I sarcastically noted, in the tradition of the muckrakers of our media today, that the first 100 articles in the two sets were identical, except for the fact that *BJ* had cut out the *Weedon* picture of Diogenes in search of an honest man.

Hardly had my review appeared than I received a letter from the *SBC* chairman saying the Committee had come to about the same evaluation of *BJ*. Furthermore, subsequently, the Federal Trade Commission insisted that the *Weedon* copyright must be indicated thereafter, as long as the two sets were so basically identical. *Britannica Junior* went on from that first unfortunate printing to major revisions that resulted in a truly outstanding encyclopedia for young people.

The following year, *Compton's Pictured Encyclopedia* sent Leora Lewis, a librarian, and one of the first of the distinguished line of library consultants employed by publishers of approved encyclopedias, to see me at Peabody. She confronted me with the challenge, for the first time, to shift my interest in encyclopedias from the negative critical crusade to positive, creative editing. Speaking as a librarian, Leora contended we had a professional obligation to help publishers build good reference books before they spent their money, rather than wait until after the mistakes were made to tell them what they should have done.

I pondered this, discussed it with several colleagues in whom I had great confidence, and finally with Carl Milam, at ALA headquarters. With his good business sense and broad professional perspective he urged me to consider the Compton offer. "It is time some of us cross the line and begin working with publishers. SBC members cannot, but librarians not serving on the committee who are qualified and interested, should."

I accepted the Compton offer to become the Company's library adviser. In 1934, therefore, began an 11-year association with publishers and editors that I shall treasure always.

Beginning with the late F. E. Compton, a nephew of Woodrow Wilson, I was introduced to a level of graciousness and ethical standards hardly surpassed by many libraries. Every one guarded my professional obligation. Again and again I would suggest an enthusiasm which appealed to them, but which they would caution must be checked first of all with ALA to see if they would consider it ethical. I began to look forward to talking with Mr. Compton on my periodic visits to 1000 North Dearborn Street in Chicago, where the mansion-like editorial offices reminded me of my picture of British publishing.

I worked directly under the late Athol Ewart Rollins, managing editor from 1922-1942. Although Guy Stanton Ford was the Editor in Chief, he was making infrequent visits to Chicago during my period of service. Rollins, a Rhodes Scholar at Oxford, and a former literary editor of the *Milwaukee Journal*, as well as a teacher of Greek and Latin, gave me my editorial baptism. Graciously, he would listen to my youthful, and often crude protests about encyclopedic decisions. And then, very quietly, he would say, "Louis, how would you like to protoype, on a small scale, your idea of how it should be done?" I soon discovered how much easier it was to find something wrong than to try to make it right. I was seeing the encyclopedia from the production side. I was beginning to understand that imperfections were not deliberate but compromises in which the choice was always between comparative imperfections.

The most challenging assignment came to me in 1936. Compton's assumed my Peabody salary for a quarter, and a little more so that I might devote myself to preparing a pamphlet on how to use an encyclopedia. It was published in 1937 under my title, "Know Your Encyclopedia." It was a cold winter quarter in Chicago. Gerry went back to teaching in Tuley high school. We rented an apartment in the St. James on the near north side. Since she had to arise earlier to arrive before her eight oclock I enjoyed the luxury of a few extra minutes in bed to contemplate the switch board operator's cruel telephone awakening: "Good morning, six o'clock, 20 below."

I trudged over to South Dearborn street, crunching hard packed snow under my storm boots. Briskly I would begin on "Know Your Encyclopedia." There are still some copies of this 48-page booklet, bound in red paper covers, available in libraries. Some dimensions in library use were introduced that were incorporated in college and school courses later. Notably, I tried to communicate my discovery of the power of the overview, and how to self-educate oneself through sophisticated use of reference tools, in general, and encyclopedias in particular.

In the process of filling assignments, I was self-educating myself on encyclopedia production.

Before 1933, Encyclopedics, a term I coined to comprise all of my involvement in encyclopedias, concerned itself primarily with consumer aspects. The first of these was encyclopedia use, beginning with myself for better grades in school and college. Next, it became part of my evangelism to help students educate themselves. I was convinced teachers underestimated the potential of the encyclopedia, because of their own inadequate instruction. I raged every time I heard a principal talk against letting pupils use encyclopedias, as did two principals, one in California and one in Florida. I knew their own diffidence with these mines of learning accounted for their inferiority complex.

So I began to teach and write encyclopedia use—in school, college and library, wherever I was on the payroll. In 1928, I did a series of four articles for *Scholastic* on "How To Use Your Library," later reprinted as a text booklet for use in schools and colleges. Part II was devoted to Reference Book use, with a major section on the Encyclopedia. Other publications on library use followed: the Compton "Know Your Encyclopedia," in 1937; the Barnes & Noble College outline paperback with Dr. Samuel Smith, the publisher's capable general editor, titled *Best Methods of Study*, which went into many editions. My section was, of course, library use. Then followed the *Peabody Library Information Tests*, two for each level—elementary, secondary, college—coauthored with psychologist Joseph Moore.

I began teaching in an accredited ALA library school in the summer of 1930, and enlarged my encyclopedias to include encyclopedics instruction for librarians from a perspective I had not had in library school. It began with the three ways of book distribution in the United States —Trade, Textbook, Subscription Book—and the implications for the librarian especially in relation to patrons. What had made me especially aware of the distribution dimension was association with library representatives when publishers, at last, recognized it was important to find out from librarians the strengths and weaknesses of encyclopedias as revealed on the firing line of reference service.

It was my association with so many innovators and innovations at *Compton's* that set me to sketching my ideas for an ideal encyclopedia. Dimensions in *Compton's* that excited me especially were the fact-index, both the amplification of the citation, and its placement at the end of each whole-letter volume; dramatic introductions to every subject; complements of caption and legend, for each illustration so that all three integrated with the text; study outlines for self-education; meticulous attention to style so that no matter how authoritative the article it might yet be understood by young people. I recall especially the numerous rewritings of the article on archaeology by the distinguished Egyptologist, Dr. James Harvey Breasted, director of the University of Chicago Oriental Institute. The first version would undoubtedly have drawn accolades from his peers. But it was perfectly unintelligible to the adult layman, leave alone elementary school pupils. It was rewritten by a Compton editor. When Breasted saw the rewrite he was furious. He tried again; the Compton editors revised again. Back and forth went the manuscript. Finally, a tenth version was acceptable to Breasted, as not violating scholarship; and to the Compton editors, as intelligible to young readers.

I went back to my Reference students feeling more humble than ever. How could I as a librarian have been so caustically critical of encyclopedists, reputable ones, with standards so high, who suffered with contributors so conscientiously. Crossing the line as I had with *Compton's* convinced me there was as high a professional ethic among editors as among librarians, and that these two groups must begin to work more closely than they ever had before. I was crusading again. There was nothing I could do to stop this churning that went on inside.

In the romantic, picturesque red brick mansion that housed Compton's in Chicago, we used to engage in deep philosophical discussions of the encyclopedia's place in our American society. The gracious F. E. Compton himself personified the care and awareness of the entire staff. Sometimes these discussions took place in his office. Managing editor Athol Rollins might drift in, or Leora Lewis, or art director Seymour Jones, enlarging the discussion on encyclopedia scope, comparative organizations of knowledge as represented by classified and alphabetic variations on the arrangement or access theme. Then we would all repair to a luncheon table to continue our animated discussion of a brainstorm one of us had for introducing an innovation.

What I try to underwrite here is that the eleven years as an advisory editor for *Compton's Picture Encyclopedia* began my own encyclopedics and a philosophy for the encyclopedia design I developed ultimately for the new *Collier's Encyclopedia.*

Perhaps the time had come for librarians to begin to produce as well as to consume reference books; to experience the decisions that editors had to make between imperfections. In June 1946 I accepted the challenge to design *Collier's Encyclopedia*, a brand new major English language encyclopedia, a librarian's encyclopedia. When I reported to the Collier editorial offices, then on Park Avenue in New York City, I was suffering from disillusionment about the United States' commitments and promises to its returning veterans. Part of my depression resulted from the postwar housing shortage. As I resumed my Peabody responsibilities in Nashville, Gerry and I could find only a room in a boarding house where everyone had to share a single bathroom. In New York, naturally, the situation was even worse. Hotels would take guests for a maximum of three nights in those days, and I shuttled between rooms in three of the city's five boroughs, pausing to leave my suitcase in the locker room of Grand Central Station.

Service-incurred ill health did not make matters any pleasanter. The CBI fevers and chills remained with me for many years. In 1946, acute strange moments of delirium would strike in the afternoon, mostly; and at night, when I alternated between quaking chills, and sweat-drenched pajamas. My left foot, which I had injured in the army, was making walking difficult. I went to see a Manhattan orthopedic surgeon, in his office. He took one look at my left foot, shook his head, whistled, and said "You have the beginning of a club foot; we may even have to amputate. It's a wonder you have ever walked at all."

I realized then the meaning of bedside manner. There seemed no excuse for that type of medical pessimism. I said firmly "That foot has done as much as thirty miles in a day, in the Burma jungle, with a pack on my back."

The surgeon looked unbelieving, "You in the army?" He examined my foot more carefully, and inquired about my civilian occupation. When I told him I was a librarian, he said "I have a twelve year old son, and he is having trouble with reading in school. It is driving his mother to distraction. Both of them are worrying me to death." I looked at the physician and felt a kinship. We were all human beings, for some reason meant to suffer and bear our crosses. Mine was housing; his was a backward son. I told him about our new reading laboratories and what we did to improve children's readings. He became so interested, and asked so many questions about the metronoscope and opthalmograph, the two instruments that were featured in reading labs then, that we both forgot about my foot.

After a half hour of discussion about his son's reading difficulties, I gave him my diagnoses and prescriptions, and the name of a reading clinic. Greatly relieved and comforted he said, "Let me take a look at that foot again. Don't worry. You should see some of the conditions I've had to work on. There is really nothing seriously wrong. All you have to do is soak it daily in water with this prescription; and perhaps wear an in-sole. We'll have you as good as new in six months."

The housing picked up, too. Ed and Minnie Wight were living in Cedar Grove, New Jersey. Ed had been acting director of the Peabody Library School during the first three yeas of my army duty. When they heard of my housing difficulty, they insisted that I bring my wife to New York and that we occupy a room in their home until we could find an apartment. I began commuting via Erie steam railroad to lower Manhattan, and then by subway to Grand Central.

What restored my Pollyannaism (and I am proud to admit that my meaning of art finds greater literature in Eleanor Hodgman Porter's "glad books" than in some of the current gruesome greats) was the Collier challenge: To design a librarian's encyclopedia from the beginning, with the financial backing of a solid publisher, and the moral support of Mr. ALA—Carl Milam. The story of how I had been selected by Ralph Smith, president of the Collier subsidiary, spurred me on. Not only I, but my profession of librarianship was on the scale. So we librarians were critical? Then do something positive.

Carl Milam's story, as he told it later, repeated itself to me as I worked. ALA and SBB had been experiencing some difficulty in getting publishers to report their encyclopedia revisions, and new ventures. Sometimes it was even difficult for the reviewers to get access to a set. "Imagine my surprise," said Carl Milam, "when an encyclopedia publisher president walked into my office one day with the startling proposition "Why do you librarians wait until after we've spent our money to tell us our mistakes? Why don't you help us before we begin? We are about to put four million dollars into a new encyclopedia. What advantage is it to ALA to withhold advice from us?"

Then it was that Milam suggested that while ALA could not officially help any one publisher there was no reason why Collier could not employ a competent librarian adviser. He suggested Louis Shores, as one librarian who had been working with encyclopedia for many years, and particularly with *Compton's*; he was about to be discharged from the army. That brought my telegram, the visit to New York, and a contract signing with Ralph Smith.

What I discovered in the Collier office was a disciplined staff that respected and feared the President. Ralph Smith had come up the tough door-to-door sales way, had worked very hard for his success, and was determined that every one who worked under him would work just as hard. The salesmen in his organization knew he could ruthlessly fire them if they strayed one inch from his line. It included a hard ethical line, which prescribed that every order taken by a salesman had to be confirmed by an accountant who called on the consumer to check that he understood the contract and had read all of the fine print.

This rigid discipline extended to his office staff. Every one had to sign a time-in book, before nine AM, or find a pink slip in his mail box, the next day. Every one signed out at five. I resented this and told Ralph Smith so. This was not my way to work, and I doubted that good editorial work went by those hours. Then, before he could argue, I demanded that I be given a key to the offices so I could get in at six in the morning, and stay as late at night as possible. He looked at me unbelievingly when I told him I had always begun my day at the university around six in the morning. To prove my point, I noted my arrival time on the time book daily at around six AM. Ralph, himself, always arrived at least an hour before the nine o'clock starting time, and was startled to find my office lit up and my head buried in reams of materials. He grinned, and said I was undermining his regimen. But he was obviously pleased. An affection developed between us, although I know I worried his stern front.

When it came time to appoint a secretary for me, one of the candidates was a young man whose father was headmaster of a New England prep school. The young man's typing was fast and impeccable. He was well read, intelligent, lured by the prospect of helping put together an encyclopedia. But he was "queer" from the business man's point of view. He anticipated the hippie. A vegetarian and pacifist, he dressed in cloth shoes because he would not wear clothes made out of slaughtered animals' hides. I will call him Bruce, here. He was devoted to me and to my wife. A talented cook and baker, he invited us to his Greenwich village apartment several times. One day he brought a cake that he had baked to my office. To his amazement I had him cut the first wedge and take it to Ralph Smith's office. Bruce and the other secretaries gasped. To them Ralph Smith was some kind of an ogre to be feared. Bruce went to the office, knees buckling on the way. What I expected, rather than what the staff feared, happened. A half hour later, the stern Ralph Smith walked over to my office, thanked me for the cake, and told Bruce it was delicious. Ralph began to admit my informality, because he saw I was getting a tremendous amount of devoted work out of my staff.

One day he walked into my office after five o'clock, and it was filled with my staff members working on a layout. I joked, "Mr. Smith, I told my staff the company has a rule that if any employee stays after five o'clock he has to pay the company overtime for the use of light and heat." Ralph Smith grinned and said, "That's right. It costs us money to keep the building open." A few minutes later, a delivery man served box suppers to all of us. Later, Ralph said, "It's good to see employees that much interested in producing work." I showed Ralph the brainstorm on maps we had worked out that afternoon, and that none of us wanted to stop. He commented, "My salesmen can sell that idea."

One day, Ralph asked me hesitantly, "Would you talk to some of my salesmen?" Then he added, "But we are having our meeting Sunday afternoon and night."

"Ralph, you know I am strictly a nine to five man. Sunday hours will cost you triple time and a box supper."

He grinned, and said, "I'm sorry, you'll have to go slumming with the rest of us and have dinner at the Waldorf-Astoria."

What belongs in an encyclopedia? I had defined an encyclopedia for myself, for my students, and in *Basic Reference Books*, as a summary of the knowledge most significant to mankind. I had, besides, already used the perspective of this definition to advise several major encyclopedias—*Compton's*, *World Book*, *Americana*, *Britannica*. In 1936 I had written an article for *Wilson Library Bulletin*, titled "The Ideal Encyclopedia." The late Clarke Fisher Ansley, designer and first editor of the *Columbia Encyclopedia* had sent me a copy with an acknowledgement that my writing had influenced him in designing that one-volume work. *The knowledge most significant to mankind*, I had defined, but how did one determine what was most significant?

I was determined not to do what so many encyclopedists I knew had done: make a list of entries in other encyclopedias and try to omit as few as possible. We would compare with the best, of course, but *after*, not before. I had introduced my own approach I had been thinking about for years. Perhaps in another book I shall detail my plan for determining the *scope* (one of my major evaluation criteria treated in *BRB*). A few unusuals are indicated here. For current subjects, I developed my list of subjects with several exercises carried out with the help of my staff. For example, I decided that since the *Wilson Readers' Guide* indexed at the time some 100 of the most popular U.S. and Canadian periodicals, the subjects of most significance to my contemporaries would be most frequently represented. We, therefore, measured by inches the number of entries in R. G. for various subjects during the past decade. The most popular subjects went into the master list of topics we were compiling for separate article consideration in the Encyclopedia, what we termed our "A-heads." We did something comparable with *The New York Times Index*, and later with *Keesing's* and *Facts on File*.

For retrospective significance, we analyzed courses of study for school systems, and syllabi in colleges and universities. Our list of A-headings was growing, on the 5 by 8 (rather than 3 by 5 cards) we were using, in those pre-digital computer days. (We went to work with RCA later to exploit computer assisted access.) Since ours was to be a comprehensive adult encyclopedia, we studied adult education courses diligently. With the ambusher in mind, I hasten to say these were not by any means all of our bag of tricks of the trade.

There were hard decisions to make. How, for example, can you measure the significance of a particular subject area? I imposed a word budget from the start. When we alloted 40,000 words as a beginning for ancient history, I was trying to balance my budget with medieval, modern, British, U.S., and other histories; and cross-culture comparisons with chemistry, music, sports and games.

The last area, incidentally, was headed by my good friend Harlan Goldsbury Metcalf. One day, Gold Metcalf came to my office with a disturbed look on his face. "Louis, you know I am grateful to you for giving me this encyclopedia opportunity. I would do anything I can do for you. But Louis, I am not qualified to advise you on this subject placed in my "Sports and Recreation" box. I took the card he held out, and read, TOPIC: *Prostitution*. I relieved his tension by telling him of the speaker who had addressed a library convention to tell them about a special library on Prostitution, and then without clarifying his antecedents, observed that the librarian of the Collection on Prostitution was a Professional.

The battles over wordage allocations with the advisers constantly reminded me of departmental budget allocations for buying library books. Among the most heated adjudications, I recall one over which President of the United States should have the longest article. The advocates for George Washington, Abraham Lincoln and Franklin D. Roosevelt were the most contentious. In the end, we decided to give the most wordage to the only president who had been elected four times, had served in the greatest world war of all times, had most revolutionized American society with a "new deal."

When the topics had been agreed upon, and the word allotments as well adjusted as possible, the advisers were next asked to nominate three authors for each A-heading article. We were entering the *Authority* criterion in earnest. I pointed out some conflict in considerations: (1) He knows the subject Nobel-winning well, but can't communicate to a layman; (2) he knows it less well but can write. Of course, we want both in our authors. But we all know professors who are outstanding in their subjects but can't teach freshmen. Our search for authors became a tremendous undertaking.

Over and above objective considerations I found I had to contend with some biases. When I arrived the cadre of advisers had already been selected from Columbia, Harvard, Yale, and especially Princeton; Chicago, Michigan, Illinois, etc., in the midwest; Berkeley, and Stanford, in the far west. But there was not a single representative from a university in the South. One of my most capable Princeton advisers expressed out loud what I fear too many from the North like to say: "Have they begun to wear shoes down there?" Nevertheless, I soon had a half dozen top scholars from Texas, Duke, North Carolina, Virginia, Florida State, and elsewhere, opening up a view of the tremendous renaissance beginning in the South.

By the spring of 1947, the first manuscripts began to come in. They were all solid in content but the variety of style worried me. We struggled over readability, trying out articles on a range of adult reading abilities. We rewrote scores of articles, braved furious telephone calls from authors, scorching letters, and even the occasional threat of suit. One of the comic episodes occurred in that first year. Our Science editor, almost on hands and knees, had prevailed on an outstanding California scientist to write for us.

One early Monday morning the Collier switchboard officer called to ask if I would accept a collect call from California. The scientist was on the line protesting furiously. "First you beg me to do an article for you; then you return it with a form rejection slip, without the courtesy of even a note." I was perplexed. Apologizing and asking him to direct the manuscript personally to me, I had an investigation made. What had happened was that the boy in the mail room tossing letters from the incoming mail toward various bins missed the encyclopedia compartment and the manuscript went to the *Collier's Magazine* by mistake. When it arrived in the Magazine's editorial department it was treated as an unsolicited manuscript, found wanting for their popular demand, and routinely returned with a printed rejection slip. It took considerable diplomacy to keep the scientist our friend. For weeks after, the magazine editors would josh me, *"Collier Magazine* rejects will be sent to the encyclopedia hereafter."

The incident parodied the point that just because a man knows his subject, it does not necessarily follow that he can communicate to a layman. But our editorial work steadily became a cross between stimulating and sensitive human relations with scholars whose feelings could be easily hurt. Many of our articles, however, represented an extraordinary combination of authority and readability right from the start.

Styling was only half of my criterion. The other half was objectivity. Bias could creep into controversial articles while the editor was absorbed with readability. Some areas were particularly sensitive. One of these is religion. No editor wants to offend any faith or denomination. At one time, two major U.S. encyclopedias—one adult and one for young people—withheld a biography of Jesus Christ until all Christian denominations were satisfied. Our own article on baptism had been rewritten as many as fourteen times. Early, I appointed what I called a "Faiths Advisory Board." Although the top three members represented the Roman Catholic and Protestant Christian, and Jewish faiths, scholars of the Islamic, Buddhist, and other faiths were referred to as necessary.

But of all the advisory committees, the librarian advisers were the most important to my objective of designing a librarian's encyclopedia. The big departure was to be in bibliography. Encyclopedia tradition required each article author to submit a short reading list which was put at the end of the encyclopedia article. It had always seemed to me that the titles were more an evidence to the writer's peers that the author knew his research literature than a help to the layman to carry on his self-education in the subject by helping him progressively go forward from the point where the encyclopedia article left him. Bob Kingery, the first librarian advisor I appointed, agreed, and since he was then head of reader advisory service at NYPL we worked out together a design for a new concept.

We would ask every author to submit a bibliography with his article, not for use at the end of article, as was customary, but as a basis for compiling a bibliography to be placed in the last volume of the encyclopedia. When we had refined the design I went to the publisher for an additional $40,000 with which to employ Bob and six other readers advisers, each with a subject area specialty—science, social science, literature, etc. I submitted copies of the author's articles, including their bibliographies, to the readers advisers working with Bob. Over a period of five years they developed an annotated bibliography of some 10,000 titles classified under 150 subject divisions, that was eventually indexed by the Encyclopedia's 500,000 entry analytical index.

The names of the librarians who worked so creatively and with such dedication can be found at the beginning of the 24th volume of *Collier's Encyclopedia*. It was an encyclopedia departure and I can understand some of the differences expressed by some librarians. At the time when the first dissenting review appeared I was dismayed and depressed. It had required an additional expenditure by the publisher when it would have been so much easier and less expensive to have done what every other encyclopedia had done—put the author's references at the end. But then came a lift when the more discerning reviewers and librarians began to see what new ground we had broken. The biggest thrill came when one reviewer called our bibliography a basic buying list for public libraries. The demand became so great that we finally published it separately in parts.

That *Collier's Encyclopedia* was going to be more library oriented than any encyclopedia ever before became increasing apparent to the editorial staff when I called library colleagues in as every one of my critical evaluation criteria arose. One of my oldest associates is Robert Blackburn, director of the University of Toronto library. Bob became my strongest ally in overcoming encyclopedia tradition of favoring the nation of imprint. I recall one morning at our quarterly three day sessions of the library advisory board. Often, I wished so much the entire Subscription Books Committee might have heard and participate in the highly professional discussions of editors and library advisers. Bob Blackburn that morning incisively observed, "I read the major article on 'Wheat' and the impression gathered is that if it is produced anywhere else in the world except in the U. S., it is in insignificant quantities. Yet your own *Statistical Abstract* indicates Canada out-produced the U.S. last year." I was so happy to have the Collier president hear this. He commented, "Louis has been after me for years to introduce more of an international perspective into the set. But the economic fact is that we make our money in the United States and therefore we must favor subjects of interest to our customers." But the publishers steadily expanded its foreign market and acceded to Bob Blackburn and me.

Because another book on encyclopedia designing may yet be written, I conclude here the story of the designing of *Collier's* by briefly citing some innovations in the criteria of format and updating, only. I committed the publisher to the extra cost of establishing the highest ratio of illustration to text of any English language adult encyclopedia. These were not just window dressing, but an extension of the text as we had pioneered the concept for young people in *Compton's*. First, it meant the extra expense of printing text on machine-coated paper so that illustrations would be in proximity, unlike our competitors at the time, who inserted pages at signature ends that would take half tones.

Having convinced the publishers of this innovation, I next moved into an art program such as no adult encyclopedia at the time had. We employed a top ornithologist to team with an artist who had specialized in painting birds to produce the most extensive series of plates yet, beyond even what the young peoples' sets had done. We did the same for costumes and for other pictures that were clarified by color. I became interested in the transparency overlay as part of my audiovisual crusade and brought the idea to editorial meeting several years before any encyclopedia, including ours' was ready to invest. One set came out just ahead of us, primarily because we were unwilling to settle for the less adequate press work in the United States and went to Berlin for our first set of human anatomy.

Updating was another problem that had plagued encyclopedists from time immemorial. Before *Collier's*, periodic revision, that is a major refolioing about every ten to twenty years, was the standard practice for the major sets. In between, the publisher issued an annual, or a quarterly paperback. Continous revision was being talked about, but until the terminology report there was no agreement among publishers and librarians as to what such revision represented. It became a yearly printing with from 5 percent to 20 percent revision of the total text. Mostly we concentrated on the quick changing fields—science especially, and technology. We set up our revision program right from the start.

At the time, encyclopedias had already begun the ten-year free reference service to its owners. Under this plan any owner could have ten questions answered each year for which there were no answers in the encyclopedia. To meet competition, *Collier's* inaugurated its reference service as soon as our first volume appeared. But I immediately set a plan into operation for assisting our updating. I put into our editorial budget salaries for a staff of reference librarians to answer owners' reference questions and maintain records on these questions as we do in library reference departments. One of these reference librarians I appointed

Quiet World / Crusades

Analyst. His job was patterned on the model of the Intelligence Analysts I had set up for analyzing AACS histories. For recurring questions we developed mimeographed answers and reading lists. When the recurrent frequency reached a certain level the material was incorporated in the next yearbook; if interest persisted, an article was introduced into the encyclopedia.

After the War, when I began my assignment editing *Collier's Encyclopedia*, Ralph Smith wanted me to stay on full time in New York. Simultaneously, Deak Sheridan Campbell wanted me to start a graduate library school for him at Florida State University. It seemed impossible to do both, but I was in love with both challenges and wanted to try. They agreed to let me. I chose to reside in Tallahassee and commute to New York, beginning in June 1947. These have been nearly 25 years of the most exciting work any librarian ever had, I believe. My decision was probably influenced by that quiet which committed me to librarianship. New York City has always been too staccatto an existence for my rhythm. It belongs to those who want to be "where the action is" if that is the kind of action one wants. Tallahassee and the South fitted my meditative mood better.

Ralph Smith and I had developed an affection for each other. It tugged at my heart to tell him where I wanted to reside. He gave me a continuing contract at a very modest retainer plus travel. On that last morning in June an incident occurred that had its origin in the establishing of my own regimen the June before. Ralph asked me to have breakfast with him and with Chairman of the Board Tom Beck. One does not say no to his two top bosses. As we lingered over a second cup of coffee I fidgeted and pointed out that it was nearly nine and that I had not signed in yet at the office. Finally, they let me go, and I was signed in at 9.07 AM.

The next morning my secretary handed me the customary pink slip with the worded lecture that the Company disapproves of tardiness. Outside my door Ralph Smith and Tom Beck were laughing.

The first major periodic revision of *Collier's Encyclopedia* was begun ten years after the original printing. I called it "The big R," and it was a massive undertaking, with complete refolioing and an expansion from

20 to 24 volumes—from 21 to 25 million words. But before that, between June 1947 and December 1959 I served as senior library consultant in the continous revision of the encyclopedia which resulted in a new printing each year. This began my 25 years of commutation between Tallahassee and New York which mounted up a half million air miles, mostly on Eastern Airlines; but also on National. I had begun the round trips during the 1946-1947 residence in New York, when I made monthly trips to the campus to design the new library school. The University had set up a $1500 budget to cover my air fare. It was not enough, and I supplemented out of my personal funds about $500, without presenting a bill to the University. Furthermore, the University paid me no salary for my work, because the State of Florida appropriation that year pinched the new university, converting from a woman's college. To my amazement, the following year my income tax was pushed into the next bracket because the $1500 travel had been marked as "salary."

Then in 1947/48 the commutations began from the Tallahassee residence to New York. The Company paid the travel generously, and offered to cover travel to library conventions for me, so that I could allocate the library school travel budget to my faculty. Even at an average of 12 commutations a year for 25 years the total mileage would be 600,000.

A major reason for my decision not to accept Ralph Smith's offer for full time was our dislike of New York living. The city violated my philosophy of quiet. I fell in love with Tallahassee. That year the song sang of that bit of the Southland, "green and grassy." And Tallahassee is *South*, although so much of Florida is "Yankee" and Miami, with its hot pastrami sandwiches seems, in places, to out-Bronx the Bronx.

I experienced the quick contrasts made possible by air travel. On many a winter commutation, I would leave Tallahassee in a blazing Florida sun with temperatures in the 80's. Two hours later the captain's voice might inform us, in flight, "Because of snowdrifts on the runway we may not be able to land at Idlewild." But the cultural contrasts were not as great as New Yorkers like to tell themselves when they justify their sardine can existence with "advantages."

I have heard more good music in Tallahassee over these years than in New York, principally, of course, because it was more accessible on the Florida State University campus. Theatre at FSU could not be ignored even on Broadway. The Asolo Theatre, an Italian 18th century edifice transported and reconstructed in Sarasota by the Ringling Museum, housed performances by the talented FSU playmakers. One summer the

New Yorker observed that the outstanding theatre during the hot months was the Asolo Theatre. About four Broadway plays a year were first performed at FSU, with leads from Broadway and supporting cast from Asolo. Several times I had the experience of seeing a play on Broadway Wednesday night, and then the very same play on Saturday night done by our FSU theatre. Forgive me. I thought the FSU performance fresher, and more inspiring, in most comparisons. And as for sports, my bias is for college football, much as I watch the professionals, and Florida State's Seminoles have been one of my weaknesses. Besides, FSU has the world famous student circus, the one which has had several hour-long CBS performances and which toured Europe for CBS.

So much for the cultural comparisons. Deaning in Tallahassee and editing in New York were almost equally exciting. On my monthly visits, I met with the editors to review manuscripts, to implement policies, to work out assignments for our library advisers, to help plan the next yearbook. Part of my responsibility was to work with our library consultant John Carroll on plans for library conventions, especially ALA annuals and midwinters. Owner queries or complaints also were brought to my attention for correspondence. From time to time Ralph Smith asked me to help out with personnel problems in the editorial staff, and to address the salesmen so that they would be better informed about encyclopedia content. It was this attachment to Ralph, personally, which influenced me to turn down a most extraordinary and generous offer by the Chairman of the Board and directing genius of the Grolier Corporation, Fred Murphy.

In 1950, he invited my wife and me to spend a gracious week-end at Ormond Beach, Florida, with him. We dined, and walked, and talked along the beautiful beach. Mr. Murphy showed keen understanding of encyclopedia problems and appreciated some of the innovations I was proposing. Above all, he agreed with my contention that too many of the works that were beginning to flood the market looked like somebody had just matched topic for topic in some previous set.

Before the week-end ended Fred Murphy made the most generous offer to me I have ever had. As editorial director I would shape and redesign all of the encyclopedias, eventually, now owned by Grolier. I was to begin with *Grolier Encyclopedia,* the American version of the British *Harmsworth's* that had not succeeded in obtaining an *SBB* recommendation; assist the editor of the *Book of Knowledge*; and eventually the *Americana.* Because I preferred to work in Tallahassee, rather than in

New York, editorial offices were to be established near the university.

I still have the contract in my file. It promised more money than I have ever received, which included an over-write of ½ of one percent on Grolier Encyclopedia sales. It was not an easy decision to say no to Fred Murphy, who had been so kind and considerate. Grolier was offering me three times as much money as I could hope to receive from Collier and Florida State combined.

It was a strenuous week in June. Depression was in the air because of the developing Korean involvement. My personal health was suffering from recurrence of the war fevers and chills. To my hotel on successive nights came Bob Kingery and Wayne Shirley to discuss Fred Murphy's fabulous offer. Both wanted me to stay with Collier, although both offered to join me at Grolier if I decided to accept Murphy's offer, and if I wanted them. I think they knew that without them I wouldn't go anywhere. Bob felt that both Collier and the University were underpaying me, and often lectured me about not holding out for more money with both of them. I had resolved I would never ask for a raise; they would have to volunteer it.

Ralph took me to Ebbetts Field, the next day, to see the Brooklyn Dodgers play. Any one who recalls Brooklyn's intense fans recalls the color of "dem bums." After, Ralph and I walked up and down the park in Washington Square, where his apartment was located, and talked. Ralph's eyes were wistful. "Louis, Fred Murphy's offer is beyond anything I can get the Company to do right now. Perhaps later. This is a good company. They will reward you eventually. The Company wants you to finish the encyclopedia. (Only about half of the set had then been published.) Above all, that encyclopedia has become the goal of my business life. I want to see it completed under your direction before I die. Louis," he added with an affection, and a voice that had a tremor he tried to control, "you are the encyclopedia for me, and without you I don't think I can go on." I remember saying without hesitation in Washington Square Park. "Don't worry, Ralph. This encyclopedia is in my blood, and largely because of you. I will tell Fred Murphy I cannot accept his offer."

When the 20 volumes of *Collier's Encyclopedia* finally appeared, we all awaited the reviews, and especially the one in *SBB*. I had convinced Ralph Smith, regardless of business reluctance to reveal advance information on new products, that we must inform librarians. I complimented

Ralph for calling on Carl Milam, and told him how other publishers had been so secretive that librarians had to find out about new reference works from citizens who purchased. "Imagine, Ralph, how a doctor would feel to find out about an important new medicine, first, from his patients." He agreed to let me inform librarians by letter of the new encyclopedia long before laymen. My first letter to librarians drew a compliment from one of the top Grolier executives. "All of us admired that master stroke," he said. But I had not written it for the business reason he indicated. I wanted my fellow librarians to know about new reference books before their patrons did, and I wanted to share some of my plans with colleagues whose opinions I respected.

The reviews brought tears to my heart. They were overwhelmingly laudatory. The *SBB* review, especially, was gratifying, because it was discerning, understood what we were trying to do even though some members of the committee apparently did not endorse entirely some of our departures, like the bibliography.

After that, continuous revision became my highest concern. We must update promptly, selectively, and coordinately. There had been several turnovers in the editorial directorship of the Collier books division, and vacancy in the post of editor-in-chief. Upon my recommendation, and after several long distance calls, Everett Fontaine, director of ALA publishing these many years, was named editorial director. Our selection of editor-in-chief was equally outstanding. W.T. Couch, for several years head first of the University of North Carolina Press, and then of the University of Chicago Press, became editor-in-chief. I worked with Everett and Bill very closely during the next decade.

Tragically, Ralph Smith was killed in an automobile accident, and there were several shakeups in the company's top level direction because of his death, and the decision to withdraw from the magazine business. Almost from the beginning of my association with the company I had been asked to advise on their other publications. One of the first was the *Collier Atlas*, which I helped to lay the foundation for in my work with the Rand McNally cartographers in preparing the encyclopedia maps, which subsequently became the *Cosmopolitan Atlas*, as well. Next, was the *Woman's Home Companion Cookbook*, for which I discussed with the editor a librarian's indexing idea for recipes, and the organization of the three major parts of any cook book. A household book was next, with attention to home repairs most frequently encountered.

John Wister undertook a garden book for us that involved some advice on arrangement. All of this led, eventually, to an even greater involvement, beginning about 1959.

There was another major change at the top, and plans for an ambitious expansion of the century-old company which eventually absorbed the century-old New York Macmillan Company. The upheaval affected the editorial staff, as well. Everett Fontaine had retired as editorial director, and Bill Couch, weary of the turnovers, and somewhat in disagreement with new Chairman of the Board, suggested that I be approached to assume the editorial direction, at least until a permanent head could be found.

At this point, the Collier subsidiary was given by far its most knowledgeable president. Raymond C. Hagel had been associated with McGraw-Hill for some ten years. He was besides head of one of the most successful Madison Avenue advertising agencies. I met him at our first editorial advisory committee in which he assumed the Collier presidency. I was immediately convinced that for the first time Collier had a president who could hold his own, intellectually, with any editor or adviser. I felt excitement as I heard him probe fine points in encyclopedia design with an elegant vocabulary.

Toward the end of the year 1959 the Collier Company recognized the achievments of the top 75 salesmen by inviting them and their wives to a week's vacation in the expensive Boca Raton Country Club. In addition, each wife was presented with a diamond bracelet. The week's entertainment must have cost the company many thousands of dollars. I naively asked our comptroller what about Uncle Sam? Does his internal revenue service approve? He indicated they encourage us to do this. Look what it means to the government. To earn this vacation for himself and his wife every salesman here has at least doubled his own last year's sales, and the entire sales force trying for the same prize boosted our sales record by millions of dollars. Right now Uncle Sam is smacking his lips over the increased revenue this year from our company.

Raymond Hagel invited my wife and me to share in this week. To a librarian and his wife used to modest living a nightly charge for a room of about $60 was rather overwhelming in 1959. The elegant menus, the ice sculpture in the drinks, the attentiveness of the hotel staff contributed to a luxurious feeling. Again I was impressed with Ray Hagel's facility in communication. His talk to the sales force was a masterly combination of Shakespearian English, Madison Avenue sales psychology, and football folksiness that had even rough-and-tumble salesmen like the door-to-door variety enraptured.

Perhaps because I am physically small myself I have tended to believe that men small in stature tend to strive harder intellectually; Napoleon was, of course, the epitome of small stature brilliance. My own General Ivan Farman, in World War II, to whom I dedicated *Highways in the Sky*, was about my own five feet seven in height. And Ray Hagel is in our height category. In many ways, Ivan Farman and Ray Hagel had the same stimulating effect upon my desire to create something extraordinary.

At the Boca Raton sales convention, Ray invited me to his room. He offered me the editorial directorship, and with the most flattering recognition of my contribution to the development of the encyclopedia since its beginning. I wanted to accept as much for the opportunity to be associated with such a brilliant mind as Ray's, and for that mysterious attraction I have felt toward certain people, all of my life, as for the encyclopedia, into which I had poured my very life blood, since 1946. I thanked him, indicated my commitment to building a great school of library science at Florida State University, and asked if he would consider letting me fill the post only for the period necessary to complete the major periodic revision I urged and he supported. I further induced him to come to Tallahassee and talk this over with my President.

When I returned to campus from Boca Raton, I immediately reported the offer to President Strozier. His reaction surprised me. Robert Strozier had succeeded Doak Campbell. He had come to us from the University of Chicago, where he had been a very successful dean of students, and where subsequently he became a leading candidate to head the institution made famous by Robert Hutchins. Bob Strozier responded immediately. "Do it Louis, please, for Florida State University." Apparently I looked puzzled. He said, "You know we had a very profitable relationship with *Encyclopedia Britannica* at Chicago. I'd like to establish a comparable relationship for FSU with *Collier's*."

When Ray Hagel arrived on campus, Bob Strozier had the red carpet out. I was excited and pleased with their conversation both in the President's office and in the elegant presidential mansion. Bob Strozier was a distinguished French scholar, decorated by the French academy. It was another case of mutual attraction. Our personal affection went beyond the respect we had for each other's academic fields. Indeed, had it been academics, only, I might have been repelled. Bob belonged to that tribe of professors who wore their liberal arts commitment on their sleeves.

My wife recalls to me often the scene in our living room. Ray Hagel and Bob Strozier negotiated an arrangement for my services during a year's leave of absence. Bob Strozier drove a hard bargain: the Company would assume my salary, I would devote every other week-end to the school, and Collier would set up a budget for my commutation travel. I enjoyed the bargaining but was not too concerned about the fiscal arrangement. I have always been reluctant about money. Again, mystically, finances have loomed as one of the obstacles of chaos in my search for the constant. Fortunately for me, my wife early accepted the responsibility of treasurer. She spoke up. Jokingly she reminded the two men her husband was not on the auction block to be sold as slave labor. And she secured some modest additions: an apartment in mid-Manhattan at Company cost, while we continued to maintain our Tallahassee home, and more salary than the University was paying.

Ray Hagel had assembled the editorial staff for me at my request. Since the retirement of Everett Fontaine and the resignation of Bill Couch there had been declining morale on the staff. Very briefly I outlined objectives for the Big R, the major revision of the encyclopedia. Even more briefly I reviewed the history of the work since 1946. Only a half dozen of the staff members had been with the encyclopedia as long as I.

A major undertaking was under way. We had invited a new group of subject advisers to review critically the entire 21 million words, recommend for their respective areas of competence deletions, additions, updatings, revisions, etc. We were going back over some of the scope approaches of 1946, especially in the perspective of some thirteen years later. As I expected the changes in science, technology, social sciences called for far greater attention than in the humanities. Indeed, so many of our literature, philosophy, and religion articles received such enthusiastic praise that we decided to revise them very little.

I set up a schedule for each editorial area. The top editors performed conscientiously and developed some young personnel for the staff who became superb rewriters, copy readers, indexers, analysts. Our art department attracted increasingly talented young people. We broke the nine to five New York routine frequently, editors missing that all important 5:15 train to Westchester or Westport, Connecticut, to stay behind and work out an editorial brainstorm that had developed late in the afternoon.

Occasionally, Ray Hagel would look in upon us with a smile of encouragement. He was an extraordinary company president. His quick mind would take in the editorial problem and often come up with the embryo of a solution. He was captivated by my idea for identifying the men who wrote the U.S. Constitution. I recalled how the signatures had fascinated me as a schoolboy. I decided to identify the signatures with the individuals in the picture and with legible printing of the names. My layout can be found on page 237 of the seventh volume.

Ray was also attracted to my variation on the chronology most encyclopedia yearbooks include. I called ours for the 1961 *Collier's Yearbook* "1960 Retrospect." The layout idea had come from a cloth calendar sewed for our kitchen wall by a friend of my wife. He got down on the floor late one afternoon after nearly everyone had gone home with me and with two cartographers from Rand McNally to plan how to map the new African nations so as to show their relations with former political divisions. When the Soviet Sputnik was first to photograph the other side of the moon, we pulled all kinds of strings to get that photo.

Not to prolong this chapter further, I will save for another book the story of designing an encyclopedia. It has been most exhilarating fun as well as hard work these 25 years. It has made me hang my head in shame many times as I recalled my youthful condemnations of encyclopedia publishers. I have wanted all librarians to witness first-hand how conscientiously publishers and editors suffer in their quest for the perfect reference book. My quarter century of association with Crowell Collier and Macmillan has been a noble reenforcement to my commitment to our library profession of destiny.

11. Library-College

Thomas Carlyle first came into my reading world with *Heroes and Hero Worship*. Before that he was a name to learn for the high school examination in English literature, and a writer for whom H. G. Wells did not seem to care too much, largely because of Carlyle's inadequate attention to Marat in the bathtub, in his *French Revolution*. The title of Carlyle's Hero book attracted me, however, and I read it in college on my own.

Originally, the book had been written by Carlyle as a series of six lectures to be delivered during May 1840. His theme could be stated briefly as faith in leadership by those of superior spiritual insight. In Carlyle's opinion such individuals of vision are the natural leaders, the heroes of world history.

I recall that I was stirred by my reference instinct to look up the meaning of the word hero. What spurred me on in my investigation of the word's meaning was the fact that Carlyle had added to the three basic meanings found in most dictionaries—divine strength, marked courage, devotion—the appealing characteristic of sincerity.

I went back to my beloved mythology and reread the story of Hero and Leander. In Greek legend, she was a priestess of Aphrodite at Sestos. Beloved by Leander, who swam across the Hellespont every night from Abydos. She was overcome when one night her lover was drowned. In grieving devotion, Hero, also, drowned herself.

The Heroes Carlyle chose to feature in his series of lectures related to six inspiring areas of human effort. Relating to Divinity, he chose Odin; to Prophesy, Mahomet; to Poetry, Dante and Shakespeare; to Priesthood, Martin Luther and John Knox; to Ruler, Oliver Cromwell and Napoleon Bonaparte. But the essay that interested me most was the one "The Hero as Man of letters," in which he featured Samuel Johnson, Jean Jacques Rousseau, and Robert Burns.

Of course, the oft quoted line at commencements, and library dedications, caught my inner eye: *"The true university these days is a collection of books."* Even more, the paragraph in which that sentence appears seemed to express my inarticulated learning philosophy. By my college sophomore year, I was convinced that I learned best when I library educated myself. In that very paragraph Carlyle wrote there is nothing a professor can do for his student except teach him to read.

The lecture "Hero as Man of Letters" was delivered on Tuesday May 19, 1840. I consider that the birthdate of the Library-College idea, which has now grown to a world-wide movement. Over 300 U.S. campuses are experimenting with higher educational dimensions that can be described as along the Library-College Way. There are a score or more of Library-College type institutions in Canada; Australia has manifested keen interest, even as far away as Tasmania; and there is a revived interest, in the United Kingdom, birthplace of the idea. Library-College Associates, Incorporated, publishes a quarterly *Library-College Journal* at the University of Oklahoma, and there have been nine conferences, at least, on the Library-College idea. Robert Jordan, Sister Helen Sheehan, Dan Sillers, Howard Clayton, and many other leaders in the movement have generously given me much credit for the idea. But I acknowledge my debt to Thomas Carlyle, who must be considered the father of the Library-College. *Heroes and Hero Worship* was among the most influencial books in my reading life. Let me delay the chronicle of the Library-College, itself, until I give one specific evidence of Thomas Carlyle's impact on my undeniable romanticism.

In my battered Heath textbook-like edition of *Heroes, Hero-Worship, and the Heroic in History*, edited by Herbert S. Murch, (Heath's English Classics, 1915) there is this marked passage among many (p. 137)

> If Hero means *sincere man*, why may not every one of us be a Hero? A world all sincere, a believing world: the like has been; the like will again be—cannot help being. That were the right sort of Worshippers for Heroes: never could the truly Beter be so reverenced as where all were True and Good!

Perhaps in what follows you will see my worship of the heroic in philosophy, in music, in literature, and in other things. But above all, for this chapter perhaps you will see how Carlyle's heroics shaped my higher educational philosophy.

Library first, and school next were my earliest loves. Later, of course, it was college. I write this and it somehow falls short of conveying the mystical attraction these two institutions have always had for me. They have been filled with romance these many years, and in combination they have produced an effect deep inside that can only be described as ecstasy.

To our unbelieving world of protest, perhaps the only way to communicate an abstraction is to introduce a bit of exhibitionism. Early, I was guilty of wanting to excel in reading, and writing, and arithmetic. In the very first grade, I began remaining standing last in spelling bees. I attribute my spelling proficiency to continuous and absorbed reading. My themes startled my teachers, and enthralled my classmates, because they never told it like it is; always my papers converted even the most prosaic assignments into sheer fantasy. I could not help it that I saw everything as happening on "Mulberry Street," long before that children's classic appeared.

Some times my more practical teachers were exasperated and crushed me with low grades. I recall telling a fifth grade teacher, once, "Anybody can tell it like it is; it takes courage to dream it like it should be." Years later, I heard these words as I thrilled to one of the few Broadway performances that measured up to my meaning of art—*Man of La Mancha*.

Even in arithmetic, I confess, I rather egotistically gloried in adding up a long column of figures before any one in class. This facility in addition has persisted through library life, and helped me before the computer age arrived, or my libraries could afford even a manual adding machine.

Even more demonstrative than my spelling, writing, and adding was my reading. With unbecoming impatience I seethed as my first grade teacher struggled with my classmates while they read, out loud, from the reader as much as one sentence at a time. When my turn came, I raced through page after page. It was so easy compared with my library reading. I recall that first triumph in school even to this day. My teacher let me read, and then exclaimed, "What a joy. Where did you learn to read like that?"

"In the public library," I boasted. Long after, when I was a public library assistant, I objected to the position of that library: let the schools teach reading, we will supply the books. "Let the public library teach reading," I contended, "because we can teach it better than the schools. The motivation is in the better collection we have, the teaching skill in those wonderful childrens' librarians. But above all, the library's superiority to the classroom is in the independence and meditation encouraged by the library climate."

This first grade reading triumph was one of the earliest in a series that added glamour to my love of school. Among some others that followed was a fourth grade sensation. In the public library I had set myself the task, one afternoon, to memorize the names of all of the U.S. presidents. Next morning, in history, the teacher asked who was the 16th president of the United States. I raised my hand, since child after child could not answer when called on. Realizing that the teacher's well-laid plan to dramatize the beginning of the study of Abraham Lincoln might be foiled, I volunteered. And then show-off fashion, I asked "Would you like to know the name of the president Lincoln followed, and of the president who followed him?"

Before the teacher could answer I gave her the two names. Then I added, I can name all of the presidents in exact order. Now my teacher was excited. She asked me to come to the front of the room for my performance. When I finished the children clapped. My teacher did even more. She handed me a note to take to the eighth grade teacher.

Now eighth grade in elementary school in our "unliberated" school days was comparable to Valhalla. When I entered the eighth grade classroom, heart pounding violently and knees buckling, I could barely gather enough courage to hand the note to the teacher. She read it silently and then addressed the class "Here is a Fourth Grader who knows all of the presidents of the United States." I quaked as I began with George Washington, but by the time I reached Martin Van Buren I was reciting like a trooper. I closed with the 26th president, Theodore Roosevelt, amidst a burst of handclapping.

There were several of these triumphs in every school year, and I confess they added some icing to the learning I relished. Unlike most of my classmates, Friday brought me sadness; Monday, anticipation. The summer vacations were long and less exciting than the school year. There was more make-believe in the five weekdays than in the two that formed the weekend.

In College, I really began to cultivate the Library Arts. They included some techniques I developed for myself as an undergraduate, to earn better grades, of course, but even more significantly for me, to arrive at what Count Keyserling later identified as "creative understanding." In high school, I had begun to understand vaguely that I could library educate myself better than I could learn in almost any other way. College influenced me to identify the components of this library learning and bring about a kind of *gestalt* to my evolving learning mode; or as the groovy group would say, "put it all togethah" (Never pronounced *er*).

As I look back on my undergraduate days in Toledo, I recall that these devices topped my library arts for learning, the inevitable prelude to the Library-College. First, I had become enamored with the *Encyclopedia Overview* before the first day in class of any of the courses for which I had enrolled in any term. To anticipate what might unfold in the next sixteen weeks sharpened my appetite for the subject as almost nothing else. Furthermore, it put me on the edge of my armchair to concur with or to refute the orientations the encyclopedias' distinguished authors had provided. Frequently, I came introduced to differences among authorities, to variations on principles and theories, to comparisons with developments abroad, and occasionally with discoveries of ultra developments, or with conflicts and contradictions that needed resolving. My learning in class never could be passive.

Second, I met the *Harvard Classics* in college, accidentally, when I was library browsing. President Charles W. Eliot put into eloquent words something I was groping to express about library learning. He wrote in his "Editor's Introduction" (v.50)

> My purpose in selecting the Harvard Classics was to provide the literary materials from which a careful and persistent reader might gain a fair view of the progress of man observing, recording, inventing, and imagining from the earliest historical times to the close of the nineteenth century.

This excited me as almost no previous browsing had. I enthusiastically endorsed "The best acquisition of a cultivated man is a liberal frame of mind or way of thinking; but there must be added . . . acquaintance with the prodigious store of recorded discoveries, experiences, and reflections which humanity in its intermittent and irregular progress from barbarism to civilization has acquired and laid up."

The *Fifteen Minutes-a-Day* Reading Guide clinched another component of my Library Arts College which preceded the Library-College. Why, I asked myself, cannot I library educate myself with a systematic reading program of more than 15 minutes a day? I calculated I could cover the undergraduate curriculum through library reading, on the Eliot plan, in half the four years required for a bachelor's degree. In the end, I proceeded concurrently with Toledo's class-centered curriculum, and my independent study.

The idea of an independent study college tempted me through graduation. In September of 1926, I hitch-hiked back from NYPL, during a brief vacation, by way of Yellow Springs, Ohio, where a former faculty member of the University of Toledo, Dr. William M. Leiserson, famous labor arbitrator, was professor of economics. Antioch College had just begun its innovative revival under Arthur Morgan, later TVA architect. The two most publicized features introduced into the college founded by Horace Mann were the work-study cooperative with industry, and the so-called autonomous courses.

I visited Dr. Leiserson's autonomous economics class on the opening day and was thrilled by what I observed. Here was my library arts college.

He overviewed the subject, like an encyclopedia article did. Then he distributed stencils containing syllabus, bibliography, project suggestions and instructions; his office number and hours. "So long," he waved, at the end of the hour. "The next time we meet as a class you will ask for it. Happy researching."

I read and thought about library arts college, independently, for my Master's classes at CCNY, and for that thesis on the "Municipal University" I was preparing to submit in partial fulfillment of degree requirements. I went back and reread Upton Sinclair's *The Goose Step*, an expose of U.S. higher education deficiencies. Bombastic articles, like the one by Kenneth Roberts in the *Saturday Evening Post* on "Murmuring Michigan" satisfied my marching spirit. I could identify campus problems as vehemently and vindictively as the self-righteous violents of today. But always I asked myself what I had to offer better. It was easy to declare I was against war, against discrimination, against pollution; for motherhood, love, and the global village. But when I got right down to sketching ways to avoid the evils and gain the goods I always ended up with other imperfections, injustices, inadequacies. I accuse the contemporary protest of lacking the courage to prototype solutions and expose their advocacies to the same criticism they expose the so-called establishment.

Dissatisfied with my own still unstructured design for the college of tomorrow, I continued my study of solutions in the past. I discovered the *Each one teach* idea in Dr. Laubach's world literacy movement had been anticipated in the 18th century Bell and Lancaster systems; and immediately appropriated them for the library arts college I was designing. Slowly, a higher educational architecture was evolving.

I began my doctoral work at George Peabody College in Nashville when I assumed the librarianship of Fisk University, across town. Among my professors in the department of higher education was the dean of the graduate school, Shelton Phelps, who later became president of Winthrop College. For my term paper in his higher education class I sketched my "College of Library Arts." He was excited about it, and first asked me to read it orally to the class. Then he suggested its publication in *School and Society*. About the same time, I was invited by the College and Reference Section of the American Library Association to prepare a paper on the future of the college library twenty years hence, since this was the general ALA theme at the Chicago World's Fair convention in 1934.

The discussion that followed my reading of the paper "The College of Library Arts: a possibility in 1954" was overwhelmingly dubious. The more sympathetic received it as a bit of education fiction, produced by a loyal ALA member as a concession to an assignment. But the more pragmatic attacked the idea vigorously, fundamentally from the position that librarianship was ancillary. It was the faculty's responsibility to teach; librarians had enough to do to supply college professors and students with the necessary sources.

I dissented. *School and Society* accepted my essay, and it was reprinted. With conviction, I set about sketching the architecture for the new college, in which the library became the only academic building. Recently, I rediscovered my 1935 notes on the college of library arts with the crude sketches of floor plans. What I had visualized was a circular building in which the stock was arranged by Dewey, the Zeros meeting the 900's to close the circle. People accomodation envisaged a private carrel for each student, and a larger one for every faculty member. Librarian colleagues opposed this more then than now.

The Library Arts College marked time for the rest of the decade. Other concerns crowded it out of my priorities. By the end of 1935, Basic Reference was dominant. When the first edition was published in 1937, I pursued the updating urge with *Wilson Bulletin*, and launched "Current Reference Books" in 1938. I was directing an ALA accredited school, and I was driving to innovate—with work study co-ops; with undergraduate articulation, years before any of the other ALA schools were even willing to discuss the problem, and we, with Rockefeller aid held the first articulation conference ever, probably. The audiovisual bug had bitten me, and I had introduced the first AV course in any accredited library school, in 1935.

There were just too many evangelisms. My doctoral dissertation on the "Origins of the American College Library" had prodded me to awake the profession to the importance of library history (the title of my opening essay for the new ALA Round Table much later). And my involvement in library service to Negroes, as we then labelled it, continued to torment me.

To add to the diversions from Library-College, the Hitler aggressions in Austria and Czechoslovakia angered me as much as the Ho Chi Minh chauvinisms later. When war finally came with the invasion of Poland in September 1939, all of my professional involvements dropped their priorities. Even the challenging chairmanship of the first ALA-ACRL Standards committee, with its stimulating membership and cause, dimmed before the Nazi threat to humanity.

Quiet World / Crusades

The Standards Committee work helped me design my Library-College library. I kept the score card in front of me all of the time I sketched what must go into a learning resource center for the independent learning mode I advocated. But beyond the library itself, an education developed that reenforced my near-frenzy to have the library at long last assume its instructional leadership in higher education.

I went to war out of the Peabody Library School classroom. Through the four years of struggle for personal survival, in CBI jungle first, and stateside just before VJ day, the idea for a library that is a college kept thrusting its way into war missions. I found myself talking with some of the college soldiers interested in education. One of them, a sergeant in CBI, son of an industrialist, wanted to help finance such a college, but, alas, he was killed in action. Among other things, I recall mentioning to him first, one time in our jungle camp, that CBI had always meant *Cumulative Book Index* to me. Since I was probably the first librarian assigned to the China-Burma-India theatre of war, perhaps I can claim another first for Joseph Kane's *Famous First Facts*, in the repetition of this CBI counterpart countless times by librarians who had or had not served over there, since.

War did not end for me until February 1946. The college was at the top of my post-war priorities. With closest friend Otis McBride, and my wife, we set out to discover a friendly home for our idea. Perhaps Otis did not quite share my enthusiasm for the library arts idea; but he was excited about the administration of the college, and I hoped that under his astute presidency I might design the academics for an institution of higher education which was basically a collection of books.

We tried the neighboring Tennessee community of Lebanon first. Cumberland University, there, except for the law school, was not flourishing. But the moment was later when Baptist consolidations occurred. Since we had Florida in mind from the start we used our Peabody spring vacation to tour both coasts. Beginning in Tallahassee we renewed our association and friendship with Doak Sheridan Campbell, who had been our graduate dean at Peabody, and who was now president of Florida State University. We told him of our mission, to which he listened sympathetically, and then offered suggestions. He ended by promising faculty positions in his growing institutions, if our plans did not materialize.

Of all the prospects, two seemed most promising. The owner of a resort hotel in Miami, which he had acquired at a war-surplus bargain price from the government wanted to establish a boarding college for daughters of wealthy parents. Our conference with the business man was discouraging and depressing. He wanted to realize "big," as he put it, on his investment. No fancy ideas on education, he warned. Show a profit from the start and make big money yourself. Lose money, and you are out on your ear at any time. "If this is too rich for your blood," he concluded callously, "say so now."

Furiously, I recall with shame, I shouted "NOW!"

But Sarasota on the west coast was different. We almost anticipated New College, there, by some two decades. The most pleasant contrast was Karl Bickle, United Press correspondent who had retired in Sarasota. He was captivated by our college idea and undertook to introduce us to several influential citizens, including the president of his bank, who made an exciting suggestion for a campus. Mr. Crosley's estate near the airport half way to Bradenton was up for sale. Perhaps the Crosleys might consider bequesting the estate to a college to bear the family name.

Excited by the prospect we all drove out together to look at the mansion and the grounds. It was perfect for a beginning. We sketched the remodelling quickly, estimated the investment, got the bank's assurance of a loan if the estate were acquired. We began communication with the Crosley representative in Cincinnati, by wire, phone, and mail. The next few days were optimistic ones as we went back to the estate again and again to design and redesign facilities for the new Crosley College. I was certain the creator of Shelvador would want to add the lustre of an innovative college to his name.

The response, when it finally came, was crushing. The Crosleys would sacrifice sell for $90,000. Even if we had had access to that kind of money, our Sarasota friends assured us, the price was high for the depressed real estate market of 1946.

We returned to Nashville. The dream was over. I had to face the realism of readjustment to librarianship after four years of war. The library world had changed. Picking up the broken threads alternately aroused and depressed me. I went to the ALA convention in Washington and sat alone in a far corner of the auditorium at the first general session. I was suffering from the self pity so many GI's felt who had been overseas and had created an illusion for themselves that the victory would terminate all of life's problems. Deep in compassion for myself in an isolated seat in that ALA meeting room I was startled to find myself approached by Viola and Ralph Shaw. He feigned offence. "A snob.

Just because you are a war hero. Too good even to acknowledge a job offer." He had written me about two. My heart was touched. That was the Ralph Shaw he did not let enough librarians see. Every one knew and respected that brilliantly sharp mind, that inventive talent with hardware. But not enough of us knew that basically human person. My associations with Ralph Shaw that go back at least as far as his Gary days had not been as many, probably, as others have had. But at a dozen points in my life, at least, Ralph had helped me turn corners even as the often unsung blocker on the football team does for the hero rusher. That Washington Conference was one of those turning points for me. Ralph probably doesn't even remember it. I did not consider the jobs he suggested but I took a new interest in life.

The gloom of my Peabody disappointment, several other unexpected rejections, the lack of housing for us in the post-war shortages, and all of the other causes of despair seemed to melt away after reassurance by Ralph and Viola that the four years at war were not all lost. I returned from the convention with two exciting offers—from Crowell Collier, and from Florida State. I took them both. And all of these encouragements revived my Library-College desire.

Wakulla Springs is 18 miles south of Tallahassee. It is a garden spot, a bird sanctuary, a wild life refuge. As a tourist you look through the glass bottom boat to the bottom of the crystal clear water the guide tells you is 180 feet deep. Fish cavort for customers as if they were paid to act, and indeed, one named "Henry" obeys the guide's direction to vault above the surface. On the beach, alligators lounge; and in the trees are almost extinct bird species like the limpkin. Because of the natural jungle setting, we are told, some of the early Tarzan films were shot here. In the gracious Wakulla Springs hotel, owned by the Dupont wealth, a major impetus to Library-College was given by the colloquium held there in the spring of 1964.

Leading up to that event was a series of higher education experimental involvements. Along with my effort to develop a graduate library school at Florida State University there was a broader commitment as a dean in the university to extend some frontiers on the campus. FSU, since its founding in 1851 (1857 officially) had run the course of seminary for men; coed Florida State College; and with the passage of the 1906 Buckman Act, Florida State College for Women. When I arrived on campus, September 1946, the Buckman Act was about to be repealed, with the arrival of the first 500 men. The state was committed to establishing a second state university. There was a climate of exhilaration for experiment and innovation. An adventurous and creative Council of Deans accepted the President's challenge to add some dimensions to the idea for an American university.

Each dean worked with his own school. My heterodoxies in the awkwardly titled *School of Library Training and Service*—aptly student-abbreviated by the nickname that has stuck, SOLTAS—implicated the campus as well as the school. In the Library Education chapter these innovations will be enlarged. Perhaps the pioneering that rippled deepest in the university, those early days, was the commitments to audiovisual instruction, not only for all librarians in training, but for teachers in training, as well as students in other divisions. The immediate result was the assignment to the school of a university-wide audiovisual service, as well as instruction.

In 1947, I suggested to the new graduate council that no master's or doctor's degree should be granted until a post bachelor student evidences enough library and bibliographic sophistication to search and research in basic sources. The suggestion appealed to a majority of the Council with the inevitable assignment to activate a program for the bibliographic instruction of graduate students. In 1947 I introduced the exciting "500" course which the Council promptly established as a requirement for every candidate for the master's or doctor's degree in any discipline at Florida State University. For if the independent learning mode was to bring student success it would have to be fortified with a bibliographic sophistication far beyond that we had yet been able to communicate to the present generation of both students and teachers.

For some time earlier a considerable part of my own campus unrest had resulted from growing impatiences with excessive specialization. The union-like selfishness of the disciplines disturbed me. I listened to a demagogue-pedagogue declare in faculty meeting "but the student comes first." Some of my colleagues would respond with head nods or applause to this platitude when it was obvious that what really came first to this faculty member was Chemistry, or Physics, or History, or Economics, or English Literature. I simply refused to accept an interpretation of Genesis in which God was a chemist on the first day; an economist on the second; a philosopher on the third, etc. This was what we were asking our students to be on successive hours during any college day. A *gestalt* was called for in the curriculum. The General

Education movement in colleges which developed right after world war stimulated me to work on some new dimensions for Library-College.

And that is how Wakulla came about. Out of our General Education struggles with faculty members who were above all loyal to their specialities, Dr. Stickler and I began talking Experimental College for the university. We reviewed what Glenn Frank had done with his experiment at the University of Wisconsin. Then we compared notes on Antioch, Stephens, where Stickler had served on the faculty, and at perhaps a score or more colleges where general education influenced curriculum directions.

The FSU experimental college epic can be said to have begun right after the third quarter of the Florida State-Houston football game. Reluctantly, three deans—one, of the college of arts and sciences, the second, of students and the third of the library school, all rabid Seminole football team boosters, tore themselves away to meet the departure time of National Airlines flight for New Orleans. The ultimate destination was Lubbock, where rendezvous was to be made with an assembling Southern Association committee scheduled to evaluate Texas Technological College.

By the time we returned to the campus, we had decided. We saw Hugh Stickler first, and then added the academic vice president, the dean of the graduate school, and the university librarian to our *ad hoc* Experimental College Committee. No matter how much we differed on dimensions we were in agreement that higher education need reforming at FSU, and in the nation. Perhaps we were anticipating the subsequent campus unrest. All of us understood that the United States was confronted with an entirely new higher education challenge—college for all.

We began to meet one night a week, rotating the meeting places in our homes. I look back at this idyllic first year of excited dialogue on some new dimensions for collegiate instruction in which something important was hardly communicable. We could never make the CBS evening news "direct . . . and in color." We neither were nor are particularly photogenic. We were ourselves averse to marching and could not have hoped to attract marchers. But we did a dialogue about our shortcomings, suggested ways to overcome them, and finally sat down to the drawing table to design a prototype college for tomorrow. Somewhere around midnight the lady of the house would come in with tasty refreshments.

Then came the idea for the Wakulla Colloquium. We would invite ten experimental and innovative colleges to describe their heterodoxies; we would be the eleventh, but we would be the only college that had not yet launched its experiment. The idea grew, and the president of the university began attending our meetings. Through the efforts of the graduate school dean we interested the Southern Regional Education Board, and they agreed to finance the Wakulla Colloquium.

The ten invited to Wakulla included five small private colleges, one medium-size private university, and four large public multiversities. Each institution sent as its spokesman the architect of the experiment. Academic vice presidents and deans predominated, but the not-yet opened California state university at Santa Cruz was represented by its president. Professors of various disciplines came, also, and there were several librarians, including Bob Jordan of the Council on Library Resources.

In between keynote and summary, the five small private colleges sketched the fundamental unit in the "True University." Antioch's autonomous courses, as amplified by Sam Baskin, confirmed the essential learning mode. The new facilities at Stephens, which I subsequently confirmed with a visit to their new learning resources quadrangle, strengthened my architectural designing for the Library-College library. I was aroused by Florida Presbyterian's interterm in which classes were completely replaced by independent library study. What I saw in the Parsons report by librarian Lee Sutton was the kind of courage that would enable the United States to realize a world history first—college for everyone. In effect what Parsons was saying to the elites was "Sissies. Anybody can educate the superior student. I dare you to do something about the potential dropout." Parsons was doing this kind of salvaging despite some disparagement by the regional accrediting agency. What New College would do was still conjecture. But I heard their projections in Sarasota with memories of our own disappointing near-success in that city.

It was most important to invite the universities engaged in experiment along the Library-College way. At the Chicago meeting in November 1969 I learned with regret how important it was to spell out large university suitability for the Library-College idea. Despite the fact that several of us emphasized the cluster college organization, two of the most intelligent librarians at the Chicago L-C meeting reviewed the conference unfavorably because they were unable to apply the idea to a multiversity. If anything, I believe the Library-College can save the large campus from the unrest inherent in the impersonality of numbers.

In succession, the middle-sized private Pacific University, and the three huge state universities in Michigan—Ann Arbor with its Dearborn campus, Lansing with its residence halls, and Wayne with its exciting Monteith—revealed the potential of the cluster organization for Library-College. Even more convincing was the projection for the new University of California at Santa Cruz. Although a 27,500 student body was contemplated, no single college in the cluster would have more than 1,000 students.

From Wakulla I came away more convinced than ever that the Library-College idea could be the salvation of a steadily deteriorating campus climate in the United States. Our committee struggled valiantly on campus, as did successive committees on the FSU Experimental College, but with discouraging results. Always the Faculty Senate, like most such bodies, could not see the forest for the trees. Behind it all was a sense of insecurity the specialist revealed in what he saw as a threat to his narrow expertise. Again and again a senator would arise to orate as faculty senators can do even more eloquently at times than their Congressional counterparts. Especially when the senator declared self-righteously, "but the student comes first" it was apparent he meant "do anything you want to as long as you build the program around the most substantive of all disciplines—mine."

But more significant were the experimental and innovative ripples on the national college scene that followed. Despite the television networks accents on the activists, and the media celebration, generally, of campus unrest as an evidence of "generations apart" (the CBS series' unrepresentative title), the generations together—faculty and students—on over 500 campuses I recorded in our *Journal* department experimented and innovated with some new dimensions. Many of these were along the Library-College way.

A series of conferences on innovation highlighted the campus positives that press and television suppressed and even intimidated by refusal to accord as much attention as the media consistently gave to the negatives. If I mention only four, of many, it is because I participated in them and they advanced the Library-College movement. The first of them occurred in Jamestown, North Dakota, where dynamic President Dan Sillers took to Bob Jordan's enthusiasm for Library-College. In December, 1965 about 40 Library-Collegers assembled at Jamestown College to design a prototype for that campus. The book *The Library College* (Drexel Press, 1966) contains the papers of the Jamestown Workshop. Among these, the Jamestown Charter, prepared by a committee under the chairmanship of B. Lamar Johnson states more succinctly than anywhere what Library-College is (p. 195ff.)

> The purpose of the Library-College is to increase the effectiveness of student learning, particularly through (though not limited to) the use of library-centered independent study with a bibliographically expert faculty.

And if one wants to know who the Library-Collegers are, the directory will reveal some of the names associated with some of the most creative dimensions.

After Jamestown came Magnolia, Massachusetts, in May of 1966. About 80 experimental and innovative colleges were represented by their presidents, deans, librarians, and classroom faculties in a range of disciplines. Among the exciting experiments described was Stafford North's transparency-tape presentation of the Oklahoma Christian library-centered program. Besides the fact that 100 percent of the student body could be seated at one time in the library in exclusively assigned individual carrels with dial access to a range of media formats, there was the learning mode of classroom independence. Other colleges from all sections of the nation presented a multisplendored array of experimentations hearteningly repudiating of the negative unrest the media so vindictively communicated as to send us all back to our drawing boards with renewed fires. The Magnolia Conference had been conceived by Sam Baskin of Antioch, after Wakulla, and financed by the U.S. Office of Education. Subsequently, the Union of some 20 experimental colleges was activated, with headquarters at Antioch, and the journal *Change* was launched.

But the Library-Collegers preceded that journal. Bob Jordan had already begun the general editorship of the *Library-College Newsletter*, each monthly issue edited by a different Library-Colleger. I edited three or four issues myself. We were inevitably moving toward some kind of organization and a printed journal. In December of 1966 strong impetus to the movement was given by the Drexel Library-College conference in Philadelphia. John Harvey, who had been a delegate to the Jamestown workshop, conceived the Drexel meeting.

The response was overwhelming. Over 200 delegates played generous registration fees to finance the meeting. Chancellor Harvie Branscomb keynoted the meeting with his brilliant "Teaching with Books" perspective on higher education. That was followed by a series of papers in all of the sessions of the nearly a week of meetings. I contributed one of my many essays on the Library-College, and was touched to be introduced as the "father of the idea." But you know I acknowledge Thomas Carlyle as the originator.

After Drexel we did organize as Library-College Associates, Incorporated. Dan Sillers was elected our first president. Howard Clayton, then of the State University, Brockport, N.Y., and now of the School of Library Science, University of Oklahoma, assumed the *Journal* editorship. Now in its fourth year, the *Library-College Journal*, in my biased opinion, is the most exciting professional reading of all education and library journals. Howard Clayton has performed editorial wonders with no subventions thus far from foundations or other donors. He has just announced *Omnibus* as a newsletter revival and supplement to the *Journal*.

The Library-College movement is spreading. At least 300 colleges report experimentation and innovation along the Library-College way, not only in the U.S., but in Canada, and in the UK, and Australia and New Zealand. During the summer of 1970, John Levett of the Tasmanian College of Advanced Education toured the U.S. to study Library-College, and those of us who had the opportunity to talk with him realized how deeply he understood the implications of Library-College for Australia's new colleges.

If another tangible is wanted for my mystical belief in librarianship as the profession of destiny, the idea that Thomas Carlyle introduced over a century ago is proof. Surely, in Library-College the librarian as hero emerges.

12. Media Unity

The generic book is *the sum total of man's communication possibilities*. I am averse to the term "non-book materials." There cannot be such a thing as a non-book. We cannot prove historically, or in any other way, that only printed pages bound in a hard cover can be called a book. In the concept of the Generic Book, a 16mm motion picture is a book; so is a transparency overlay, filmstrip, slide, or microform; a tape or disc; a museum object or picture; a community resource; a programmed communication—print, machine or computer assisted.

This philosophical concept that began evolving in my Peabody librarianship as early as 1933 got me in trouble with the "establishment." It will probably elicit from the sophisticated, now, "there is nothing new in this concept." Perhaps the concept of the Generic Book is not new now; nor the unity of print and so-called audiovisual materials; nor the common cause of librarians and audiovisualists. But from 1946 to 1960, at least, and possibly right up to the AASL-DAVI Media Standards of 1969, the schism between library science and audiovisual education gaped. Extremists in the two professional organizations of school librarians and audiovisualists opposed each other with feud-like persistence. I was caught in the crossfire for nearly two decades, beginning in 1946, when I began my crusade for unity.

The literature will attest the unpopularity of my position in those early years. For verification of the struggle, sample the gracious debate Ole Larson of Indiana University and I undertook for the late Paul Reed, editor of *Educational Screen*, Spring, 1955. Or look at the symposium I chaired for the million-circulation *NEA Journal*, May 1958. Two school superintendents—of San Francisco and of Grosse Pointe, Michigan—were far from committed to the idea of combining separated audiovisual centers and school libraries.

In 1946-47 academic year, when I began designing a library school for Florida State University, a top dimension was audiovisual competence for every librarian. Furthermore, in cooperation with the school of education, it was proposed to prepare all teachers to teach with books—generic books—more competently than ever before. Even more ambitiously, it was hoped to interest an increasing number of undergraduates in the other professional schools of business, journalism, music, social work, and above all, the college of arts and sciences, in print and audiovisual resources, *per se*, in addition to incidentally, as had been the educational defense of some before.

Philosophically, the fundamental principle was the concept of the Generic Book. It developed out of dissent with the forced separation of something called audiovisual material from the rest of the book. I could understand such separatism among the audiovisualists who were not library educated, and suffered from an inferiority complex in the presence of print. But it was painful to listen to librarians talking about "non-book materials." It was easier to sympathize with librarians, men as well as women, who like me had not been born with a talent and love for machinery. But this seemed insufficient cause for separating us into two camps, we who were struggling to convince education that it had for too long underestimated the power of the generic book in learning.

So I began, for myself, in 1946, to determine what was "audiovisual" and what was not. Or, to assume the terminology that was anathema to my professional thinking, what was book and what was "non-book?" In 1946, the 16mm motion picture was the epitome of "audiovisual." To librarians committed to the separation it wasn't the film itself so much, but the threading of the projector, the splicing of the injured film, the replacement of the bulb, the dozen of other mechanical things that might go wrong, especially in those early days, when even "experts" were frequently embarrassed by "no show."

But when I compared library science and audiovisual texts, I found certain formats were claimed by both. AV books exalted something called "flat" *pictures* as though a new medium had just been discovered, like an element in chemistry's Periodic Table. But when I walked along the long hall from the school's separated AV Center to the school library, I discovered the identical picture of Chinese peasants farming rice, called "flat" in the AV center, filed by Sears subject heading in the library's vertical file.

The AV book made much of something pontifically identified as "Realia." But these turned out to be, mostly, library museum objects —models, mockups, stamps, coins, even butterfly wings. There was always a chapter on "Exhibits" and "Display." The AV textbooks almost never referred to what libraries had done with bulletin boards and alluring displays to invite reading.

A considerable portion of the audiovisual textbook devoted itself to maps and globes. In my opinion, the AV books did a better job than had been done in either reference or book selection. When I revised *Basic Reference Sources*, I gave particular attention to some of the approaches to geographical sources audiovisual literature had opened.

Throughout the two decades of reconciling librarians and audiovisualists, I found myself extolling audiovisualists at library meetings; librarians at audiovisual meetings. To many librarians I appeared to be a renegade who had sold librarians down the river to audiovisualists. When I talked with audiovisualists, in groups or individually, I was one of those librarians who especially threatened audiovisualists by attempting to subsume them in the library world. Neither was an objective appraisal of the opportunity that existed if only we would combine our efforts.

I continued to espouse the generic book philosophy in both camps. To the audiovisualists I pointed out that what they had renamed *discs* were phono recordings in the librarians' professional vocabulary. In 1928, for example, when the AV movement was still called visual education, the Carnegie Corporation had given a million dollars to college libraries for the purpose of starting or developing record collections. When radio made its appearance, many libraries began stocking transcriptions of programs, as well as announcements and reviews of features to be broadcast. There simply was not the kind of Berlin Wall the separatists tried to create between AV and LS. Regardless of the physical makeup of the medium, it was still part of my generic book.

Which led to my next steps in the theory I was developing about the Generic Book. One of these was the complementary consideration of reader maturity. It seemed to me, early, that almost as important as the classification by *subject*, which Dewey, and LC, and Brown, and Billings for the Astor-Tilden-Lennox Reference Division of the NYPL, had all done so ingeniously, as well as Bliss and Ranganathan, later, is the classification by *level*. To some extent this had been accomplished by the public library's divisions of children's and adult departments, at first, and later, Young People's. The classification of adult books by "easy" and "hard" etc. (not with those adjectives, necessarily) was along the way to a *level* classification, complementary to subject. The later K-6, 7-9, 10-12, and even 13-14 for junior college, appealed to me. I even tried a few dimensions of my own for the pioneering effort in *Collier's Encyclopedia* (much later) of gathering contributors' bibliographies together into a graded reading list for users who wanted to self-educate themselves by proceeding independently from the point where the encyclopedia left off.

When I had thought about level and subject as complementary bases for classification of library materials, I came to the inevitable conclusion that there was still a third and underestimated element in classification—*format*. Even though the audiovisual movement was only in its beginning, I was stirred by its implications. At least two decades before Marshall McLuhan burst upon the media world, I tried to communicate the same message in my many shorter writings, and in my 1960 book *Instructional Materials*. It is: *the* FORMAT *of a medium may affect communication of various* SUBJECTS *to individuals of varying* LEVELS *of maturity*. My later membership on the ASCD national commission on Instructional Materials provided me with an opportunity to discuss this with McLuhan.

As early as just before World War II, I began to play with the idea of developing a *format classification*. After my return from the war, I did, indeed, outline the format classification which became the heart of Chapter I in *Instructional Materials*. Even more importantly, for the beginning of my crusade for unity, was the use of that crude beginning of format classification to convince reluctant librarians that there was no such thing as a "non-book." In 1935, I introduced the first full audiovisual course for librarians in any ALA accredited school, I believe. The evidence can be found in the 1935 *Peabody Journal of Education*, where there appears an article by M. L. Shane, with whom I taught the AV course. Years later, when I showed the article to one of my most critical audiovisual colleagues in Florida, who had bitterly denounced my efforts for unity, he came to me blushingly apologetic. "Louis," he said, with a grin, "All along I had assumed that like most librarians you didn't have a clue about what audiovisual means. Do you know that I wasn't even born the year you offered that AV course at Peabody?"

"Howard," I remember responding. "You are still more nearly right than you know. I'd hate to have to thread a Bell and Howell in your presence. What you could teach me about hardware would fill several elementary AV textbooks."

The Peabody course in audiovisual education offered in the library school in 1935, I consider the beginning of my crusade for unity. But like the other professional crusades started in the Thirties, AV succumbed to Hitler's threat. My rage at our isolationism and Hitler's aggressions crowded out all peaceful concerns. Nevertheless, when I finally got into the war in 1942, the army revived my audiovisualism more than any of the other crusades. The military began instructing us with the most advanced AV of the time—16mm motion picture—on many subjects: chemical warfare; survival; tropic; desert and arctic climates; and unforgettably, the dire consequences of promiscuity. The army used slides, also, and charts, and filmstrips while regarding radio and phonograph record as basic. It used all of these audiovisual media more imaginatively and creatively than I had ever seen them used before in civilian education.

From the start, I suggested to my three Florida State faculty colleagues that we must provide for the audiovisual education of our students. Our first course, offered equally to beginning librarians and to beginning elementary teachers, was our trailblazing *315*. We converted it markedly from a conventional course in children's literature that recognized the print format, only, to a course in "Instructional Materials" that brought other formats into the students' horizon, not as ancillaries, but as peers. Children's records, pictures, objects, boards of all kinds—not only bulletin—but peg, flannel, magnetic, and even the newer term "chalk" instead of "blackboard." We began to think "graphics" as materials production for children and teacher created generic books.

Enthusiastically, we began redesigning the specifications for our new library school library. It would be a prototype Materials Center that we hoped the schools of Florida would adopt. It would serve not only as the library school library for librarians in training, but at the request of the dean of the school of education, also as the curriculum library for teachers in training. This made good sense, especially, as our basic *315* course was to prepare both librarians and teachers.

We began stocking this new concept of a library which we now officially named the Materials Center. Beginning with what we had, we placed all of Agnes Gregory's collection of children's books, plus such children's book as had been acquired by the university library. It was a good core collection because of the university librarian, the late Louise Richardson, whose devotion to the art of book selection had been reenforced by her love for Agnes and an appreciation of Miss Gregory's profound knowledge of the literature for children.

Because some of my colleagues, both library and education, insisted that the curriculum and library science libraries be organized separately, I conceded in the interest of gaining friends for our heterodoxies. Not, however, without indulging with them in one of those "corninesses" with which my long-suffering faculty colleagues have had to put up all of these years. Since Lucky Strike cigarettes were then featuring in their advertising *LS/MFT (Lucky Strike means fine tobacco)*, I sullenly paraphrased for the organization of our new Materials Center LS/MFT means *library science and materials for teachers.*

After we had gathered the print, we began the audiovisual splurge. From my Air Force reserve I acquired free: two 16mm projectors, beat up, of course; an opaque; a record playback; two slide projectors (both 2 by 2 and 3¼ by 4); three screens; a motion picture camera; a Leica we considered quite a windfall; and later, a filmstrip projector, and assortments of surplus property accessories, like a film splicer, outlets, wiring, etc. Included were even some army films, among which was the notorious one on venereal disease.

Academic year 1946/47 was excitingly strenuous. Once a month, I commuted between New York and Tallahassee. In the Park Avenue offices of Crowell Collier, I helped design a new encyclopedia, one that would reflect librarianship's hopes and dreams for the 'backbone of reference,' as the late, great Isadore Gilbert Mudge had once called my favorite reference book. On the campus of Florida State University, I worked with Agnes Gregory and Sara Srygley on designs for an innovative school in librarianship.

We occupied the new quarters at a former Air Force base, Dale Mabry Field, upon my assumption of full time duty in June. Into the concrete structures went all of the materials we had been assembling—children's literature, textbooks, curriculum materials, audiovisual equipment and materials. Only librarians can understand the exhilarating fatigue that accompanies moving into new quarters—even shabby barracks ones like ours. In addition to the usual unpacking of books and arranging them on the shelves, setting up the card catalog, establishing a circulation system, organizing for acquisition and preparations, and much more in conventional library service, there was the whole new frontier of audiovisual service, especially from the heterodox approach, for 1947, of the generic book.

In that summer, the famous Florida Leadership Training programs was launched for supervisors, principals, and superintendents. We added librarians and audiovisualists we hoped to "integrate" into a new breed "Instructional Materials" supervisers and specialists. We induced Amo de Bernardis of the Portland, Oregon schools to serve as visiting lecturer. He was the first audiovisualist I knew who was excited about the unity concept and who tried to apply the idea to his own instructional materials program, and help us "structure" (as this word began to capture pedagogical vocabulary) a new curriculum.

We could not afford, as yet, a full time position for professor of audiovisual instruction. But by Christmas, the money was in our budget, and I recruited the audiovisualist I wanted most—Charles Hoban. With his father, and Zisman, he had written the best AV textbook then available. Charley was even better than their book. He captivated his students —teachers as well as librarians.

From the start, we were philosophically and sentimentally drawn to each other. It was comforting to me, also, that this deep thinker in media philosophy shared my ineptness with the hardware. We both had to be saved from embarrassment in maintenance and in operation. But over a beer in a nearby tavern or in the neighboring airport we would dig deep into the concept of the generic book. I had known many audiovisualists and a few librarians who were whizzes with wrenches and hammers, who could take a projector apart and put it back together so as to improve the manufacturer's original product. Neither Charley nor I had that talent or inclination. But we loved to talk theory, and the literature of the other formats.

Charley introduced me and the library school, and teachers in training, to the documentary film. Under Charley's direction, we activated the Tuesday night Preview. Students and faculty, not only in library science and education, but from journalism, music, business, arts and sciences came to look at four new films, argue about them, vote to rent or purchase. The range represented science, social science, humanities, as well as education and libraries. But the documentary involved all of us. Favorites included John Grierson's *Drifters*; R. H. Watt's *Night Mail*; Robert Flaherty's *Nanook of the North* and the *Louisiana Story*. When Julian Bryan, creator of documentaries, came to the school, it began a long friendship. He is not only a creative artist, but a gourmet who has tantalized my wife and me with goodies on several occasions.

In addition to film, we plunged right into recordings, beginning with discs, and, when they became available, tapes. That year I purchased its predecessor—the wire recorder. We started right in recording everyone and everything, so captivated was I by its potential. Once we hid the wire recorder in our kitchen while my wife was hostess to a ladies's bridge game. Then we played it back to them and the ladies became hysterical over the interminglings of their conversation about clothes, babies, men, recipes, and bridge hands. More seriously, my interest in oral history was born, as the movement itself was, by the invention of the magnetic tape. We pioneered "Listening Posts" in our Materials Center reading room. It was a miracle to us then that a student could read Shakespeare silently, and hear John Gielgud do it out loud, without disturbing any reader. We added listening booths, and a language laboratory; taped bird sounds and industrial noises. Progressively, we were applying my theory of the generic book.

With a twinkle in his eye, President Campbell said to me one day, "Don't be selfish. Share this AV with the rest of the campus." What he wanted to do, really, was unify the audiovisual program for the university. Several of the science faculty had purchased projectors out of their departmental budgets, and had refused to share, confronting the President with demands from other departments to duplicate quite expensive equipment.

At a meeting of faculty department chairmen, I sketched a plan for a campus-wide AV service from the library school, in which all of the resources of the university would be pooled. Since we then had the largest collection of AV materials and equipment, all of the other departments quickly agreed, except physics, which insisted it required exclusive access to the Bell and Howell it had purchased out of departmental funds. I did not object. But hardly six weeks after the activation of the university AV service, the physics chairman phoned me frantically. They had an important film showing for a distinguished group of visiting scientists and the projector wasn't functioning.

I went rushing over, not only with my maintenance man, but with the library school's own new projector, which we immediately set up and put into operation for the assembled audience. We took the inoperative projector for servicing, and the next day restored it. Shamefacedly the physics man said "We would like to join the pool."

The service mushroomed, partly because of my over-enthusiasm. I saw more and more opportunities. To the football coach, and director of athletics, I went one day, and offered the Air Force motion picture camera, and the new photographer I had just added to our staff to photograph football games and practice for study by the coaches and players. Common as this is today, in 1947 this procedure was quite unknown. For botany, we stocked and rented time lapse motion pictures, once that world had been opened to the professor in a most tactful way. With music, business, education, and a range of the social sciences and humanities we developed AV programs that boomed our business.

Each time I reported new triumphs, I suggested budget increases for faculty, staff, materials of all kinds, print as well as AV. The service was enabling us to build the library school when student recruitment was still quite small. We could not possibly have justified the size faculty I felt we needed to build a distinguished school for ALA accreditation without this early AV involvement. But over and above these financial considerations was the passionate belief in the generic book concept, and the necessity to prepare a new breed librarian and teacher better to prepare the next generation.

As soon as we had activated the application of the Generic Book concept on the Florida State University campus, we began thinking about missionary work throughout the state. The summer 1947 Leadership Training Conference provided an initial impetus. Captivated by our approach to the "unity of library and audiovisual service," several of the supervisors and principals participating in the Leadership Conference invited us to bring extension courses to their county school systems.

In the fall of 1947, we offered the first of the extension courses which resulted over the years in orienting nearly 10,000 teachers, administrators, graduate students, and parents, in our gospel of learning through a range of media formats. Incidentally, we began the recruitment of some of our most creative library school students through a planned summer-extension schedule that led to the master's degree for many teachers and librarians in service.

These extension classes began our missionary work in the state of Florida. Standards were gradually revised to anticipate, by more than two decades, what AASL-DAVI produced in 1969 in its media standards. Steadily we were revolutionizing the school library into a Materials Center; we were metamorphosing the professional profile of the school librarian into an "Instructional Materials Specialist." That is what we began to call them in the library school, as "Instructional Materials" became the professional term for the generic book, before *Educational Media* was finally adopted.

Our next goal was a certification for personnel that would unify audiovisual and library as our Materials Centers were doing, and as we were preparing librarians and teachers in our library schools. It wasn't easy. Florida had then a school librarian certification, much like that found in the regulations of most state departments of education. There was no special certification for audiovisualists, who were beginning to make their presence felt. They felt very strongly that they deserved and needed recognition to gain any support for the audiovisual cause in Florida schools. For the most part, the audiovisualists were teachers of science and social science, of shop and physical education, who devoted part time to maintenance and operation of audiovisual services, mostly 16mm motion picture, filmstrip, and slide projection; but also, materials production, photography, and manipulation of various kinds, from dioramas and murals to puppets and dramatization; radio and even television beginnings.

In Florida, I was content when a school library added a staff member responsible for AV, even though in many cases the individual had no library science training. But we moved to cross the format boundary line. Indeed, one year Elenora Alexander, one of my Peabody Library School students, tried having, not an assistant supervisor of libraries and an assistant supervisor of audiovisual services, but instead, divided responsibilities by level, that is, an assistant supervisor of elementary instructional materials, and an assistant supervisor of secondary school materials. On the building level, she experimented with responsibility division by subject—librarians of science, social studies, and language arts materials.

In Florida we experimented and innovated along these lines, also. But even before, we moved through state meetings to bring media workers together—audiovisualists and librarians. We introduced, possibly the first joint AV-library luncheon at state teacher conventions. As a result, the two groups reorganized, and changed their names, respectively, to Florida Association of School Librarians (FASL) and Florida Audiovisual Association (FAVA). In 1950, these two groups voted to have a joint annual meeting in the FSU Library School. At these meetings, we developed the climate for several unity successes.

The first of these was the first joint certification for audiovisualists and librarians in the United States. I served on the committee with the Teachers Advisory Council to draft the specifications for the certification, which has been titled for all of these years "Instructional Materials" (Library-Audiovisual) and for which we developed the educational program under which a teacher, librarian or supervisor could qualify. It wasn't easy, and the obstacles were not all created by audiovisualists.

As a matter of fact, libraries, and organization librarian were the hardest nuts to crack. Traditional librarians in the state resisted bitterly any coalition. Jealous of the only ALA accreditation in Florida, FSU had to walk tight ropes to articulate the Florida certification program with the ALA master's. This will be especially apparent in the Library Education chapter. In the joint meetings, too often the resistance to integration came from traditional school librarians.

One of the stumbling blocks was terminology. What shall we call this new breed professional? we dialogued. Audiovisualists, mostly men, resisted being designated by the feminine title of "librarian." And librarians were not about to abandon their professional identification. In one of my endless efforts to reconcile, I suggested seriously that since we all deal with instructional materials we call ourselves *Materialists*.

This brought instant protest, with the observation by one librarian that our financial support and salaries indicated that we were anything but materialists. In desperation, I then offered that we are all involved with media; why not call ourselves *Mediums?* At least, the burst of laughter, and the promise to begin holding seances relieved the tension.

Despite the strains that developed at times between the two groups, we accomplished much. After the triumph of joint certification, came sufficient awareness for an extraordinary appropriation of one million dollars by the legislature, earmarked for Instructional Materials. This had never happened before, certainly not in Florida. It was a tribute to the united front.

As soon as the money was approved in the spring legislature of 1954, the FSU library school went to work on plans for a series of Instructional Materials Clinics on selection and utilization of the generic book. We enlisted co-sponsorship from the state Department of Education, and from FAVA and FASL. The University supplemented our budget, as did the General Education Division for whom we carried on our extension classes. Seven Clinics were scheduled during a pre-school planning week in August and September, at strategic centers that would cover the state geographically, from Pensacola to Key West.

The structure of the Clinics resembled a touring troupe of entertainers for fairs. In the cast were several of us from the library school faculty, the state school library supervisor, some local leaders in the Instructional Materials movement, and a star speaker. Equally distinctive in our touring show was what I called our "Medium Fair," a selection of the generic book output for that year to be examined by the participants before spending the money allocated to their respective school systems out of the extraordinary legislative appropriation for Instructional Materials. Just as the materials producers provided displays of their best, so the manufacturers put at our disposal the latest models of their equipment. Around the lectures, we scheduled previews, pre-auds (as they were beginning to be called then), and demonstrations of material production.

The attendance at these Clinics was astounding. Each pre-school year, 1954-1956, the seven Clinics attracted over 1500 educational workers of all kinds—superintendents, principals, supervisors, teachers, and of course, librarians and audiovisualists, proud of their joint sponsorships of these dramatic events. Several of the Florida newspapers supplemented their news stories about the clinics with editorials on the significance of the materials Center idea. It wasn't long after that the even fancier name for library—Learning Resource Center—replaced Materials Center in the pedagogical evidence of being "advanced."

Implicit in the concept of media unity is a new kind of individualized learning to replace the traditional classroom teaching approach. In November 1954, the Florida Education Association *Journal* published my essay under the title "How to Tailor Learning to Meet Individual Needs." Perhaps that was the first article in which I made the point that for the first time in the history of education it was now possible to match individual differences in students with individual differences in media. Hereafter, I predicted, the art of the new breed teacher will consist of sensitively fitting media to the learner and the learning situation involved. To do this, the teacher will have to know his students individually better than he has in the past. But even more, he will have to know books and libraries, that is, the generic book and materials center, or learning resource center, more sophisticatedly than ever before. To paraphrase Harvie Branscomb's title for college professors, school teachers will have to begin to *teach with media.*

If this was to come about, if a new generation of teachers was to revolutionize the learning mode, as required by the trend to universal education, at least two important innovations must occur. The first of these would have to happen in teacher education, which would have to stop teaching teachers about books and libraries, about media and media centers, *incidentally,* and begin to teach teachers about the generic book, *per se.* We had made a start in Florida by having our basic materials course made a requirement for elementary teacher certification. We were working on the secondary teacher requirement.

The second innovation called for was in the education of the librarian. We had made a start at Florida State University in being the first library school to require that all of our librarians be audiovisual competent. But much more was needed. Philosophically, the school librarians must get rid of their ancillary complex. In the chapter on school librarianship I shall reveal how my library soul was tortured by the repeated vindictive declarations of some school library leaders that librarians must study more pedagogy—must *follow* the school curriculum and the school's philosophy. With my mystical belief in the destiny of our profession, I raged against this one-way interchange between school and library. I felt very strongly that librarians took more education courses, knew more about professional education, than educators knew about librarianship.

For a change, I wanted school librarians not to *follow* the curriculum, but to help make it; not only to learn the philosophy of the school, but to teach the school some things about an educational philosophy the pedagogues had overlooked, or failed to discover in the history of education.

13. Library History:
The Quest for the Constant

On my desk, as I begin this chapter, are all three printings of my *Origins of the American College Library 1638-1800*. Whatever evaluation of *Origins* librarianship and history will ultimately settle, some librarians and historians have cited this book as the beginning of the current library history movement. Certainly, before, library history had been comparatively neglected by librarianship. Indeed, even library education and library investigation treated history as a second class area for research as late as 1929, when I was admitted to the Graduate Library School of the University of Chicago. Yet, the history spark that had been struck inside me by my reading was fanned into a glow by at least three faculty members at GLS. Douglas Waples became my counsellor and hero in 1929-31, during my interrupted residences in Chicago. He opened the world of the scientific method to me, for the first time, and I became deeply involved in his investigation of *What People Want to Read About*. But when I mentioned my history interest, and my hope to undertake an investigation in library history he offered to introduce me to Pierce Butler and James Westfall Thompson on the faculty. Nevertheless, his own enthusiasm for the scientific approach, and my admiration for him, induced an apologetic attitude toward the dilettante study of history, compared to the bread and butter of statistics and the whole folklore of identifying problems first.

Before my GLS days ended, however, I met and talked with both Professors Butler and Thompson several times. I elected to work on my doctorate at Peabody as much because I was encouraged in my history interest there as in the fact that my financial resources and obligations would not permit the greater costs in Chicago. Before I left Chicago, however, I passed both foreign language examinations—French and German—and the course in statistics with Karl Holzinger. I was encouraged to go on to the doctorate at Chicago, but my Fisk job, in Nashville; responsibility for my mother's support; and approaching marriage suggested the doctorate, if accomplished at all, would have to be undertaken in Nashville at one of the two institutions there that offered the degree.

In 1929 I embarked on a Ph. D. program at Peabody with joint concentrations in history and higher education. The combination had been suggested by my master's program and thesis at CCNY—*A History of the Municipal University in the United States*. The CCNY thesis had come about from growing concern with college education—the concern that led to Library-College—and my very early absorption in history.

Back in the children's room, along with fairy tales, I would find myself reading biographies of heroes and tales of history. I recall my fascination with Dickens' *Child History of England*; with Crecy's *Fifty Decisive Battles*; with Marco Polo and Mandeville, among many other byroads into history reading. I began reading about Napolean, early, and the other great military conquerors of history: Alexander the Great, Hannibal, Caesar, Marlborough, George Washington, Ulysses Grant and Robert Lee.

Much as I gloried in the romantic triumphs of U.S. history, in the feeling there had never been a nation like ours before, nor could we be matched by any now, I was stirred to a new love for history when I elected a high school course in English history. New heroes entered my personal hall of fame. In succession, I dreamed I was Alfred the Great; William the Conqueror; Oliver Cromwell; the Duke of Marlborough; Sir Francis Drake; Sir Walter Raleigh; Gladstone, and Disraeli. The story of the Spanish Armada I read in some fifty versions. Perhaps that high school course in English history was the beginning of my Anglophilia, my growing conviction that the British people were the most mature of any nation in the world, and the parents from whom America inherited its talents for goodness and greatness.

My interest in history persisted through college. I indulged in historical fiction almost like an addict. Scott had really whetted me with *Ivanhoe, Kenilworth, Rob Roy, Marmion,* and the rest. A catalogue of my historical fiction reading up through the one I am reading as I write this—Mary Renault's *Fire From Heaven*, about the early life of my hero, Alexander the Great—would prevent me from getting to *Origins*.

Leading to that dissertation was my master's thesis. The fact that I was a student at the University of Toledo, a municipal institution, aroused me to investigate how many other cities in the United States supported a university. In 1926, there were only seven: Charleston, Cincinnati, CCNY, Louisville, Toledo, Akron, and Wichita. When I began my master's work at CCNY it seemed to me that being a student at two of the municipal institutions predestined my choice of thesis subject. Besides, when one of the encyclopedias called Cincinnati the oldest municipal university I was challenged to prove this incorrect. (The College of Charleston was founded in 1770—although chartered after the Revolution.)

I proceeded to study the catalogs of all seven institutions; corresponded with officers at all of them; read government publications relating to them; and thus established my own historical method. I was encouraged by Paul Klapper, dean of CCNY school of education, who served as chairman of my thesis committee. The municipal university was a rehearsal for my doctoral foray into college library history.

As soon as I had passed my doctoral preliminaries at Peabody, some time in 1930, I set to work earnestly on an investigation into the beginnings of college libraries in the colonies. In the late spring of 1933, my wife and I set out in our new Pontiac. Our first major team effort was the doctoral journey to the nine colonial colleges.

We drove, first, from Nashville, through the Great Smokies of east Tennessee, and the Blue Ridge mountains of Western Virginia, to Williamsburg. Our visit preceeded the Rockefeller launching of Restoration. But Williamsburg enraptured even without the lift that came subsequently from the ten million dollars grant. The charm of the village was exceeded only by the history of the campus and the graciousness of two librarians who speeded my mission by day, and hosted us at night.

From early morning to supper, and then to near midnight, we poured over musty minutes of the faculty, August 10, 1729 to June 4, 1784; the journal of the meetings of the president and the masters; the charter, transfer and statutes of the college; as well as memorabilia of all kinds. We were both so absorbed that the days melted away. At night we would talk over our discoveries, and Gerry would type up our notes on her portable.

Some of the incidental verifications were as rewarding as the major identifications. I had noted that a great many articles and secondary sources referred to the *Brafferton* estate. As I worked with the primary sources in the William and Mary archives, however, I was sure that Brafferton was really *Brasserton*. Immediately I sensed that some of the secondary source authors, apparently not English literature majors, had been unaware that early English printing made the "s" similar to a lower case "f." I had had this brought to my attention by one of my undergraduate literature professors, whose classes were huge, with over-enrollments by co-eds because of his reputation for concentrating on "mature audience" literature. One day, I recall, he had showed some of us an early printing of the Shakespeare lines

> Where a bee sucks
> There suck I

with that devilish enjoyment of his co-ed students' inductions.

It was with sadness that we left William and Mary. Williamsburg meant Virginia to us very much more than did Charlottesville. We always recalled what one William and Mary alumnus told us proudly: "We were over a century old before the University of Virginia was even a twinkle in the eye of our alumnus Thomas Jefferson."

And then came Harvard. By charter date, Harvard is the oldest college in the United States. It was established in Massachusetts Bay Colony in 1636, and named for its first benefactor, the Rev. John Harvard, of Charlestown, who willed to the college "the sum of 779 pounds, 17 shillings, and two pence, and more than three hundred volumes of books." I placed Harvard first in the chronology of my *Origins*, but I recognized, also, the possible claim for priority by William and Mary. In 1618, the London Company ordered the establishments of a university in Virginia and property was donated by Sir Edwin Sanders and others, which consisted of "a communion set, a *library* and large sums of money." But an Indian massacre put an end to this start, and the college was not permanently established until 1691.

Between Williamsburg, Virginia and Cambridge, Massachusetts, geographically, we drove to Princeton first, and arrived the morning of the outdoor commencement. Librarian James Thayer Gerould, brother of Katharine Fullerton, had graciously prepared for us in advance. He had arranged for a room in the home where Woodrow Wilson had lived. After we had unpacked, we walked to the old Princeton library for a tour. That this great man (and he was famous to me) should delay his vacation for a 24-year old unknown in librarianship made me humble indeed. Perhaps I need remind only the younger generation that Gerould's book on library architecture was the classic of that time. He had, besides, written much in international relations, on debt settlements of World War I, on the Treaty of Paris. He was prominent in the American Bibliographical Society, American Library Institute, and in numerous clubs, such as the Century.

After thoroughly orienting me in library locations he overwhelmed us by saying, "as you know we have no summer session at Princeton. The library will be shut tight until September." Then noting the fright in my face, he chuckled, took a key ring out of his pocket, and removed a key from it. "Here," he said, "is the master key to the Princeton University Library. When you have finished with it leave it for me with your landlady."

My wife and I worked in the Princeton library all alone during the several days of our stay. Perhaps this trust is another evidence of the unique fellowship of librarianship. Shortly after, Gerould came to see me in Nashville, and we talked about this trust in our profession, and about Chicago's introduction to the scientific method. When I showed him the statistical work I had been doing for Waples, he raged, like a humanist who was already beginning to fear the monopolistic trends of the other culture. Looking at some correlation coefficents I had on my desk, he declared vehemently, "This stuff makes my blood boil. It is ruining a good humanist like you." Reflecting this point of view was H. L. Mencken's satiric review in *The American Mercury* of *What People Want to Read About*.

It was Yale next. Our tour followed not the chronology of the origins, but the calendar of visits I was able to effect. Andrew Keogh and his staff could best see us the week after Princeton, so to New Haven we steered our Pontiac. I was most anxious to see the Sterling Library, because I had modeled the new Fisk University library on their tower model, but of course, much more modestly.

As I entered the monumental door of the gothic structure, I saw the reason for the *Nation's* satirical description. A pair of roller skates would indeed speed the approach to the circulation desk. Nevertheless, I was awed and inspired by this concept of a library. Even more was this so when we set to work in the archives. The ambulatory early life of the college resulted in a thrilling battle for the library before it was settled in New Haven. Each college, as we studied the archives, began to take on a personality from its origins. Governor Elihu Yale somehow clinched Yale's American beginnings as contrasted to Harvard's English and William and Mary's Scottish origins.

Providence was so close by that Brown University had to be the next stop. The distinguished bibliographer, on whose classic work I had been teethed in Columbia, Dr. Henry Bartlett Van Hoesen was the librarian. Yet this great and good man, and his wife, insisted that we should have a room in their home for the period of our investigations of the origin of the Brown University Library.

We packed, had breakfast with the Van Hoesens on our last morning, and departed with a thrill of anticipation for Cambridge. We had never before seen Harvard, although both of us, from reading, and from talk with colleagues who were alumni, shared the academic awe for Harvard. The Widener Library overwhelmed us, but after a Cook's tour, we settled down to the archives about which I had been in correspondence with the assistant librarian, C. E. Walton. In his absence, he had arranged for us with Mrs. Anne F. Dakin, archivist. She devoted herself to us, captivated by my dissertation.

From Cambridge to Hanover, New Hampshire. Dartmouth became my favorite of the tour. Many years later, we came back to put the finishing touches on the manuscript for *Basic Reference Sources*. What intrigued me on the *Origins* tour was Eleazer Wheelock and the missionary work with the Indian students. I saw even then some comparables in the white man's wrongs to both Red and Black.

After a week at Dartmouth, we drove to New York City. With nostalgic memories I went to East Hall, first, home of the School of Library Service, to visit with Assistant Dean Edna Sanderson, and with staff members who knew me. All of the memories of 1927/28 trooped back. I had loved library school, and what it had taught me about our profession of destiny. With renewed inspiration, I drank in the words of Milton Halsey Thomas, curator of the Columbian Room, and tingled, with the pride of an alumus, over the founding of Kings College.

After Columbia, there remained but two more colonial colleges. At Rutgers, assistant librarian Russell Van Horn, and his secretary gave time and attention to all of our quests for sources and answers. Likewise, at the University of Pennsylvania, where the tour ended, librarian C. Seymour Thompson had instructed staff member, Miss Edith Hartwell to work with us.

As I look back, nearly four decades, now, there is an idyllic quality to this tour. That distinguished librarians should have given so much time and attention to the efforts of a neophyte had a profound effect on my subsequent relations with students. The littlest one was ever to me as the angel of the classic.

The tour of the nine colonial colleges shaped my library history crusade significantly. Tangibly it rewarded me with a doctor of philosophy degree before age thirty, a goal I had set for myself. In 1934, librarians with earned doctorates were extremely rare. I had known too many among my colleagues who were "all buts." Even today, we have many fine librarians who boast they have completed all of the requirements for the degree but the dissertation. I drove myself relentlessly, past midnight mostly, to write so many pages each day. With a full time job at Fisk, and later at Peabody, and still some seminar classes to attend, the inevitable effect on my health followed.

I recall the four o'clock defense of my dissertation in the spring of 1934. Fatigue and weariness undermined my desire to bubble about the tour and champion the cause of library history before my stern committee. It was the year of one of Ernest Hemingway's successes. As I sat down at the head of my inquisition table there was before me the book jacket of *Death in the Afternoon*. But I lived, miraculously through my final. Miraculously, because a few days after I came down with a high fever, nature's apparent signal for a physical collapse. Dramatically, I took my degree in that open air commencement in front of Peabody's famed pillars of the Social-Religious building in a wheel chair.

Tangible as the doctor's degree was for academic recognition and salary, it was far less important to me than the intangibles my tour of the Colonial colleges accomplished. It initiated my own historiography. I fear not too many historians will endorse my method of writing history. Nor will the majority agree with my reservations about the scientific method as an approach to the record of civilization. My doctoral work spurred me to read in the philosophy of history.

Leopold von Ranke (1795-1886), the German historian whose "wie es eigentlich gewesen" was first quoted to me by Fremont Wirth, especially sent me into deep meditation and dissent. It was Ranke who applied, elaborated and epitomized, for me, the scientific method of historical investigation. He is still considered the father of the modern, so-called "objective" historical school. Although one should not quarrel with his aim to reconstruct events and institutions of the past "as they actually were," I still was troubled to reconcile this "telling it like it is" with his mystical implication that history is the expression of the divine will.

Philosophically, I argued with myself, how can man discover the divine will by limiting himself to mortal measures of sensory phenomena. Not by the scientific method, I increasingly and mystically felt, man's great discoveries of truth and beauty had come about. Revelation seemed more than ever to transcend research, in history. Even in some of the words of two great 20th century scientists—Einstein and Whitehead—there were the haunting suggestions that their great truths came not so much by laboratory and experiment as by an unaccountable flash that seemed to have been delayed by man's stubborn insistence on his scientific method.

Whatever validity objectivity had for math and physics, and the other natural sciences, I was convinced that art must eschew all attempts at "objectivity." Instinctively, I believed the true artist was more likely to receive the divine message than the scientist. And I wanted history to be more art than science. This philosophy began shaping my historiography after the tour. I concede the possibility that because of this unscientific philosophy my history may not be as objective as our times demand. There is a possibility, however, that the pendulum will swing back to Hegel's philosophical school, at least.

We need to look back so that we might advance forward. History haunts me with a sense of lost opportunities. Somewhere in the past, librarianship overlooked some innovation, some idea, some device, some concept that got lost in the shuffles of efficiency, or overwork, or neglect, or inopportune time. These buried nuggets have to be prospected for over and over again.

The celebration of newness and change, especially by our activist times, frustrated my quest for the constant. I wanted us in librarianship to study library history more, not only for perspective, for a sense of our tradition, for a record of this underestimated profession of ours, but as an approach to solving today's problems, and anticipating some futures of destiny. I set about, with the help of many fellow crusaders, to accomplish four tangibles.

The first of these was recognition of library history by our national professional organization. In 1947, Wayne Shirley, my ALA convention roommate for a quarter of a century of midwinters and annuals, accomplished this with the help of Carl Milam. That year, the American

Library History Round Table was activated and held its first meeting. Wayne Shirley assumed the chairmanship, in which he served until 1968; and I was the secretary for all of that time. Our first few meetings attracted only a dozen or so participants. Among these early faithfuls was our other roommate, Orwin Rush, first executive secretary of the ACRL. Orwin and Wayne and I would plan for ALHRT in our hotel room. In my memory, cold winters at the Edgewater Beach color the pictures I retain.

Each of us would return to our room from different meetings. Usually, I was last. Wayne loved the fresh air, and had the windows wide open. Orwin was huddled up on the third bed, a cot placed there by the hotel. As I opened the door to our room, I would be pinned against the opposite wall by a howling Chicago blizzard gale that swept across the room from the open window. Wayne would wake, obligingly close the window, sweep some of the snow aside that had blown in, and we'd begin to plan the next ALHRT program. Orwin would awake and join us.

Our organization was informal. There were no dues. The program included two or three papers, followed by discussion. There were many reminiscences about events and people. I have often regretted that I did not have a tape recorder to start my later oral history crusade at these meetings. The range of subjects included libraries, librarians, special collections, philanthropies, library organizations, library types, kinds or work. At the opening meeting, held during the 1947 annual ALA convention, Wayne Shirley informally outlined the aims and objectives of the Round Table. I read the first paper, on "The Importance of Library History"; Stanley Pargellis presented the second paper, "Long Life to the Library History Round Table." At that very first meeting, I expressed the hope that we would one day publish a journal.

After that first meeting, Wayne and I troubled how to stir more interest in the ALHRT meetings. We had no resources for promotion. But an unanticipated treatment in one of the papers on library pioneers, by a lady librarian, who had another lady read it for her, created an unprecedented stir. Perhaps that is why she did not read it herself. It was reported in that paper that some of the library pioneers were also men with whom it was unsafe for young women to ride alone in library elevators. The content of that paper passed along the convention grape vine. At the very next ALHRT meeting, we were moved from our scheduled meeting room to accommodate the ALA members who were lined up like a movie crowd waiting to get into a movie for "mature audiences."

Quiet World / Crusades

In 1961, the Shoe String Press published *An American Library History*, selected by John David Marshall, with forewords by Wayne and me. A look at the contents will reveal some significant library history by creative library leaders. At random, I recall two that were informally spoken, rather than read: Chicago Public Librarian Carl Roden's recollections of William Frederick Poole, and Harvard librarian Keyes Metcalfe's first-hand associations with NYPL director E. H. Anderson. Ben Powell and Robert Lester, of Duke University and of the Carnegie Corporation respectively, did two papers on the library renaissance in the South. Among the library leaders featured were H. W. Wilson, by Howard Haycraft; William Warner Bishop, by Foster Mohrhardt; Louis Round Wilson, by Maurice Tauber; Carl Milam, by Emily Miller Danton; Herbert Putnam, by David Mearns; Sydney Mitchell, by Lawrence Clark Powell; William Brett, by Carl Vitz. There were two papers on Josephine Adams Rathbone, one by Nordica Fenneman, and the other by Wayne Shirley. "A Worm's-Eye View of Library Leaders" was the title of Marian Manley's intriguing paper.

Biography was by no means the only history area. These titles will suggest the range of subjects: "The Coonskin Library" by Vinnie J. Mayer; "The History of the ALA Intellectual Freedom Committee," by David Berninghausen; "Stop Thief!" by Larry Powell; "Multilateral Approach of French-Canadian Librarianship," by Jean-Charles Bonenfant; "Opening the People's Library on the Lord's Day" by Sidney Ditzion. Beyond that first published reader there are the makings of the next volume, with papers by such eminent library historians as Jesse Shera, Sydney Jackson, and others.

The second tangible was the library history seminar, for library historians. There was still just a handful of us. We had no prestige or even status in the profession. There have been three of these seminars and the fourth is in the planning stage. From the start, I enlisted our History department's interest. There was plenty of precedent for this affinity. The first president of the ALA had been the eminent historian Justin Winsor. The classic *Guide to Historical Literature*, from its inception toward the end of the last century, had been a joint AHA-ALA venture. Every head of the Florida State University History Department co-sponsored the seminars enthusiastically, and many members of the department read papers. Among them, Richard Bartlett's contributions have been most creative and policy shaping, both for the seminars, and for the journal that followed.

The first seminar attracted only sixteen library historians. The papers were published in a mimeographed volume. The second and third seminars had the enthusiasm and leadership of Martha Jane Zachert and Richard Bartlett, and they were assisted by other library school faculty members, particularly John Clemons, one of my very special library recruits, right out of high school, who later helped me develop the *500* course for graduate students outside the library school. Another one of my graduates who did yeoman service in the seminars was John David Marshall, who became my bibliographer.

The third tangible was the big plunge. With no subsidy from the University or any other source, I estimated the cost of financing a 64-page quarterly, with cover. This was not a new undertaking for me. I had launched several library journals before. When I became president of the Florida Library Association, I undertook to publish and edit *Florida Libraries*, in our School. When I became president of the Southeastern Library Association in 1950, I decided the time had come for this nine-state organization to have a quarterly journal. We launched *Southeastern Librarian*. When the *AASL Journal of Education for Librarianship* began running a year behind and floundering I was asked to take over as chairman of the publications committee, and again I became involved in financing.

On the basis of these experiences, and others with library journals, I estimated we would need 300 subscriptions at $10 a year, plus some advertising, to pay for the printing and distribution of up to 1,000 copies, four times a year. We launched our campaign for subscriptions, first. Using the ALHRT rolls, seminar registrants, libraries that had named library historians. We watched the mails bring in a half dozen subscriptions daily, at first. I said to Marguerite, "As soon as we reach the 300 mark interrupt me no matter who is in my office, and no matter what I am doing."

One afternoon Marguerite came in with the announcement," We have passed the 300 mark."

"We're in business, Marguerite," I said. "Bring the gang together as soon as possible."

The *Journal* appeared in January 1966, on schedule. The format was disappointing. We had taken the lowest bid. It came from a small printing establishment with limited resources, and among other things, a font of type without italics. Volume one, number one looks amateurish. We shifted to another type style in issue two, and to another printer later.

Our last department in the journal was reserved for Oral History.

It had a very special interest for Martha Jane Zachert, who has contributed significantly to the development of our program at Florida State, as well as to the movement throughout the United States. For me, Oral History developed into a crusade within my larger crusades of library history and audiovisualism.

Before 1946 I had been captivated by listening to older people recount their first-hand experiences with historical events, in associations with notables. I had worked out my own system for note taking, on my opportunity to talk with some of my literary heroes—Louis Untermeyer, Edwin Markham, Philip Wylie, Aldous Huxley, and others. From witnesses of the Dempsy-Willard fight, the world series of various years, of football games that involved The Four Horsemen of Notre Dame, Red Grange, I gathered notes for my sports essays. I interviewed Judge McCord to obtain evidence that Florida State had a good football team before the Buckman Act took away all of its men and converted Florida State College into Florida State College for Women, for forty years.

But in 1947 I acquired a wire recorder for the new audiovisual center we were building in the library school. The Oral History possibility immediately suggested itself, and was confirmed by the movement at Columbia, led by Allan Nevins. (Years later in his California home I wished I might have taped the father of Oral History on Oral History.) I began using our wire recorder in a crude innovative cross between my audiovisual and library history crusades.

The Oral History movement grew and attracted some 100 universities and libraries by the time of the first Oral History convention on 1966 at UCLA's Lake Arrowhead Camp. I read one of the papers there, and mine attracted the attention of the *Wall Street Journal*, as well as a request for publication in full by the *Library Journal*. I had suggested two new dimensions.

Up to that time, the standard operating procedure was to tape the interviews, transcribe, submit the transcription for correction and approval to the subject, and then destroy the tape, preserving only the transcript. I urged the preservation of the tape as well, insisted the tape was really the primary source, and potentially supplementary documentation. I illustrated with tapes that revealed nuances in the interviewee's voice that were subject to different interpretations.

My second dimension was a proposal that the time had now come for Oral History to become visual. Just as the tape recorder's appearance in 1947 had started a new era in Oral History, so the appearance of the video-recorder must begin an age of Visual-Oral History. I illustrated with four clips from EBF films, furnished by my good student Dr. Wayne Howell, then corporation vice president. One of these clips was of Frank Lloyd Wright discussing an architectural principle. I first played the sound part of the film alone, giving the interview with Frank Lloyd Wright much as the Oral Historian would have it from a tape. Then we accompanied the sound with the visual on the screen, and some of my colleagues gasped at how much more was told as they saw Frank Lloyd Wright point to the features he was describing orally. A comparable effect was accomplished with the clip of Pablo Casals performing on the 'cello when the visual reenforced his oral discussion of techniques and effects.

These were the four tangibles of my Library History Crusade. But Round Table, Seminar, Journal, Visual-Oral History were only means to my philosophical end. What attracts me to history is not that superficiality of change and newness our superficial protest celebrates. Man's noblest investigation has ever been his search for constants. Somehow, we in librarianship must call mankind back to the eternal verities. We must begin by looking back more often at our past so that we won't repeat the same mistakes, if we can benefit from the trials and errors of before. Above all, there is the possibility that serendipitously we may discover in our history a great truth that has somehow been subsumed in the frantic clamor for change that stampedes us these days. Hence my crusade for library history.

IV Library and Society

14. Library Communities

Librarianship has typed libraries four ways. By the communities served predominantly, libraries are identified as (1) *Academic*; (2) *Public*; (3) *School*; (4) *Special*.

Comparative librarianship, on all of the continents of the world, had helped develop a perspective on the library's ultimate role in society. There have been enough lessons in Britain alone to reenforce several of the crusades begun in the United States. But there had also been enough eye openers to cause turnabouts in previous thinking. Dramatic examples can be illustrated by the confidential Reference service of England's cities like Leeds; by the mobile county service of York; by chemist Urquhart's documentalists, who anticipated the America Information Science movement; by Britain's deep and profound consideration of the library's epistemology—what we know through the classification of subjects.

Although the Fulbright mission was basically Reference, it was inevitable that the three other major divisions of library work—Acquisition, Preparations, Circulation—should contribute their comparatives. In this way I arrived at the augmentation of my definition of Comparative Librarianship as even more than geographical comparatives among nations, but as possibly intra-nation comparatives among the four kinds of library work.

Furthermore, the vast odyssey among the libraries of all the continents had indicated clearly a major area of Comparative Librarianship might well consider comparatives among the four Library Types. I had been fortunate to study all four types and to serve in all of them, although more briefly in School and Special libraries than in Academic and Public. Let me, therefore, summarize in this chapter my developing philosophy about the roles of each of the library types, for their respective communities, and their part in the total library impact on world society.

Louis Shores

ACADEMIC LIBRARIES

The crux has already been presented in the chapter on Library-College. Certainly for the instruction half of the Academic mission, a library-centered independent learning mode is definitely in the trend to universal higher education.

PUBLIC LIBRARIES

Of all four types I am most indebted, personally, to the Public Library. Awe and affection entered my four-year-old body the first time I stepped into that Cleveland branch. If there is anything at all to transmigration, or reincarnation, or metempsychosis I found it in that first visit to the public library, I believe. One of my favorite short stories is Rudyard Kipling's "The Finest Story in the World." If Charlie truly was a Greek galley slave whose soul had transmigrated to Britain's near-20th century, then I might have been a scribe at Edfu whose soul had reincarnated in Cleveland's public library about the year 1908.

Part of the awe came from that feeling of having been in a library before—long before. It comes to me every time I enter the stacks and smell the mustiness of old bindings. It comes to me especially when I am pressing the sheepskin bindings of the earlier volumes of the Congressional Set. There are other times in the library, especially in the reading of some strange line or even word that something stirs me to feel I have been here before in just such surroundings of books of some kind. Perhaps my first sense of reverence for the public library stems from this supernatural sensation, from this element in my whole mystic feeling about library quiet and its strange destiny for me and for mankind.

My second attachment began developing almost at the same time. The awe of reincarnation seemed to suggest that in the library I would re-establish communication with that eternity from which I had come to this temporal existence. My second attachment could be described as a sort of excitement rather than awe. As if I had discovered a way to adjust quickly to this new strange existence on earth. If the awe promised to keep me in touch with the ultimates, the excitement suggested there would be a way to adjust to the proximates for a soul that apparently didn't think much of telling it like it is on this tiny insignificant planet.

There is, of course, nothing scientific in these first paragraphs. I wish that those of my colleagues who can find no philosophy in library literature might discover here one librarian's reeling gropings with some beliefs not all together pragmatic. The excitement, since it promised adjustment to the here and now, became rapidly tangible. I began to feel even before I was admitted to public school that I had discovered an independent way to educate myself.

This then became the ultimate role of the public library: independent study for all. I saw in the public library a revolution in education. Let the colleges and universities, the high school in my boyhood, and even the upper elementary grades, snob-like restrict themselves to an elite. Let them try as they might, by barriers of all kinds—economic, academic, sex, race, religion, national origin, geography, vocation, family—to bar the way to highest literacy through their formal educations. It would not avail hereafter as it had in history in the past. The public library would throw open the gates to all. Not only literacy but higher literacy would soon be universal.

As the public library began to help me outdistance my school mates from the very first grade I began to ponder this strange power. It was teaching me something that the schools were not. It was teaching me independence. It was luring me into learning with its own tricks and devices of browsing, of ladder listing, of story telling, of reader advisories. The last were quite different from the assigned reading in school.

I pondered the difference. It began defining itself only after I had graduated out of the eighth grade into high school. We had only the eight-four plan in those days before the junior high was born. The change was abrupt—from one room for all subjects, where the one teacher tied everything together, and somewhat related them, at least by her person, to several rooms in high school, each for a different subject. In my high school freshman year I began to feel that separation of science and math from history, from English, from French, and from other subjects in the secondary curriculum. This specialization was accented in college where faculty members, fired up by their respective learned societies, made it clear in their class hours that physics, or economics, or linguistics was that one element from which God had originally created the heaven and the earth. Not so in the public library. There the soul could skip lightly across these specialists' boundary lines without passport and visa. Indeed, the public library had many alluring interstices not provided for by school and college curricula.

From time to time I had been able to spend hours on such academically ostracized subjects as UFO, clairvoyance, telepathy, precognition. I had delved into Yoga, Rosicrucianism, the strange manifestations by some *gurus* in the Far East, especially India and Tibet, like levitation and miracle healing. My teachers in high school would have been concerned; my professors iconoclastically critical. But the public library not only offered the books but its librarians with almost parental concern provided oral and written bibliographic advice.

My thinking train wound along tracks that led to my ideal school, first, and then to my ideal college. The public library, I am sure, modeled both my Library-College and my Medium School. Since the essence of both innovations is independent study, there can be no doubt that my commitment to independence in education was born and nurtured in the public library way of learning. Why can not school be like that, I asked myself first. My frustrations in some college classes contrasted with the joy of creative understanding that came to me in quiet library hours. By graduate school, I was convinced the library was the gateway to a tailored learning for all of the individual differences in the world.

One election eve in 1968, I addressed the Metropolitan Library Association in Denver. That year was the culmination of a process in which riot, assassination, violent demonstrations, and protest marches of all kinds seemed to have become an accepted part of American life. I wanted to challenge this assumption, and suggest the role libraries should have in a crisis-filled, march-dominated country.

I challenged us to revive the New England Town meeting in 30,000 U.S. public libraries. To begin by inviting marchers off the streets and into library meeting rooms. There to communicate their protests. To offer to devote our library graphics departments to make more artistic signs and placards of any slogans they want to communicate. Above all to provide sources for documenting their causes, suggesting solutions to their problems.

I suggested that we voluntarily declare a moratorium on marches for one year. Marches of all kinds were to be denied permission—patriotic, sacred, entertainment, as well as protest. The New England Town Meeting has been described by many political scientists as the form nearest to pure democracy. Every time some one, or some group, felt impelled to march in protest, he or his group could apply to his neighborhood public library for a town meeting or a neighborhood meeting, or for a chain of these meetings, depending upon how widespread the problem was.

The structure for these meetings could be adapted. As an example, intolerable conditions in a neighborhood slum might impel the residents and sympathizers to march. Instead they would ask for meeting space and time in their neighborhood branch library. With the help of the library staff, the organizers could expect assistance in assembling facts to document the protest; graphics for communicating these facts dramatically, in print and on radio and TV; on bulletin boards and in exhibits and displays all over the areas involved or affected.

These meetings would be more than academic discussions. They would be organized for action, for speedier action than the disorders had accomplished. This action would be accomplished by the democratic forms provided by our constitution, including initiative, referendum, and recall of public officers who would not act as the people wanted them to.

As preparation for this action, each library meeting would identify the problem and document the causes. But unlike the marches, the meetings would not stop with the problems. Immediately, solutions would be offered and each in turn evaluated and compared with other proposals for remedying the ills. When the meeting had agreed upon a solution it would be taken to the people for vote, in the neighborhood, the city, the state, nationally, as desired. The vote could be on immediate institution of the reform, or a prototype experimentation with several possible solutions. Perhaps out of these meetings would come offers from various segments of the population, of industry, of government, and of other institutions to contribute to the solution.

Meetings of this type occurred even during the height of the last decade's disorders. In my home city part a slum neighborhood was replaced by model housing. Rabid citizens whose patience had been exhausted by most trying surroundings for themselves and their children were induced by a few of their leaders to postpone physical communication until they had met with city officers and representative civic leaders. Identification of the problem was readily acknowledged. After which every one settled down to designing the most expeditious solution.

Salutary was the spirit of admitting shortcomings in one's self as well as in others. Landlords admitted exploitation. But tenants also admitted neglect of their homes and streets. Once it had been decided to demolish the slum and rebuild with model housing and a park, voluntary contributions began. A banker offered finance; the city agreed to street repaving, park and playground facilities; a contractor to an advantageous contract; labor to some para-union considerations. But the tenants themselves worked out their own community contribution to beautification, to maintenance, to home making education, to insure that the neighborhood would not deteriorate to slum conditions again. Temporary housing was offered during the construction by a number of agencies and private citizens. To compensate the exhibitionists who enjoy physical communication, a master march and dance was planned for the completion of the project.

What my Library Dream challenged the protesters to do is to communicate through the American public library. What it challenged us professionally to undertake is to provide a truly non-violent form of communication in our public libraries. As a public librarian I felt responsibility for the disorder in our cities. I believed it was our professional destiny to show people how to reform society more expeditiously and less violently than the militants. The activists might appeal to the TV networks as better show business than quiet libraries. But if we in libraries showed the way, the people might yet turn from the superficialities the networks celebrated to the solid documentation libraries offered.

I believe the public library can strengthen national minds all over the world as no other single agency can. I believe the library can toughen the fibre and beautify the tone of man's thinking in a way that none of our mass media can, alone. We in the library are the sum of all media. We acquire, organize, and disseminate the best of all media formats, subjects, levels. We in libraries offer the sum total of man's communication possibilities through the generic book we select.

One day we will overcome our ancillary complex and realize our high destiny. When the libraries of the world unite to strengthen all national minds there will be no more war.

SCHOOL LIBRARIES

Most important is the new breed School Librarian. From the beginning of my professional career I was strangely drawn to the school library. Perhaps it was my complex about the "underdog." I resented the second class citizenship the school librarian seemed to be relegated to by many professional librarians. It seemed to me unwarranted that my beloved public library should feel on the defense about the developing school library. I agreed it was unfair for any municipality to maintain a double pay standard, compensating the public librarian even more inadequately than the underpaid school librarian. But rather than foster a separation it seemed most important for school and public librarians to unite in their common mission to strengthen our national mind. From this union could come bargaining power for better status for both school and public librarians.

Even more was I troubled by the double standard for classroom teachers and librarians. In many school systems there was a preferential salary schedule for those who centered their effort in the class instead of in the library. Part of this was the librarian's own ancillary complex; her repeated accents on supporting the classroom teacher to the exclusion of her own educational dimension.

It seemed to me that the School Librarian must do both. Support the classroom teacher, by all means. Indeed, use this support to stimulate her colleagues to teach with books and libraries more creatively than most classroom teachers knew how. If Chancellor Branscomb had indicated in his study for the Association of American Colleges that too many professors were not teaching with books adequately enough, an even stronger case could be made against classroom teachers in American elementary and secondary schools. Teachers were not to blame as much as the teacher education that had for so long inadequately prepared teachers in the potential of library teaching. School librarian support of the classroom teacher might be used to compensate for the teacher education deficiency.

But in addition to supporting the classroom teacher the School Librarian as a faculty member has a professional obligation to experiment and innovate with the learning process from her library vantage point—to accept Chancellor Branscomb's challenge to librarians to come up with an education of their own. It seemed to me that we School Librarians should venture in each school to demonstrate library learning in comparison and even in competition with classroom teaching. Why not two controlled groups of children, one taught by the conventional classroom, the other exclusively by library independent study, bibliographically counselled by the School Librarian?

Always much opposition came from some School Librarians who claimed there was "too much to do." For a very long time this "too much to do" was insistence that each school library had to classify and catalog its own books. Even when LC and Wilson cards were introduced there were School Librarians who insisted that each school must adjust these processes to the individual school requirements. What disturbed me was the knowledge that some school librarians were converted classroom teachers who had hoped to escape "discipline" problems by devoting themselves to classifying, cataloging and tó making a federal holiday out of neatly labelling, pocketing, shellacing, and doing all of the other processing. I could not possibly disagree that cleanliness was next to Godliness and that library housekeeping contributed to better working conditions. It was before the day of the paraprofessional, or even the parent aides, or WPA workers, and there was no money for clericals. Student assistants were not paid.

My school library writings are charged with my evangelism for a new breed librarian. I was convinced that the School Librarian could, if she would, give our children a better education than Classroom Teachers who had been inadequately sophisticated in books and libraries by their teacher education. When the audiovisual bee stung me in the early thirties I saw from the start that the proliferation of formats would reenforce the School Librarian's effectiveness with the independent study dimension in library learning. Philosophically, from my own learning struggles, I had arrived at that fundamental measure of quality education later stated in a USOE "Dimensions" pamphlet by Winslow Hatch:

> The degree to which a student can study independently is a measure of quality education.

When my pointed suggestions that experimental programs in independent study be established in both elementary and secondary schools made no headway I resorted to dreaming about futures. At one Pennsylvania education meeting I read a paper describing a library-centered school in 1984. At the Indiana school librarians conference in Turkey Run State Park I described a Medium School in the year 2000AD. *School Libraries* published several of my futures, the last under the title "Just Suppose" in which I imagined what would happen in a school if there were no classrooms at all; only library carrels where pupils began studying independently under the librarian's direction right from the start. Many considered this impossible for most children. But I recalled I had begun that way in the children's room of the public library, pre-school, and I was convinced that every child should be given a chance to learn that way. If my four-year-old blue eyes seemed always filled with the wonder of learning, as several teachers and librarians used to remark to my mother, then why should not all children be introduced to the opportunity of wonderful browsing in a library; of pursuing the Fourth R?

Later, when the professional fad of delaying reading until "readiness" captured some educational thinking, I was driven to some extreme evangelisms in my speaking and writing for educational audiences. I insisted, wrongly or rightly, that such delay was a denial of the child's right, from birth, to explore vicariously all of the wonders of mortal existence. I contended passionately that a book should be put in the baby's crib as soon after birth as possible. Perhaps as early as eighteen months babies would be reading in wonderment the pictures of picture books and communicating in infant words some startling meanings colored by their more recent experiences with the infinite.

My ultimate for the School Librarian was "anchor man" that TV newsmen epitomize. My ultimate for the School Library was for it to become the school—the Medium School.

When schools library-center their learning, they are *Medium Schools*. As I look back now to the elementary schools of Cleveland, Ohio, where I began my formal education, I realize that I was subconsciously reaching for an ideal school which would be primarily a library. My public library beginnings even before I entered kindergarten had undoubtedly conditioned me to an independent study mode. I was captivated by browsing, a term I did not meet until much later. All I knew was the excitement of exploring on library shelves and confronting unexpected discoveries. I began remaking my elementary school into a library.

After browsing and reading I discovered a third component in my developing library learning mode. Later I called it the Fourth R— Reference. The encyclopedia opened the door. Somewhere in my school days it occurred to me to look up the subjects that were causing me trouble in the classroom. The incident about magnetism in high school physics was illustrative.

Out of this first encyclopedia learning experience developed two more techniques. The first of these I call comparatives. I discovered that an obtuse (for me) treatment of a topic by my textbook or by my teachers could be clarified and amplified by another approach that more nearly related to my background. I therefore practiced consulting the index in a half dozen other textbooks in the library and in the encyclopedia. Whether it was repetition, or, as I suspected, an approach more nearly tailored to my development, the important point was that these comparatives were helping me to learn better.

The second learning technique the encyclopedia suggested was the *overview*. That high school economics class with the pretty teacher started the habit of overviewing the subject of every class in which I was to be enrolled the coming term. This device enabled me to anticipate; to shake my head in approving awareness if the teacher followed the encyclopedia's unfolding; to challenge intellectually when the instructor departed from what my overview had taught me to expect. I submit this is creative learning. My independent approach *first* seemed a better learning sequence than a pre-digestion by the teacher ahead of my own confrontation.

These components—quantity reading, browsing, comparing, and overviewing—began to shape my developing ideas for a reform of education on all levels. By the end of my undergraduate college days the Library-College concept was emerging in my own campus unrest. Subsequently, my dissent with elementary and secondary education evolved into the Medium School.

In pedagogical literature I had met repeated references to *Individual Differences* in learning. I agreed with that. But I despaired at the neglect of the library in serving these differences on all educational levels. I wrote impatiently about fellow librarians who were forever exhorting school librarians to follow the cirriculum, to support the school's objectives, to be better informed on professional pedagogy. I tried to do all of these things, as I think most school librarians have. But I did not think those in pedagogy were reciprocating by letting the curriculum follow the library, by shaping the school's objective somewhat by the library's potential for learning, by being better informed in the literature of librarianship. Some librarians agreed; but others wrote sharp dissenting letters to the editor on some of my heterodox school library writings.

I persisted in my advocacy of a library-centered learning that would more nearly adjust to individual differences than the classroom centered teaching that was standard. During my second graduate year at Peabody I wrote a major paper on the idea of a library-centered education. I called it "The Passing of the Classroom" and explosively predicted that the classroom teacher would be replaced by the library teacher. Out of this paper evolved my Chicago ALA address on the "College of Library Arts" which was subsequently published by *School and Society*, and which some have cited as the beginning of the Library-College movement in the United States. Out of that Peabody paper evolved also the "Medium School" idea which was published as an article in *Phi Delta Kappan*.

The Medium School is a school in which learning is library-centered. In place of recitation and the textbook, instead of the teacher teaching and assigning, the Medium School encourages browsing, reading, viewing, tasting, smelling, (even dreaming) among many different kinds of media, *first*. It encourages independence from the start, as rapidly as the pupil can manage it.

Necessarily, in following a chronological account of my personal struggle to learn, from my earliest library and school days, I have not presented an orderly description of my evolving concept of library-centered elementary and secondary education. I will try to conclude this section with an overview of my ideal Medium School.

Classrooms are converted to mini-libraries. These are replicas of the building Materials Center, or Learning Resource Center, or Media Center, or what ever name you choose to give the library. At this point we will not dialogue on the variations. The classroom center, or Echelon, as I described it in my book *Instructional Materials* (Ronald, 1960) includes two collections—Permanent and Rotating. The Classroom's Permanent collection includes materials for the appropriate level, and includes:

1. *Encyclopedia, Dictionary, Almanac, Atlas* (basic reference books)
2. *Reading books* (appropriate level)
3. *Magazines and newspapers* (appropriate levels)
4. *Globes* (terrestrial and celestial)
5. *Maps* (wall, stand, seat: world, national, state local; appropriate level)
6. *Pictures*, charts, objects, dioramas, etc. appropriate
7. *Discs and Tapes* (appropriate music, recitations, etc.)

The Classroom Center includes at least the following equipment:

1. *Boards:* chalk, peg, magnetic, flannel, bulletin
2. *Projectors:* overhead, opaque, slide, 8mm motion
3. *Audial:* disc playback, tape recorder, radio set.

The Rotating collection relates to the curriculum or cocurriculum unit to which the class is committed at the time. It is charged to the room from the Building Center, and will include supplements to the Permanent classroom collection of materials, equipment usually too expensive to duplicate for each room, such as 16mm motion pictures and projectors, videotape recorder, additional encyclopedias, and other expensive hard covers.

To illustrate Medium School learning as it might be undertaken for a fourth grade unit on Mexico: The library teacher accompanies the class to the Building Center (School Library, Learning Resource Center, or any other designation the school considers best describes its aim). Pupils are asked about the "Half of Knowledge" first, for which there has been progressive preparation from pre-school with a new dimensional approach to teaching library use. "Where would you start your investigation of Mexico, first?" the teacher asks.

The first hand recognized might respond by getting up from his chair, walking to the set of *Compton's Pictured Encyclopedia* and depositing on the large library table, designated for the gathering of sources, the "M" volume opened to the page headed *MEXICO—A New Nation With an Ancient Heritage*. Another hand precedes an excursion to the filmstrip corner and the deposit of a little tin can labeled *Mexico*, which the child located through the catalog. In turn each child's hand that is raised is followed by a walk to the medium format that probably last communicated best. There is an obvious greater sophistication about "knowing where to find it" than conventional fourth graders display.

When the table is piled high with materials, the pupils make proper charging records, and transport on book trucks, super market fashion, all of their shoppings to their own classroom center, where shelves just cleared of materials related to a previous unit or project await the new "Rotations." The children set to work on their own selections first, and then on some of the alluring sources selected by classmates. The children dialogue with each other freely about materials and issues. At one point in the course of the unit an "Each One Teach" dimension may be introduced, when fifth grade pupils who had the unit last year are invited to dialogue with the fourth graders, reenforcing the principle that one learns best when he has to teach it to another.

SPECIAL LIBRARIES

Telescoping the several definitions offered by general dictionaries and encyclopedias, and especially the library glossaries, like ALA, Harrod, Massa de Gil, *et al*, a Special Library can be defined as a library that serves the special interests of research and investigation in the pure and applied disciplines. Mostly special libraries are components of government, industrial, commercial, philanthropic, or learned society agencies, although they may also be departments in academic and public libraries.

My own special library experience over the years had begun as law librarian in the University of Toledo during my last two undergraduate years. It had been strangely timed with a sudden interest in going into law that had been stimulated by the successful debating season of the university intercollegiate team, especially in the dramatic finale against the communist local. Periodic revivals in law librarianship were aroused by several colleagues and especially by students, some of whom switched from law to librarianship and some *vice versa*.

My next special librarianship was in medicine at Meharry Medical College, when, in 1930, as Fisk librarian I was asked to assume that additional duty. Soon I discovered another natural affiliation between two professions. I became especially enthralled by the great physician Sir William Osler, whose bookmanship surpassed most librarians. Think of a great physician being an authority on a relatively obscure 17th century essayist. Although Sir Thomas Browne was himself a physician he was also a name in English literature, and Osler had collected one of the best libraries about him. And then it had been my good fortune to work with the physician Dr. Rogers who had been one of the architects of Medlars. The medical library experiences I had strengthened my growing Special Library philosophy.

Other Special Library experiences included brief staff or consumer experiences in Education, Social Sciences (especially in the New York Public Library Economics Division under Roland Sawyer, and in the London School of Social Work). Major attention to Armed Forces Libraries, especially at Air University, Maxwell Air Force Base, Alabama, where I served as Chairman of the Board for seven years, and the world-wide SAC conference contributed another dimension to the overall Special library philosophy I was developing.

With diffidence, I suggest that Special librarianship may yet lead the way in scientific investigation by offering to specialists some generalist perspective. Special librarianship can do this by interrelating the disciplines more effectively than the specialist often can. After all, the librarian has a background in our epistemology, our classifications of knowledge, with that extraordinary class designated "generalia."

Perhaps Special librarians can begin with our colleagues in Information Science by recalling the greater significance of values than retrieval of isolated facts. There is a gestalt in the very essence of librarianship that tends to fade as the specialists absorption with minutiae accelerates. Even in Special librarianship the intrinsic generalism of our discipline and profession offers a leavening for investigations.

15. Organization Librarian

Before the libraries of the world could unite the librarians had first to be united. As I look back over my organizational effort in local, state, regional, national, and even international professional associations I realize how much of an evangelism this desire for professional unity was. Although I was in the vanguard for recognition of the special interests of academic librarians and school librarians, of reference workers and of audiovisualists, of library historians and exponents of comparative librarianship, and of a half dozen other special causes, I always tried to call these specialists back to our common professional mission. I believed our high destiny was to disseminate the noblest deeds, the deepest thoughts, the most beautiful communications man had been capable of. To fulfill our destiny we must not be divided by special interests.

Perhaps I began my organizational crusade at Columbia library school during the academic year 1927-28. There I gained my first knowledge of Organization Librarian. There I was taught about ALA, and began my membership in it. I was informed about other library associations, local, state, regional, and even international. But my thoughts were all about ALA. How could we become as important in

American life as the American Medical Association or the American Bar Association or the National Education Association?

I had my baptism in Organization Librarian at the 1928 ALA convention. In company with several of my Columbia classmates—Charley Mohrhardt and Ralph Ulveling, who began then to stand for the Detroit Public Library, and with some other tyros in the ways of conventioneering—I wandered about wide-eyed. I try now to relive my own captivation and wonderment of that first convention. The exhibits, much more modest then than now, absorbed me early and late when meetings were not scheduled. Perhaps at that first meeting was born the idea of giving the exhibitors more recognition at conventions than was the custom then. I believe I was one of the first, if not the first, under my presidency of the Southeastern Library Association to introduce the institution of presenting each exhibitor individually at the first general session, by having him announced as he walked up the aisle from the platform. Perhaps the signing up for prizes to be drawn at the last general session was originated previously elsewhere. I treasured my relations with exhibitors, from the start, and was grateful for the many kindnesses they showed me throughout my professional life. Bringing the exhibitors into the organization was also part of my intense desire to unite us.

It was Mr. ALA, Carl Milam, I am sure, who suggested me for my first ALA committee assignment. *Constitution and By-Laws* both flattered and frightened me. I wished I had devoted myself in college to political science, especially when I sat down to my first meeting. The committee chairman was Perry Danton. Librarians had warned me of his brilliance, some with sympathy for having to begin my committee work under a genius who could be intellectually brutal. I discovered at once how literate and intelligent Perry is. But from the first hour, I liked his human warmth. Perhaps I should speak only for myself, but I have felt empathy for Perry from then to this day. I have turned to him when I needed intellectual assistance that was beyond the ordinary. Even recently when I was asked by Crowell Collier and Macmillan to assist on the new *Encyclopedia of Education*, I turned to Perry for contribution and for advice. Committee work on the ALA constitution was the best possible orientation into Organization Librarian.

What little parts I played in the two ALA reorganizations that followed were aided by my committee initiation. Beginning with the Third Activities Committee I brashly orated to Carl Milam my model for ALA reorganization. He challenged me to write it out. It was published in the *ALA Bulletin* for December 1938 as "Proposal for the Pyramidal Reorganization of the ALA." Although I had several articles published in other professional journals, this was one of my first major writings for the *ALA Bulletin*. Some of my suggestions were represented in the Third Activities Committee thinking.

More of my thought and effort, however, contributed to what I consider was the major issue that threatened unity to our national association. College and university librarians were in revolt against a professional organization that they contended was overwhelmingly committed to just one type. They referred to ALA as a "Public Library" association which diverted dues from members in the other library types to advance public library objectives, predominantly.

As in so much protest, the case was often overstated. Some of the vindictive academic librarians threatened secession, in writing and in impassioned speeches on the Council floor. I wanted more recognition for college and university librarians, but not at the price of splitting Organization Librarian. From the start of the organizational debates I was attracted to the leadership of one man—Charles Harvey Brown. Director of libraries at Iowa State University in Ames, Dr. Brown had been among the first to promote science in a heretofore predominantly humanistic profession. He had a brilliant mind that often communicated sharply and with biting satire in his distinctive voice which had undoubtedly been cultivated to overcome a speech defect. Because his repartee could become withering at times, librarians were reluctant to meet him head on.

He became one of my early professional godfathers. Perhaps my youthful admiration of his keen intellect and my worshipful attention to his professional observations, which at the time stimulated my thinking more than any librarian I then knew, encouraged a mutual affection. He listened to me thoughtfully one day at ALA when I expressed myself spiritedly on unity. "We are so few in numbers compared to physicians, lawyers, teachers, that it would be a shame to let this schism between academic and public librarians divide us so that we would not have a united voice to represent librarians in the national councils of professions." I had the satisfaction of hearing Dr. Brown declare my position on ALA Council floor, subsequently, much more articulately.

However outdated the work of the Third Activities Committee may appear to the contemporary revolters, that reorganization of ALA in the late thirties accomplished at least these two important reforms; (1) recognition for another library type in addition to public, as major; (2) preservation of the unity of the national library association. Now that the academic librarians had been authorized major status what would they do with it?

Academic librarians had previously been given a section in the American Library Association. It had been called the College and Reference Section. Possibly because of my association with Charley Brown I was elected to the charter Board of Directors. The late Willard Lewis, librarian of Penn State University, was elected the first secretary. Willard and I were once referred to disparagingly by one of Dr. Brown's antagonists as "Charley Brown's errand boys." We told each other after this remark was relayed, "It's an honor to be an errand boy in so creative a cause for such a good and great man."

Willard and I initiated some firsts for Organization Librarian. At my suggestion, we activated first ever "Hospitality Desk" for ACRL. ALA was growing into impersonality. Willard and I set up a schedule at our desk, from early morning late into the evening, taking a great number of the hours ourselves. We helped tyros at ALA meetings; bewildered librarians trying to find each other or to make appointments; a crude placement service for employers and prospective employees; even a "lonesome" service for librarians who had no one to eat with, or sit down beside at meetings. When public librarians began coming to us with opening sentences like "I wish we public librarians had something like this," we began to feel that perhaps these errand boys were contributing something. Always we assisted any ALA member, whether he also belonged to ACRL or not.

It was not all housekeeping. I was deeply pleased that when the ALA HQ decided to set up a first committee on Academic Library Standards that I was named chairman. All of us spent many hours in meetings and at home on our specific assignments. I learned tremendously from this first chairmanship of a major ALA committee. I wondered how I had been chosen, I, still a very young and inexperienced librarian, to head a working party, as the British call it, of such distinguished library leaders. Among the individuals who influenced my selection, I am sure, was Carl Milam, who appreciated my devotion to unity, and to a strong ALA. Equally influential was Charles Brown, the recognized leader of the academic librarians. I have treasured his words on several occasions: "Louis, I can't stand these library politicians who declare platitudes pontifically. You are one librarian who thinks deeply enough to make me stop and review what I stand for." I knew I did not bat in his league, but I was pleased that he would listen to some of my vehemences when my evangelisms overcame me. Indeed, it was Charley Brown who once exasperatedly fired back at me, "You should have been a preacher instead of a librarian."

Before our work was complete I went to war. Vice-chairman Eugene Wilson carried the committee work forward. When I returned from the China Burma India Theatre I glowed with pride over the publications with the title-page words "Adopted by the ALA Council, February 1943." For a Committee Hall of Fame, if ALA should ever establish such an institution, I nominate all of my colleagues on that pioneer Standards Committee, who carried on to completion while their chairman was in a distant theatre of war. When "Century One" is written, the title I first suggested in the *Journal Of Library History* for the history of the first 100 years of ALA, every member of that Standards Committee will undoubtedly be mentioned at least once.

On that first ACRL Board I had an opportunity to contribute to some innovations. I was among the first who pleaded for a journal of our own, and *C&RL* resulted. The greatest of all resistance to my crusade for audiovisual librarianship came from the academic librarians. School librarians, first, and public librarians, next, had become receptive. University librarians, particularly, tended to belittle these "non-book" materials as unworthy of "liberal" education; as somehow identified with vocationalism and trade school. But I persisted, tenaciously, got myself appointed chairman of an ACRL Audiovisual committee, finally approved by my fellow directors. Having championed the journal from the start the editor let me edit an audiovisual department and write some articles on the place of AV in academic libraries. Finally, since Reference had been given major recognition in the title of the new Association, I was able to begin my efforts for fuller recognition of the information function in libraries. Eventually this led to the Reference Services Division at the next major reorganization of ALA.

Both ACRL and ALA committee work provided me with a range of assignments in Organization Librarian. Perhaps my responsibilities were not even average, but no member, I am sure, was more excited and pleased over appointments. Sorting them out in the period before the next major ALA reorganization, publishing and editing activities stimulated me as much as any organizational effort. I had my share of satisfactions, and some disappointments. My term on the ALA Publishing committee was a critical one in which we not only examined all serial publications by the Association and the Divisions but projected some new projects, and considered others like audiovisual undertakings in film, filmtrip, tapes, slide, transparency overlay, etc.

Included was a term on the ACRL Monograph series in which significant doctoral dissertations came under consideration. Althought not part of ALA, the Association of American Library Schools was having some deadline and financial problems with its *Journal of Education for Librarianship*. The quarterly was running exactly one year behind. I accepted the chairmanship of publications, and began my search for an editor, since Harold Lancour, the founder and editor had found it necessary to give up the responsibility. Most fortunately, Bill Katz accepted the invitation. His fine journalistic background and his creative talents were perfect for a journal that was in difficulty. First, I imposed rather autocratically, I am ashamed to reminisce, a catchup schedule giving Bill one year to produce eight instead of four issues so that we would be back on schedule. He met the schedule and maintained it with quality content as well.

My long membership in AALS and my success as chairman of publications which included responsibility not only for *JEL* but for *Who's Who in Library Service* and some projected publications inevitably brought me an invitation to be candidate for president. I had declined one time. The second invitation came while I was on leave in New York. Sara Vann as chairman of the nominating committee came to see me. It was very hard to decline Sara. I know what a thankless task serving on a nominating committee can be. The encyclopedia was absorbing much of my attention, and at the same time I was commuting to the library school every other week. This schedule, I knew, would prevent me from giving my best to AALS. There was another reason, very personal. I did not want to oppose my dear friend Jesse Shera. Even though by all odds he should win the election easily I knew how fickle the electorate could be, in Organization Librarian as well as in American politics. As it turned out Jesse lost the election. He won it in a second try.

I have always opposed the idea of the same nominating committee submitting two slates. I opposed the changeover in ALA Council, when I was a member; and I opposed it in the regional and state associations of which I became president. When I finally agreed to accept the AALS nomination for president I faced almost as heartbreaking an opposition. The late Leroy Merritt, who had done so much in the Intellectual Freedom movement was my opponent. Leroy was my type of librarian—quiet and capable, modest yet courageous. The election result was close and Leroy won.

It was time to re-do the Third Activities "re-do." Whatever else may be said about ALA I want to declare one member's opinion that Headquarters earnestly tried to reflect membership desires. The Herculean task was aggravated by the restless sixties with its breathless, bouncing demands for change, above all. As history looks back it will undoubtedly ponder the causes behind a decade's fierce suspicions of almost anything that had a history. Although librarians as a group were more deliberate in their repudiations of the past, there was still among us a considerable segment who gloried in "modernization," in resorting to reflecting the thinking of "young people" without ever specifying which young people they represented. To acknowledge these protesters' part in our profession, Headquarters tended to favor the activists at times more than the meditationists.

The new reorganization of ALA accomplished some unifications and aggravated some separations. It gave associational status to the other two major library types to match what the Third Activities reorganization had accomplished for Academic Librarianship. Of these, the American Association of School Librarians seemed particularly overdue. When AASL received comparable recognition in the National Education Association I was especially pleased that the school librarians had shown the way to the other three library types.

The reorganization also accomplished divisional recognition for several major kinds of library work. Especially exciting to me was the achievement of major status for Reference. It was satisfying, also, to see acquisition, classification, and cataloging recognized under a division called *Resources and Technical Services*, despite the embarrassment that followed in designating its membership, at first, by the initials RATS.

My most absorbing involvement from the first was in the activation of the new Reference Services Division. As already indicated, the unification of reference workers was complicated by the existences of two almost antagonistic sections, one in the ACRL and the other in the Public Librarians Division. I had been a member of both from their respective starts. Although I had become rather strongly identified with ACRL as one of its organizers and as a director in its charter board, I met less opposition among public library reference workers than did most ACRL members who tried to become members of both sections. Partly, this was due to my own public library professional origins; but mostly because my long life in education for librarianship had resulted in association and dedication to all four library types, about equally.

When RSD was finally chartered by the ALA Council, I became the new division's *pro tem* head. This automatically thrust me into the three overall committees involved in the "policing" of the ALA reorganization. The first of these was the toothpaste-sounding one called PEBCO. It had to do with fiscal allocations to the new major divisions and to other units. As *pro tem* head of RSD my primary obligation was to procure support for the reference mission. I gave this my first attention, of course, in the deliberations that began at the Edgewater Beach hotel in Chicago, that gracious landmark that has also given way to change.

Important as RSD was to my crusade for major recognition of the information function in our national association, I could not subordinate my earnest desire for unity of our profession and for strengthening of ALA. Inevitably I found myself involved in the financial struggles of other neglected areas. At the top was my concern for the new school library association. Miss Williams of California was its PEBCO representative and I sensed, or thought I did, that second class consideration was being given to this library type, as it had appeared to me had always been the case in ALA before. She told me several times after that my support and speeches in PEBCO helped AASL off to better financial consideration than it might have had. There were other places in ALA that I thought had been fiscally neglected, including our American Library History Round Table, and Library Education.

In addition to PEBCO, which concerned itself with finances, primarily, there was COO, the committee on overall coordination of functions in the reorganized units of ALA. This was a challenging and sensitive assignment for all of us. We spent hours and even days and nights listening to conflicting appeals for responsibilites by contending divisions and units. There were adjudications between RTS and RSD to be made on such areas as Government Publications, Bibliography, Microforms. For what aspects of these was Acquisition responsible, and for which Reference? In the shuffles of functions to implement the reorganization, Circulation had been overlooked completely. A place in the reorganization had to be found for those who served in this important part of library service where they could meet and discuss their peculiar problems. My work on COO over several years gave me the best perspective on Organization Librarian. More that ever I wanted to help unify us.

Perhaps because I had developed a reputation for wanting to conciliate differences, and had been good naturedly jibed about my "sweetness and light" approach on these organizational conflicts, I was one of the select group appointed to SCOR to help resolve the schism that had developed on issues of reorganization. This Special Committee on Reorganization had been appointed by ALA Council to meet in Chicago after the Conference. What added to the sensitivity of SCOR's assignment was the personalizing of the conflict, possibly more by the membership than by the personalities involved.

It was a committee assignment that tormented me more than any organizational effort I have ever known. All three of the persons were among my favorite library leaders—my kind of deep thinking people, deeply committed to our professional destiny.

Retiring President John S. Richards had been my colleague on the epoch making ALA-ACRL Standards committee whose landmark documents had been approved by ALA Council in 1943. We had, besides, been sympathetically associated on a variety of issues. I believe we enjoyed meeting and talking in the conference lobbies with that bit of extra affection that makes two people stop no matter how great the pressure of duty. On his side, I believe, was president-elect Lucile Morsch, deputy chief assistant Librarian of Congress. Besides my professional admiration of Lucile as one of that eminent small group of scholars in classification and cataloging that I had been fortunate enough to dialogue with philosophically, I had come to know her, and her lawyer husband Werner Ellinger, personally. I was more sentimentally attached to them than they probably know, because of that mysterious force that has seemed to draw me to some people.

On the other side was President Ralph Shaw. The issues, in retrospect, seem less important than the people. From previous pages it is apparent that Ralph and Viola Shaw have had a unique place in my professional and personal life. I always felt that Viola knew what was going on in my heart much more sensitively than did her husband. Ralph's brilliant mind, I feared, would reject my heart and agnostically probe for rationales behind my actions. Yet, at times I was forced to reexamine and be ashamed of my fears. His concern for reestablishing me in the profession after a four-year absence in military service is an example of my underestimation of Ralph's heart. But his devastating vindictiveness at other times, it appeared to me, left me profoundly sad. I admired Ralph so much, indeed loved him (something I would not dare say to him because of the sharp iconoclasm it might induce) that perhaps I was the one at fault in not being able to communicate with him at times.

This happened at SCOR in Chicago. ALA had invested considerable money to bring us back for our meeting. Out of habit, I decided to write out my solution, my plan for reconciliation, in advance of the meeting. I saw much good in the ALA reorganization; recognition for some of the neglected library types like School; and library work like Reference. But I was concerned that the pendulum might have swung too far toward separation, toward weakening the professional unity I wanted so much. Thirteen divisions—six by library type and seven by library work—suggested a feudalistic structure comparable to the historical period in which nations became subordinate to their fiefs. At the heart of my plan was a device to strengthen our national association by drawing the divisions together. I proposed two councils under the ALA Council, as I recall, one a Council of Library Type Associations, and the other a Council of Library Work Divisions.

Apparently, Ralph had drawn up his plan in advance, too, and as ALA president, he presided at the first meeting, a night session, as I recall it. He began the session by presenting his plan, and then somewhat impatiently, it seemed to us, urged that we adopt it, and the SCOR meeting would thus be quickly and efficiently completed. I asked Ralph if perhaps we should not give other members of SCOR a chance to present their plans or ideas. When Ralph asked if any other member had a plan and none was offered, I asked Ralph, with fear and trembling, I recall, if I might offer mine. I read it, and sat down worried, mostly because I feared I had offended Ralph. What followed troubled me even more. Several members arose to express a preference for my idea of synthesis. The upshot was a vote to adjourn and consider both plans the next day after a night's sleep.

The next day was even more trying. Ralph persisted in his effort to get SCOR to approve the plan he had offered. When Foster Mohrhardt arose to say if he had to choose between only these two plans he would prefer mine, Ralph suggested we break for midmorning coffee. As I entered the hotel coffee shop, Ralph asked me to join his table, and followed with a pleasant esoteric offer: "A Moxie for your proxy."

When Ralph and Viola had visited Tallahassee just before, we had offered them the usual refreshments on our Florida screened porch. When I mentioned that Wayne Shirley had sent me a case of Moxie, the New England soft drink, Ralph immediately asked to sample it. He had heard Wayne talk up this New England drink so often at ALA conferences that I knew he was intrigued. When he tried it, at last, Ralph was so disappointed that he declared it left a bad taste in his mouth—so bad that he could not undertake an alternate liquid refreshment. The offer of a Moxie for my proxy at the Chicago SCOR was a kindly effort at conciliation. I reproached myself. But I could not conscientiously vote for Ralph's plan because it did not accomplish what I considered paramount for professional unity. When Ralph put his plan to the vote after coffee break it was defeated. The Committee worked on and came up with a compromise plan. Ralph was obviously unhappy, not only with the committee, but as I feared, most of all with me for letting him down.

I suffered over what I thought was an estrangement between us. Perhaps this had been the epitome of ingratitude on my part for the many considerations Ralph had showed me in the past. At the next national convention in Washington, the Association of American Library Schools was scheduled to meet at Catholic University, some distance from the convention hotel. As I stood outside the hotel door despairing of ever getting a taxi, Ralph came up to me, in his inimitable way: "Louis, would you be willing to settle for second best transportation in my car?" We drove over to Catholic University together talking gaily as of old. I hope I have written of this in a way to reflect my reverence for one of the finest minds and hearts I have ever known.

When I came out of the army in 1946 I was invited to meet with a small group of library leaders in the South to explore the possibility of strengthening the regional Southeastern Library Association. Among them were colleagues I admired most, as librarians and as friends. Louis Round Wilson was still the patriarchal leader. But Mary Utopia Rothrock, formerly Knoxville Public Library director and, after, architect of the federal Tennessee Valley Authority pioneer regional library service was a leading spirit. Her successor at Lawson McGhee, Helen Harris, and University of Tennessee librarian William Jesse comprised a triumvirate from East Tennessee who spurred us all on to new perspectives. An informal meeting was called by Toby Rothrock in idyllic Gatlinburg, Tennessee, set in among the Great Smokies. We dreamed about a new role for our regional library association that would introduce some new dimensions for the nine states and perhaps offer some models to the rest of the nation. A planning committee was deemed necessary and I was asked by those present to chair the working party selected. It was a tremendous challenge for those of us who were designated the SELA Activities Committee. We met and talked, corresponded and published, and finally came up with a reorganization plan that tightened up the loose organization SELA had been since its 1920 founding. When the plan was presented at the next biennial conference there was the inevitable opposition.

I have pondered this role of negativism which appeals to so many today. To prevent something from happening tends to become a virtue among those who are too often lacking in imagination and innovation. President Skip Graham and president-elect Bill Jesse proved masterful parliamentarians, providing the activities Committee chairman with adequate opportunity to present the plan and to document it. It was Skip who eased the tension of debate which can become so heated at library conferences with his observation that "it was time for the loose SELA to get tight." The plan was approved to go into effect with the new biennium.

Little did I realize that Bill Jesse's successor as president of SELA would turn out to be the chairman of the Activities Committee. I was called long distance by the chairman of the nominating committee. In those days such nomination was tantamount to election. Only one slate was proposed by the nominating committee with privilege for floor nominations by the membership. I delayed my answer over the week-end. My wife was concerned about my health. The jungle fevers were weakening me every afternoon despite the fact that it was now 1950 and the China Burma India experience was some six years behind me. I wanted so much to contribute something to this regional renaissance that I called on Monday and accepted. I was reenforced in my decision by the fact that Dorothy Crosland, a dynamic and creative librarian at Georgia

Tech, would accept the vice presidency. Together I felt sure we could initiate the new SELA. The Executive Board that was elected, one member from each of the nine states, must have been divinely picked. Never has any president been blessed with more talent and courage.

Among the immediate challenges we faced was that posed by segregation. Many libraries had separate facilities and entrances, and Black librarians who attended SELA were segregated, not by librarians, but by hotels and restaurants. Blacks could attend meetings only after all meals and refreshments had been finished. So we eliminated social functions from the program.

There were other pioneerings in this new SELA. I had placed a journal at the top of our objectives and it was launched at the beginning of my presidency under the capable editorship of Bill Hoole of the University of Alabama. It has continued to prosper under the present creative editorship of Jerry Orne. We appointed the first paid executive secretary for SELA, on a part time basis, to begin with, and a headquarters was established at Georgia Tech where Dorothy Crosland guided the operation. Since ALA had used blue ink for its letterhead I adopted green and got an artist to design a nine-state map symbol for SELA identification. It was fun trying to model a regional headquarters, borrowing both from ALA, and from the other regionals, especially New England, which I had addressed several times, PNLA, and neighboring Southwestern coming into being at about the same time.

But we had other bigger dreams for SELA and our region. Through Toby Rothrock's efforts we contracted with the regional TVA and secured federal funds under a contract to survey the library resources and needs of the nine southeastern states served by the Tennessee Valley Authority. I know we did not quite accomplish what Toby had hoped we might. We fell far short of what I had begun to dream for the libraries of our region, first, for the nation next, and ultimately for world librarianship. With the impracticality of the romantic dreamer I am I talked my heart out trying to describe my early idea of a regional network long before the term network was ever used in connection with either libraries or Information Centers.

As I sketched it for myself and for a few deep colleagues who encouraged me excitedly, I believed fundamentally that libraries could be trusted much more than radio and television, or even the press to inform the public impartially. I was beginning even then to revolt against the mass media emphasis on show business; the self-righteous insistence that only the unusual was news. Through our balanced library selection I believed we could toughen the regional mind by informing the people more objectively and less condescendingly than our mass media insisted was necessary if the news business was to be profitable.

To finance this Southeastern Library Network I proposed that the SELA produce various media formats, distribute them through the libraries of the region, and finance them by advertising very much as print, radio and TV. Ours would be a non-profit enterprise, with incomes shared by the Association with all of its member libraries. We would produce not only artistic formats of printed bibliographies, reading lists, adult courses, etc., but radio, TV, and other media formats.

It was an ambitious undertaking. I could not sell it during my presidency, chiefly because I had not the time from my job or the physical energy.

Although the dream was not realized Southeastern Organization Librarian was strengthened. SELA is deep in my professional heart for all time.

Organization Librarian in Florida right after World War II when I arrived to assume my duties at the University in Tallahassee seemed particularly disunited. Perhaps the pattern of organization was not too different from most of the state. Presumably the Florida Library Association was the state voice for librarians of all library types. But if it was it was comparatively weak in influencing the Legislature for either public or school library support, and not particularly felt by the Board of Regents for higher education. As for special libraries, although it was the pre-Cape space period, and before industry had begun to be attracted to the sunshine as particularly conducive to specialists, there were a number of military establishments engaged in research that deserved better library support than they were getting.

Part of the reason for the ineffectiveness of Organization Librarian in Florida was due to some of the separations. Despite the fact that Florida is not a typical Southern state, there was segregation. Separate library associations for whites and blacks existed, and although the latter members could belong to the white-dominated Florida Library Association, not many Black librarians availed themselves of the privilege. Indeed there were many who militantly held out for separation. When the ALA reorganization specified that only one state-wide organization might gain chapter recognition in each state, the Black library association applied first. I joined State Librarian Dorothy Dodd who was then president of FLA in an informal conference with some of the leaders of the rival associations. I pleaded earnestly for unity among us as librarians, regardless of color, faith, or any of the other criteria that artificially prevented us as librarians from working together for the good of the Human Race. Whether my plea and my reputation in "library service to Negroes" (the Library Literature heading) contributed, the decision was for union and for augmentation of FLA membership, goals, and representation.

There were other causes for disunity among Florida librarians, too. A schism had developed between school librarians and the other three types. As a result, a Florida Association of School Librarians had been formed, which identified more closely with the American Association of School Librarians and the N.E.A., in the nation, and with the Florida Education Association in the state. School librarians increasingly used their convention attendance time and money for the FASL state and regional meetings. The fact that school librarians were placed on classroom teachers' salary schedule, which was considerably better than the pay provided by the same local governments to public librarians, widened the gap between these two library types.

As a library school dean I was committed to the preparation of all four library types, equally. If anything, I had in the early years of my deanship associated myself most with school librarians. We were preparing more students for school than for any other library type. Nearly half of my library school faculty were specialists in children's and young peoples' material and in school libraries. We had pioneered the Materials Center concept for schools. Perhaps because of this, and our housing of the FASL annual meetings for some ten years, we were able to induce an increasing number of school librarians to become active in FLA.

If school librarians were the first to introduce a schism in state librarianship they were soon confronted with one of their own. Audiovisualists who entered Florida from states like Indiana, Iowa, and New York, where audiovisual centers were being activated separate from the school library began pushing for similar separation in Florida. Florida Audiovisual Association was organized and it began to meet separately and push for separate appropriations, through FEA and in the legislature. Committed as I was to unity I contributed to the movement for a joint meeting of FASL and FAVA. It began with a joint luncheon at FEA, with each association contributing half the program, followed by dialogue which stressed the possibilities of joint effort for funds, for recognition of the "Instructional Materials" mission in the schools.

It was agreed to have a joint FASL-FAVA meeting at Florida State University Library School in the fall in addition to the joint luncheon at FEA in the spring. Out of these meetings developed the unique state certification in Instructional Materials parenthetically described as "library-audiovisual" in which all librarians were required to have minimal audiovisual education, and all audiovisualists minimal library education.

Other schisms were always threatening. Numerically, FLA, which should have been our unified strong voice for libraries in the state, never reached a paid membership of 300. Consequently when I joined two or three leaders in FLA to lobby for state aid to public libraries in the legislature we were politely refused. I believe I pleaded before appropriations committees at least five different times to no avail. "We cannot undertake new commitments" a certain legislator whom I can recall only by the memory of an eye that looked like it had been made of ice, would say. Florida was the last state in the Southeast to obtain state aid for public libraries. Perhaps because of these disappointments I wrote a strong head for the little promotion bulletin I designed as FLA legislative chairman. It read NOT FOR TOURISTS. I pointed out that in Florida's efforts to attract affluent retirees and tourists it was better to say nothing about the backward conditions in the state's libraries.

When the Southeastern Library Association survey of library resources in the nine states was implemented with surveys by the individual states, I undertook to prepare the Florida booklet. Perhaps my disappointment in the legislature was reflected in this writing also. But I felt the people of Florida needed to be stung into action about the library neglect in a state that simply had to be a show window in all cultural areas if its glamour was to draw visitors as the state Chamber of Commerce hoped.

My effort for unity led to some real challenges. I felt we needed a state library journal, and on a shoe string I launched *Florida Libraries* in the School. The first issue was mimeographed in the dean's office. Had any one undertaken an investigation of "conflict of interests," a rising educational tide, he would have revealed that the dean-editor had profited to the extent of losing several nights sleep writing and editing, and about $25 of his personal funds for postage and paper. His compensation was in the fun of editing and mailing an essay in unity. The next two issues were more professionally produced in the offset printing plant Otis McBride and I were trying to establish.

Three months after our return from my Fulbright year I learned I had been elected vice president and president-elect of FLA, at the last convention in spring, while I was out of the country. The secretary who was supposed to have informed me had taken ill. To complicate matters more, the president was in an auto accident and therefore if there was going to be a convention at all the vice president would have to do something. Memberships and dues were at an all-time low. There were no funds in the treasury to pay speakers.

I set to work on the two general sessions. For the first Thursday night I approached six major publishers of U.S. encyclopedias for a first time ever on the making of encyclopedias. Lavinia P. Dudley, that gracious lady who edited *Encyclopedia Americana* so creatively for so many years accepted first. Good friend Walter Yust, shy about attending library conventions, agreed for *Britannica*, over the telephone. With John Rowe, Walter and I had talked encyclopedia for hours over the years. No one more deeply understood the craft of the encyclopedist than Walter Yust. Everett Fontaine agreed for my own *Collier's*, and so I turned to the editors of the young peoples' sets next.

It was natural to start with Charles Ford, at *Compton's*, where I had devoted so many of my own encyclopedia years, and for whom I had just written the article on Reference Books. Charles, all six feet seven of him, a joy to work for and to associate with, readily agreed. It took very little persuasion to enlist Maurice Jones, architect of the *World Book* that took the top rung in major encyclopedia sales. The sixth speaker was the predecessor of Everett Sentman for *American Educator*, and I had my first general session at no cost to the Association.

For Friday night I wrote to an author who had replaced Upton Sinclair as my sentimental favorite. I had, of course, been excited like most of his big audience by *Generation of Vipers*. But his novels and short stories were more like my meaning of art, especially the imagination of The *Disappearance*, the happily ever after *Crunch and Des* stories, the powerful *Tomorrow* that followed, and a half dozen others. I closed my appeal to Philip Wylie in the letter in which I told him we had no money even to pay travel with the words "all of my fingers and toes are crossed."

He wrote back, "Uncross them. I'm driving up from Miami to

Tallahassee. Let's go over to Pensacola together, where the FLA convention is to be." This began the series of visits to our home by Phil and Ricky that we shall always treasure. We drove over and back in two cars. Philip Wylie's Friday night address to the FLA banquet is a red letter in the diary of our state library association. The Pensacola newspaper front-paged "Six Walking Encyclopedias arrived in town." The press outdid itself on Philip Wylie, Florida's leading author.

The general sessions were triumphs for the association because a major city in Florida became aware of libraries and the fact that there was a profession of librarianship as worthy of admiration as teachers and doctors and lawyers. But so was the opening general session on Thursday. For the first time, a leader in each library type prepared a paper to show the relationship of his type to the others and to the profession as a whole. These were some of the blows I struck for unity.

16. Intellectual Responsibility

Organization Librarian gave me no more exciting assignment than the ALA Committee on Intellectual Freedom. It suited my crusader instinct. I entered into its vigilances with fervor. Its causes were my causes *par excellence*. No wonder I got one extra year's appointment. The six years of membership ground hard on some of my eternals.

Freedom to Read was a cause I would die for physically as well as intellectually and spiritually. It was unthinkable that anyone should be denied the privilege of choosing his own reading. The Library Bill of Rights and the School Library Bill of Rights had to be to the Librarian what the Hippocratic Oath is to the physician. In addition, as a teacher, freedom to teach had ramparts of its own that I must keep an eye on. I liked the ALA motion picture; I was even more moved by the NEA film that closed with the teacher refusing to erase the word "democracy" off the chalkboard, and the closing words, "If it is to be erased, let the Board of Education erase it." I was armed to go forth with my colleagues on the Committee and do battle against censorship wherever that ugly word appeared.

There were two major causes for censorship in those days. In my low level levity, at times, I observed in Committee that both of them involved a four-letter word. Communism and obscenity dominated our agenda. How strange that both of Karl Marx' names had four letters. How ridiculous that four-letter words for coition and other natural functions should be cause for suppression.

In the first year or so of my membership on the ALA Intellectual Freedom Committee, the mission was clear cut. We went after every community that dared to suggest public libraries could not buy books that were pro-Marx or over-sexy. These were strange bedfellows—communism and obscenity—to be put to rest in the committee room of an American Library Association activity. But we were relentless. Although we recorded our personal dissents with Marxism we defended the right of the Marxists to be heard. None of us quite extolled the "honesty" of the four-letter word as some later sophisticates did. But increasingly we inclined toward *laissez-faire*. If an adult enjoyed erotica, why not? If these same choice masterpieces were also available to adolescents and younger, what then? We did pause.

I went on a censorship reading binge. Morris Ernst's *To the Pure* became a guide book I carried to and from Intellectual Freedom meetings. My Library School classes at Florida State livened into liberation testimonials, especially by the coeds. It was still the pre-sixties, and when a pretty young woman, just past her undergraduate degree, spoke out one of the milder four-letters, she knew, and so did her classmates, that she had established herself as a liberal, intellectual and well-read, sophisticate already heralding those "young people" demagogic statesmen would increasingly convert to political capital. I went along with that, longer than I did with our stance on Communism.

Strangely enough, the break came on my own encyclopedia. In the spirit of our ALA Intellectual Freedom Committee I read and refused to go along with an article on "Academic Freedom" written for us by Russell Kirk. Very largely it seemed to concentrate on his own differences at Michigan State University. William T. Couch was then our editor in chief. He had sponsored the article and we dialogued about it several times. My personal regard and sentimental attachment to Bill persuaded me to look at his side more than I might have otherwise, in view of my deep commitment to the ALA Intellectual Freedom Committee and what it stood for. Bill agreed to my point that any encyclopedia should present both sides in controversial cases.

At the next ALA, I conferred with my good friend Jackson Towne, then library director at Michigan State, about the academic freedom article. Jackson had been my colleague in Nashville. During the five years I was librarian at Fisk he was the librarian at Peabody. From Jackson I gathered there had indeed been two sides, and that only one side had been presented in our article, since it had been written by the victim of the controversy. After Bill Couch and I had agreed to balance the Russell Kirk article with another one, we were free to continue our dialogue, academically.

Bill Couch was too keen, too well-read, too fair to be underestimated. He introduced me to Russell Kirk's provocative book, *The Conservative Mind*. It helped me begin to balance my own reading on social issues, which I admitted tended to favor the left. Bill is a Southern gentleman. In all of his differences he is most courteous to the opposition. Always his questions probed. "I admire your vigilance in behalf of the left. But if you truly believe in intellectual freedom should you not be equally vigilant to protect the intellectual freedom of the right? Of the intellectual right? We have no more use for Joe McCarthy than does the intellectual liberal."

What Russell Kirk and Bill Couch had accomplished for my intellectual thinking on Freedom was to force me to reexamine my own liberalism. Fundamental in my definition of a liberal is the conviction that the individual should be left as unrestricted as possible in his opportunities for self-expression. In the Rock idiom of today every human should be free "to do his thing." Then I was caught up short when in my reading about Anarchism as a concept, about that time, I ran across these words by Mikhail Bakunin (1814-76), the Russian who ranks with Proudhon as one of the two modern originators of the contemporary movement in Anarchism. Indeed, my readings in radicalism had catapulted Bakunin to the top of revolutionary rivals of Karl Marx. My notes quote Bakunin: "I am free only in so far as I recognize the humanity and respect the liberty of all the men surrounding me."

Were we on the ALA Intellectual Freedom Committee sufficiently respecting the liberty of those who dissented with dissent, not from a reactionary Joe McCarthy Red-baiting prejudice, but from the standpoint of an intellectual conservative like Bill Couch or Russell Kirk. These men were literate and gave evidence of having read on both sides of Marxian Communism, pondered the pluses and minuses, and deliberately and sincerely rejected both the theory and applications of the materialistic interpretation of history.

I began asking myself, and John Henderson, and my other Committee colleagues, what have we done recently to protect the Conservative's freedom of self-expression? It had not occurred to any of us to consider the possibility that on social issues any other than liberals or radicals could be repressed. Above all, there began to emerge the concept of a third theme. One might have unlimited channels for communicating the *status quo* through the media supported by industrial and commercial advertising. Increasingly, liberal and radical social positions as represented by Socialism and by Communism were expanding their own outlets to embrace intellectual agencies like the ALA Committee and an increasing number of organizations incorporating "democratic action" or "civil liberties" in their chartered name. But what about those mavericks who felt "a plague on both of their establishments?" Especially, what about the intellectual moderate who philosophically as well as sociologically observed that the pendulum had now begun to swing too far to the left. There was now too much accent on change, and not enough quest for the constants.

Nor was my concern about our attention to obscenity less affected. It developed out of my aroused vigilance on social issues. As case after case was brought to the Committee's attention, censorship took on a sex pattern. Committee obligation, I reassured myself, required me to devote more of my reading time to erotica. It was just before Tom Lehrer had arrived on the scene to parody the concern about intellectual freedom that most often involved Marxist Communism and sexual frankness, although rarely in combination. Then his band "Smut" finally appeared on the best seller disc *That Was the Year That Was*.

For myself, I had come to the same conclusion after reading an increasing number of these frank novels and plays. Tom Lehrer, the Harvard math instructor who had turned from "Ed biz" to "Show biz" and had shown brilliant talent in both, declared humorously, but pointedly: "Of course we read these books, and defend them in the name of intellectual freedom. But you and I know, that the real reason is 'dirty books are fun.'"

To be perfectly honest with myself I had to admit I enjoyed reading about these "cliff-hanging seductions" one *Newsweek* book reviewer almost reflexively coupled with his conclusion that here was one of the great novels of the 20th century. Sex is an irresistibly attractive experience, I once exploded in a Committee meeting, and, of course, got an explosive response of laughter. As I recall, I went on to declare that I believe sex is here to stay, at least for a while longer. But, I continued, let's not make seduction a symbol of intellectual freedom. As a committee, we should begin to be a little surfeited with crusades for books that are mediocre by any literary standards at all. Our hearts should stop bleeding for these poor authors who have to wait three months for their specially designed fourth Cadillacs; or who are teased about their $20,000 cocktail parties.

Let's avoid these cliches the so-called liberal is building into his vocabulary. When four-letter words are introduced into a novel the *author* put them there; not the reader. Any obscenity the reader is supposed to have put into these words could not have been accomplished without the author first inserting the words there. Certainly the author has not been penalized either critically or financially. The intellectual climate is increasingly nurturing this "frankness" in our literature; making it both more profitable and more acceptable.

What we must look at as a Committee on Intellectual Freedom is what is happening to the opposition to such frankness. Several incidents had occurred to disturb my literary values. I had read a novel manuscript by a colleague and friend. It had appealed to me as a work of art. A publisher's editor had said just that in his letter of rejection, with the disturbing suggestion that a bit of "sexing up" would make it marketable. This had not been the only case. Some other writers had confided comparable editorial responses to "make the characters more honest by having them use four-letter words in their conversation." Was not economics imposing a kind of censorship on intellectual dissent with so-called frankness?

Assignment to the ALA Committee on Intellectual Freedom had a profound effect on my thinking. It forced me to reevaluate many of my values. Above all, my six years on the ALA Intellectual Freedom Committee forced me to review my esthetic values. I wished many times that Martin Ross had been at my side during my membership on this Committee. I recalled the days and nights we had spent dialoging answers to the question, "What is Art?" Always we had referred back to Tolstoy's classic by that title. But Martin was in distant California still teaching English literature and writing, while I was trying to serve as a committee member in Florida.

What I recalled most often was Martin's and my favorite line in Tolstoy's *What Is Art?*

Louis Shores

> Art is a human activity having for its purpose the transmission to others of the highest and best feelings to which men have risen.

The highest and best feelings to which men have risen. That I believed, above all, art must transmit. By such transmission, I mystically felt, we approached more nearly the solution to that "riddle of the universe" Ernest Haeckel had suggested all mankind, consciously or sub-consciously, sought. So much of the art our Committee was protecting from censorship did not remotely, in my opinion, approach Tolstoy's noble purpose for art.

I struggled with the argument of contrast. It was the contention of some of the critics who sympathized with the neo-frankness that by exposing the lowest and worst feelings to which men have fallen the rest of us would be warned and inspired to the opposite. An example in point was one of the sophisticated critics' favorites—Tennessee Williams. I had read and seen many of his plays, always with a feeling of repulsion for his work. As if to torture me it had seemed as if when I had to entertain one of the encyclopedia's authors or advisers or editors, my guest would express an interest in a current Broadway production of a Tennessee Williams play. I must have seen *Cat on a Hot Tin Roof* in this way at least a dozen times, besides having read it. I used to take my revenge on this play by retitling it *The Hot Cat on the Tin Roof.*

Perhaps, as some of the sophisticated critics contend, Williams has technical, theatre skill. The command of language some attribute to him meets that top measure for the swinger-cuteness. Williams' characters are generally brutal, depraved, or neurotic. He is not a true Southerner, in my opinion, because he commits his efforts to portraying the South as decadent and depraved, employing a low form of naturalism to grind his axe.

There is no region in the United States, or in the world that does not have its evidences of decay and depravity. All of these places have also manifestations of higher and better feelings to which inhabitants of that region have risen. Let science take Tennessee Williams, and Edward Albee, and the other realists who titillate sex-suppressed Broadway audiences. It is for Art to discover goodness and compassion, nobility and self-subordination in mankind and celebrate those; not the depravities. I do not believe that man will necessarily tend to contrast if he is shown the depravities. Rather, I believe one reason realism is so popular today is because it comforts depravity in real life. Says the Broadway admirer of *Glass menagerie, Night of the Iguana,* or Albee's *Tiny Alice* or *Who's Afraid of Virginia Woolf,* "I am not quite that bad yet and therefore I can sin a little more." I have listened to self-appointed experts, just before the curtain rise, expound on the "symbolism" and "allegory" of *Tiny Alice* with what sounded like a guilty conscience for liking this celebration of some of the lowest and worst feelings to which men have fallen. My appreciations of allegory and symbolism are certainly on a different level.

I write these first two strong dissents and I realize their wording is as omniscient as the virulences of some Broadway critics who bounce out of a romantic musical like *Half A Sixpence* and write in their morning column "If you like that sort of thing." Well, however low I may fall in the opinion of those "who know art" I must honestly declare that for me such musicals with the courage to see sweetness and light in mankind come nearer to Tolstoy's meaning of art than do the celebrants of depravity, however much more profitable the latter may be, or likely to receive Pulitzer Prize, Oscar or Emmy.

Let the musical comedy moderate us into consideration of my literature choices. I know this will evidence my naive taste to the critics who espouse a more sophisticated and realistic fare. I go back to the Tolstoy answer the question "What is Art." It must transmit to me what I consider man's highest and best feelings. Musical comedy has done this better for me than the theatre of Tennessee Williams or Edward Albee, or most of the realistic drama that has won so much recognition in recent years.

Comfort about my theatre choices is confirmed by the record of Broadway long runs. Nine of the ten top all-timers on Broadway have satisfied my answer to the question What is Art? Leading in long run performances at this writing is still the old favorite *Life With Father,* followed by *Hello Dolly* and *My Fair Lady.* Only number two (in number of performances)—*Tobacco Road*—strays from the noble in my meaning of art. Otherwise there is joy in seeing that the top ten includes three of my most sentimental favorites—Oklahoma (number six); *Man of La Mancha* (seventh); *South Pacific* (ninth).

What does this prove for me? Despite the critics' preference for sophistication; for realistic "telling it like it is," for the "courage" in exposing abnormalities, deviations, addictions; for "anti-hypocritical" frankness which appears to have as its current ultimate performing on stage as stray dogs do on curbstones; in the face of review exhortations for realism, the majority of theatregoers hunger for a kind of wholesome reality. Somewhere in *Man of La Mancha* Don Quixote's romanticism responds to Aldonza's realism with the line, it takes less courage to tell it like it is than to dream it as it is in heaven. And this I believe is the mission of art—to dream it like its in heaven.

Let me write toward the close of the chapter about a few of my choices. Among the novels of this century committed to reforming our society that have communicated protest, and desire to correct injustices more effectively than any of the current marches or diatribes, I would begin with Jack London, Edward Bellamy, Frank Norris and Upton Sinclair. The *Iron Heel*, though violently revolutionary, was salvaged for me by its prophetic overthrow of a fascist dictatorship. *Looking Backward* is really a look forward from 1887 to the year 2000. In keeping with my meaning of art I have always liked writings which identify solutions more than those which only identify problems. Bellamy did this by the novel device of preserving a man in hypnotic sleep for 113 years so that he might compare problems of his day with solutions of a century later.

Frank Norris' novels about wheat (*The Octopus, The Pit*) though more problem identifying than solution celebrating have less of the contemporary vindictive *live sadly ever after* at the end. It is powerful writing Frank Norris does for reform, but with less wholesome optimism than Upton Sinclair, whose greatness will one day be rediscovered. *The Jungle* not only revealed the exploitation of Lithuanian workers in the stockyards, but positively induced some Congressional investigation and action. Similarly *King Coal* exposes savage labor conditions in the Colorado coal mines.

There is much more social reform fiction in my 20th century choices than almost any other type. John Steinbeck began "infecting" me in the sense of that word as Tolstoy uses it to answer the question, beginning with *Grapes of Wrath*, a powerful epic of an Oklahoma family driven from the land by poverty and drought; and continuing through *Tortilla Flat*, a haunting story of California's Spanish peasants; and past the depressing pathos *Of Mice and Men* to even such lighter fiction as *The Wayward Bus*.

So much has been written about racial and religious prejudice, and I have been so deeply involved educationally and emotionally, that to undertake an indication of choices in this segment of contemporary literature would result in a lengthy catalogue. James Baldwin's *Go Tell It on the Mountain* tells the story of a Black evangelist family's struggle for salvation in the Harlem ghetto that reawakens my own early emotions at Fisk and therefore emerges first in retrospect. Next, Alan Paton's *Cry the Beloved Country* must be my number one choice as both the most effective social essay and the epitome of the answer to the question what is art? Perhaps because of my own South African involvement, my crisis in Johannesburg in the midst of such touching librarian hospitality, and above all, because it recalled me to the comparative perspective at the heart of my comparative librarianship crusade, I was moved more by *Cry the Beloved Country* than by any other writing in the vast literature on this heartbreaking cruelty of White Man to Black Man. Never shall I forget the searing words, What if after all of these years of injustice the White Man remorsefully begs forgiveness and the Black Man can no longer forgive?

What is Art? And what is intellectual freedom? And what is the role of libraries and librarianship in preserving freedom and disseminating "the highest and best feelings to which men have risen?"

I believe our high destiny is to serve as a balance, as a medium among media, providing the golden mean in our intellectual climate. In a totalitarian state we must crusade for freedom. When freedom verges on license we must evangelize for responsibility. Through it all, we must have the courage to advocate our quest for the constant, for the eternal verities, for John Keats' Truth that is Beauty.

17. Library Education

To realize our high professional destiny we must plan now for the education of the next generation. In 1963 the ALA activated a "Commission on a National Plan for Library Education." If membership on the Intellectual Freedom Committee influenced my professional outlook most, I will have to say that invitation to serve on the National Plan Commission excited my hopes for professional destiny more than any assignment I have ever had in Organization Librarian.

Perhaps even now I can boast of having headed ALA accredited library schools as long as any one. Four or more decades of involvement in library education on all levels have helped me develop a plan of my own. I have written much on many elements and aspects of library education that have appealed to me as crucial. Inevitably, this long involvement in library education, plus my evangelistic complex, have caused some biases and accents not always accorded priorities by my colleagues.

The statement on "Objectives" prepared in the ALA Library Education office and issued on January 8, 1943, in advance of the Commission's first meeting, could not possibly have satisfied all of us. Of the six "other desirable outcomes" besides the overall general ones, these coincided with some of mine: (1) a representative *philosophy*; (2) a significant *role* for library education that would be recognized by library practice; (3) substantive discipline acknowledgement for our core of knowledge; (4) articulation, not only of *levels*, as the LED document indicated, but of what I called *peripheries* as well; and with general and other professional and specialized educations; with governments, and with other forces that contribute to a national and a world mind. The fifth and sixth objectives—research and public relations, primarily—were important to me, but secondary to the Plan itself.

My very rewording and reaccenting of the LED memorandum will indicate my revolt against the dominant philosophy of what I call *ancillarianism* in both library practice and library education today. Of course I believe libraries must support other worthwhile endeavors in society, and in education; but no more than these endeavors must reciprocally support each other and libraries. With the bias for our profession which the late novelist Jan Struther expressed so well, I apply another novelist's much quoted line in *Animal Farm*. All professions are equal in society; but some professions are more equal than others; and liberalizing on George Orwell's liberalized English, librarian-ship may be the most equal of all in this staccato world of ours. With everyone trying to out shout everyone else, what with marches, demonstrations, theatricals, and other exhibitionisms, the time is about here when quiet will be listened to above the din of spectaculars. I submit that Library Quiet is about to have its day. Signs point to librarianship as the profession of destiny.

It is for this destiny that my plan for the education of the next generation of librarians would point. Specifically, we are in a position to toughen the shabby minds that now communicate physically because they are inarticulate intellectually. Fundamental in our philosophy of library education is a commitment to library sophistication of all mankind so that each of us may independently document our positions on life's issues. As a profession, we must introduce people to the generic book, to the sum total of man's communication to date. We must educate humans, from the cradle to the grave, in that half of knowledge—knowing where to find it.

This suggests a new perspective on what we have called in the past "teaching library use." Key to this new approach to teaching the laymen of all ages how to use the library is independence and individual differences. Recognition that one measure of education, of literacy, of the mentality necessary to cope with the vital issues of living is the degree to which an individual can study independently refocuses the teaching of library use, from earliest infancy to latest maturity.

To accomplish the library education of all people, for a greater world literacy there must be a reorientation of librarianship itself. Again and again we have accused ourselves in our own professional literature of overcommitment to pragmatism. If we appear to contend, philosophically, that the practical effect of the way a thing works is the only criterion for truth, may that not be due to the tendency, professionally, to favor library practice over library education? Have we not, overly, committed education for librarianship to preparing the next generation for library practice as it now is? My position on library education's role is that it must not only prepare students to serve in libraries as they now are, but encourage experimentation and innovation, and that library practice must be more receptive to learning from library education as well as insisting that library education learn from practise. Only in this way can practice recognize the full significance of education.

Perhaps I have departed most from the wording of the LED memorandum's third objective. More important than the pooling of knowledge by specialists, in my opinion, and the experience of practitioners, is the prior recognition that librarianship is based on a substantive discipline of its own, without apology or ancillary status. Too many of us tend to equate specialization with substance. Like History and Philosophy, the Library discipline brings unity to knowledge by cutting across specialists' restrictive boundary lines. Just as there is a history and philosophy of art, there is also a library of art; even as we speak of a history or philosophy of science or sociology, or any other discipline, so also there is a library of science or sociology, or any one of the other specialized fields recognized by our educational curricula. When I speak of a library of science I do not mean just the collection of books that is arranged on the shelves by Dewey 500's, or by any other classification system. What I mean is the perspective of the generic book on these fields in relationship to other specialities, and the rest of knowledge. This perspective the library discipline, through the generic book, accomplishes even more nearly towards some ultimates than even those two other generalistic disciplines of History and Philosophy.

Finally, *articulation*, the "in" word of library education since post-World War II, I claim some fatherhood for. Efforts in the 1930s to interest the Association of American Library Schools in articulating our ALA accredited schools with the mushrooming undergraduate programs in teachers colleges received a "no problem" response. Finally, in 1941, at Peabody, we staged the first articulation conference. Since, a series of conferences have resulted in some criteria for undergraduate programs. But articulation involves much more than undergraduate-graduate library science programs. There are other articulations: lay library education—education for librarianship; education for librarianship—education for the other professions, especially teacher education; library-education—peripherals education, such as Audiovisual, Informations Science, Archives, etc., and integration of state, regional, and national library education plans with the growing trend to state systems of higher education.

Our library education role in the high destiny of librarianship is to help develop the mind and spirit of mankind. A specific, practical way is to introduce humans to the generic book, to the record of man's noblest deeds and thoughts. We cannot begin too early. Pre-school as far back as the cradle, or even prenatal, if there is really something, as I mystically believe, to surrounding the expectant mother with good books, and good minds, and noble spirits. Teaching library use should certainly begin pre-school, if for no other reason than to speed the so-called reading readiness that has captured the thinking of so many child psychologists and teachers.

The particular reorientation advocated here is that even in pre-school library use teaching, the aim should be to develop independent study. Library advisory and browsing methods are ready made beginnings. Match individual differences in children with individual differences in media—print and nonprint, if such a distinction is still possible in the steadily merging formats. This independence can result in a greater readiness for all school work when the child enters formal education for the first time.

"It is surprising," wrote the editors of *Scholastic* in the Foreword to a series of articles I wrote and published in pamphlet form as *How to Use Your Library*, "how many otherwise intelligent adults regard the library as a fearsome and complicated mystery, like the stock exchange or the grand jury, and consequently never go inside its doors. The only way to remedy the situation is to rear a generation of library-wise school children. . . . a student who is not at home in a library may as well resign himself to educational failure. . . . Moved by these considerations the Editors asked Louis Shores to prepare a series of articles on the 'inside' lore of libraries for the benefit of students. . . . he has consulted with and received valuable suggestions from . . . Dr. C. C. Williamson . . . Miss Mary E. Hall . . . Miss Estelle M. Slaven. . . ."

Perhaps of the many writings in library education credited to my byline, the next landmark should be the *Peabody Library Information Tests* I developed in co-authorship with my colleague and close friend, Dr. Joseph Moore, then a young assistant professor in psychology at Peabody, later head of the department at Georgia Tech. We went to work on the tests during the first year I joined the Peabody faculty, in 1934, trying out the college level instruments on his and my students. After that we proceeded with the high school and elementary school instruments in the schools of our Peabody graduates. Revisions were frequent before we were ready to let the Educational Test Bureau, which had a Nashville office, publish the first preliminary edition. For a number of years the Peabody Tests enjoyed nearly exclusive markets in the testing field. Despite prodding by the publisher and our own inclination Joe Moore and I became involved in so many other things we simply could not get back to the tests. But they were a landmark in advancing library instruction from K through college.

I was not satisfied with the degree of library sophistication I found in our non-library school students at Peabody—the next generation of teachers. Surely, if these teachers continued to use libraries as gingerly as they had in the past their students would do no better. I began to take more and more time from my main job of preparing librarians to contributing to teacher education. What better place than Peabody, I told myself. It had been established to provide educational leadership for the South. If we could send educational leaders into the schools and colleges of the region who were library indoctrinated, just think of what we could do for our regional mind in the South, and then for our national mind, as my other colleagues and friend at Peabody, Michael Demiashkevich, had taught me in comparative education. Indeed, I was already pushing him to think more about a World Mind that would study war no more.

I began to consider where and how to infiltrate libraries outside my library and library school shop on the campus. It began in instruction in the English department, my own under-graduate major. At Fisk I had introduced an elective one-hour course in library use. Very few chose that class because it did not fit in with the requirements and credit patterns. The same thing had begun to happen with the course I introduced at Peabody. It was impossible to make it a requirement, first because of College resistance, and second because our teaching load was already so heavy that the library school faculty, small as it was, simply could not handle the hordes of frshmen who would be compelled to take the course.

A unique solution suggested itself during a coffee dialogue with the chairman of the Freshman rhetoric courses, required and offered in many sections, as in most colleges. We agreed that library use was an important part of Freshman English. Our Library School faculty was too small to offer the necessary instruction to all of the Freshman, but we would feel honored to work with the English faculty on a week's unit in the Freshman Rhetoric course.

We met to plan the unit together, English and library school faculties. Then the English teachers began the library instruction. I observed individual classes, and taught units on occasion. Joint faculty meetings to follow up on our planning were held once a month. The plan appealed to most of us, students as well as our two faculties.

Pleased with the Freshman program I turned to other points in the education of teachers. The professor of educational administration invited me into his basic class for school principals to teach a unit on what every school principal should know about his library. It was the early thirties and I hope you will believe the naivete of the questions. I was flattered that they called me by my first name and let their hair down about their librarians who kept them in a state of constant defense. It was obvious some of the principals had a fear of the library and did not want to expose their ignorance. I assured them in that class anything goes, and I began by revealing my ignorance about golf terminology with the question "What is the difference between a double bogey and a double birdie?" Which put the golfers into stitches of laughter, and at their ease.

Said one, "My librarian is one of those perfectionist gals who scares the life out of me when she talks about her accession record. What the hell is an accession record? To me it's like your double birdie and double bogey." I sketched quickly the differences among the three basic records of catalog, shelflist, and accession book; when the last was still a must. This brought all kinds of hilarious testimonials, and surprise on the part of one principal, an ex-football coach, when I explained Decimal classification and the range finders in the stacks. He remarked, "And I thought *973* meant that was the number of books on those shelves." (Before you doubt that, remember this was the 1930s and we had an administrator in attendance who boasted "the first time I was ever inside a high school was when I became principal of it.")

From Administration courses I moved to curriculum instruction and research. Rockefeller's General Education Board had just established the Division of Surveys and Field Studies at Peabody, which began to consult with and advise state departments on curriculum development. When Dr. Doak Campbell became director he invited me to work with the teams on library development. Always library-minded, Dr. Campbell early became an educational leader who promoted library development in the South. It was largely because of his commitment to libraries that I followed him to Florida State University when he became president there.

My first-hand experiences with teaching library use in college and school resulted in numerous publications. Perhaps two should be cited here. When Dr. Samuel Smith, long time general editor for publisher Barnes and Noble, decided to undertake for their notable *College Outline Series* a book on *Best Methods of Study* he asked me to join him and a third author (who changed) in collaboration. The first edition of the book appeared in 1938. It went in to several revised editions and multiple printings. I wrote the major chapter on library use and contributed suggestions to other chapters.

Right after World War II, "General Education" for the first two college years developed into a considerable campus movement in the United States. As a member of the Florida State University faculty committee on general education, I exerted considerable pressure on my colleagues to provide more library instruction for students than the Freshman orientation week unit allowed for. A one credit course was introduced, and we innovated with various new dimensions in content and learning mode, including educational television. In the latter, for example, my Reference class students undertook with me a weekly series called *Find the Answer*, intended to glamourize the Reference books on our open shelves that students, and professors, too, neglected. In 1950, publisher Wm. C. Brown Company of Dubuque, Iowa published *General Education: A University Program in Action*, edited by W. Hugh Stickler, James Paul Stokes, and Louis Shores. I wrote the chapter on the "Library in General Education" based on our efforts to place the library more strategically in the student's college learning the first two years.

When I was also appointed, later, to the university's Graduate Committee, I resolved to work for greater library orientation of our master and doctoral candidates. Before I began grinding my library axe I proceeded to make myself useful, first, in the areas of more immediate concern to my committee colleagues and to the president. A new subcommittee on the Doctoral Program was activated, on which I accepted a working assignment, which resulted in my being designated to write the draft for the revised doctoral regulations. With very little change my draft was approved all the way up to the University Senate and the President. This included approval for the recommendation that our doctors' degrees at Florida State represent the highest library sophistication required by any graduate school in the United States.

I accepted the challenge to implement this. For both master and doctoral candidates I recommended a required course in *Library Searching* to be offered in the first term of residence, either by the department itself, to comply with the outline of content I proposed, or if the department did not or could not offer such a course, the student be required to take the general course offered for the Graduate School to all graduate students (except library school students) by the Library School. A student might exempt by taking the Graduate Library Searching Test to be offered each term.

But this was only half of my library recommendation for graduate degree candidates. The other half provided a capstone. Every master's thesis and doctor's dissertation would require in addition to faculty committee members' and graduate dean's signatures, the approval of the Graduate School's bibliographer on library searching, and bibliographic form.

I began the program for the University and the Graduate School in

1949, assuming the duties of bibliographer on top of my overload as dean and professor in the library school, and encyclopedia editor in New York, plus a mobilization reserve assignment in the U.S. Air Force. It worried my wife. There was so much to do and so little time to do it in that fervor overcame my fatigue. I began teaching the "500" course, myself, checking the theses and dissertations at home at night, and conferring with the graduate students from other departments in between scheduled appointments with my own students.

The "500" course as I first conceived and offered it was intended in no way to be a glorified Freshman library use course. When it deteriorated at times to just that I was depressed. Inevitably, the graduate students who could not exempt on our qualifying test brought a range of library sophistications. This necessitated some Freshman library use review at the beginning. But the focus was always, for me, where in the general sources are help on my thesis or dissertation. The second half of the course concentrated on the individual student's special sources. As the graduate student body began to approach 1,000 and then far exceed that number, it was necessary to increase the number of sections. This enabled us to group the graduate students in sections that concentrated on sources in the natural and social sciences, and in the humanities. Some of my colleagues on the library school faculty took sections of the "500" course, and further relief to my heavy load came as several departments undertook to offer the course for their majors.

June 1934 I became the youngest head of an ALA accredited library school, according to a *Library Journal* feature that portraited all of those in the U.S. and Canada directing education for librarianship. My youth embarrassed me at times, in the deliberations with older heads at AALS meetings, and especially in the presence of some of my very pretty graduate students who were in my chronological generation and were frequently intellectually and professionally too mature to be talked down to as teachers do to students at times, much like parents with children. Despite my sensitivity on some personal relations, however, I knew early that I wanted to concentrate on the professional education of the next generation of librarians.

I came to the headship of the Peabody Library School with at least fourteen years of practice in all four types of libraries—eight in public, nine in academic, one in school, two in special, overlapping, of course, to come out the right total of years. For three years, for example I had two jobs, one academic, the other special; for another year, one public, one school. Under ALA pressure Peabody was forced to separate the two jobs of college librarian and library school director and I was given my choice. There was no doubt about my decision.

Our quarters, then, were the top floor, which had an open well overlooking the library's main lobby on the floor below. It was before air conditioning, and the summers were excruciatingly uncomfortable, as the students, augmented by Peabody's large teacher enrollment, absorbed every bit of circulating hot air. Teachers' offices, three classrooms, and the school's library surrounded the open well.

The new dimensions we developed under my direction, most significantly, were a new informal faculty-student relationships; a work-study "co-op" innovation for library schools; articulation of ALA graduate with unaccredited undergraduate programs; placement procedure. There were, also, some experimental approaches in curriculum, in teaching-learning method, in library-library school practice—education liaison, and some other implementations in certain areas like my own Reference, where the Basic Reference concept was developed and where I launched the first of my three major current Reference Literature reviews—namely, *Current Reference Books* for the *Wilson Library Bulletin*.

Perhaps because my chronological age was so near that of my graduate students I placed at the top of my earliest effort establishing community rapport between faculty and students. We dialogued informally and in periodic student meetings. The College owned Knapp Farm, where the house had been converted into a rough club house. There we picnicked frequently and carried on a sort of professional retreat on extra-class concerns. My wife, there, began her match-making, for which she has had an enviable reputation, and which later caused many to say my deanship was merely a front for my marriage bureau operations. One of our bachelor friends who was accused of crossing the street every time he saw my wife approaching, jokingly told her out of the really deep affection he had for both of us, "no bachelor is really safe in Mrs. Shores' company. If he isn't careful, he will be married before he knows what has happened." Despite the fact that matchmaking is not a criterion for ALA accreditation, we are both very proud of the fine families we started at both schools.

More tangible was the attention given to student placement. During the Great Depression, announcement of a library job created something close to stampede. Unemployment was rampant, generally, and especially among teachers. Librarians were at the bottom of the teachers wanted list, quite the opposite of the sixties when school librarians at one time moved into the number one position of teacher demand. Accordingly, my effort in the thirties was to open library demand in schools that had never even thought of employing a librarian. I cultivated the administrators who came to Peabody in the summer to work on master's and doctoral degrees. Frequently I induced a principal to employ one of my library school graduates as a teacher of English or history, and librarian part-time, which usually developed into full time.

Partly, from the desire to open up work opportunity but mostly because I was attracted to the learning potential, I introduced the work-study co-op into library school, I believe, for the first time anywhere. I had been introduced to the plan as it had been originated in the University of Cincinnati School of Engineering by Dean Schneider when I was writing my master's thesis on the municipal university. Cincinnati had been one of the nine municipal universities of the time, and serendipitously I had been attracted to their work-study co-op. I had also experienced the Antioch version of it on my visit to Yellow Springs. I had tucked away into one of my innovation corners the desire to introduce this into library education. Peabody gave me my opportunity.

There were two patterns of work-study co-ops in my experimentation. Distant libraries like those in Springfield and Memphis were calendared by terms. Each co-op team had two students. When student A was in library school, student B was on the job in Springfield or Memphis. The following quarter term the students changed, with B in library school and A on the job. The library filled one position on its staff, paying the two co-ops the equivalent of one full time salary. Each co-op with half of a full time salary was able to pay his college expenses, and travel. The calendar was so set up that the student on the job did not leave for his study term until he was relieved by his co-op, so that the library experienced no break in service. The alternations meant the student took six quarters instead of three to complete the requirements for his BS in LS degree (which was then offered for the fifth year instead of the master's.) Usually the library offered both co-ops permanent positions and this also helped placement.

The other co-op work-study calendar alternated morning and afternoon-evening schedules. Student A studied in the morning while working in the afternoon; student B did the opposite. The following term they reversed schedules. This plan was undertaken in the Peabody College Library when I was still college librarian as well as library school director, and was continued by my successor in the library. It was also very effective in a special library—that of the Vanderbilt Medical School across the street. Mrs. Eileen Cunningham, designer of the medical classification that bears her name, was enthusiastically attracted to my proposal. When I was at Fisk she had generously helped me start the Meharry Medical College library, not only with advice but with many valuable duplicates from her own collection. Together we planned the work-study programs for a group of students who committed themselves to medical librarianship.

Early I became concerned about a number of our matriculants, usually teachers in the summer session who had taken library science courses in unaccredited undergraduate programs. These students came to us with a miscellany in Reference and Cataloging, in school book selection and administration, and even in such subjects as history of books and libraries, teaching library use, and school libraries. What to do with these students as I counselled them in their objective to acquire an ALA accredited degree at Peabody, troubled me. I wrote to BEL (the Board of Education for Librarianship) at ALA headquarters. I had taken the problem to the Association of American Library Schools several times. Each time the response had been we don't have that problem in our schools up north; next subject. About the third time I persisted with my concern at AALS I received some unexpected help from Joseph Wheeler and Harold Brigham. Both arose to plead for some staff members with undergraduate library education who were serving extremely well on their respective public library staffs at Enoch Pratt in Baltimore and in Nashville. Somewhat irritated, the heads of some of the older library schools insisted that transfers from undergraduate unaccredited schools should be made to take courses in Reference and Cataloging over again, because their undergraduate programs were below the standard required for ALA accreditation.

I disagreed. Every time one of these teachers came to my desk for counsel my heart bled. We were trying to recruit for librarianship, yet we were discouraging good recruits by our vindictive penalizing of students who had prepared themselves for their school library work in undergraduate programs.

Edward Allen Wright, our first research professor, became interested in my concern with articulating unaccredited undergraduate and graduate programs. As a result he directed for me the first conference ever held, I believe, on the subject, in 1941, to which we invited delegates from the faculties of both kinds of programs to dialogue. After the war, articulation began to arouse the schools up north, as well, and the ALA Committee on Accreditation assumed the leadership in a series of conferences that led to guidelines for undergraduate programs developed in cooperation with the association of colleges of education. Although I was pleased by this recognition of the problem, I wanted a fuller articulation which would enable students to do the first half of their accredited master's work at one of the undergraduate schools. This had to wait for Florida where my attempt to develop a state plan for library education was aborted.

In the Peabody years my own plan for a library education that would more adequately prepare the next generation for our professional destiny was undoubtedly advanced. There I introduced audiovisual instruction into the preparation of librarians at least a decade before librarianship became concerned. Basic Reference as a concept really emerged at Peabody, and I was able to launch *Current Reference Books,* in Wilson Library Bulletin, which Frances Cheney has carried on so creatively since 1943.

In March 1946 I came back to Peabody after four years in the army. Physically still feverishly ill from stubborn jungle fevers; mentally uncertain whether I could recapture my library commitments after a four-year separation; and morally suffering from the veteran's depression and inferiority about return to civilian life; I nevertheless plunged into the Peabody problems.

There was just one post-war academic quarter for me at Peabody as I have already told. Then began the 25-year commutation between New York and Tallahassee to design a comprehensive innovative encyclopedia and an accredited innovative school of librarianship. I arrived on the Florida State campus in early September 1946. For this new state university President Doak Campbell planned new professional schools to supplement schools of music and education, which already surrounded a strong college of arts and sciences with the oldest Phi Beta Kappa chapter in the state. The first was to be a school of library science. Since Doak Campbell was known as the educator who most promoted libraries on all levels, it was natural for him to think of this professional school first. He and Otis McBride recruited me by long distance telephone and letter. It was like old Peabody days when Dr. Campbell was dean of the graduate school, Otis director of placement, and I head of the library school. The only difference was that Otis had been hired as dean of men at a woman's college.

I found an undergraduate library science department doing solid work on the top floor of the library. It had been founded by librarian Louise Richardson. Two of the three faculty members are still members of the faculty a quarter of a century later; the third died, tragically, during that first year of my commutation. We three—Agnes Gregory, Sara Krentzman (now Sara Srygley) and I began designing the curriculum for the new school to be opened July 1, 1947.

We decided to continue the undergraduate program and work out some new dimensions in articulation. The continuity of these two programs was our first exciting innovation, not entirely accepted at first by ALA. We designed four basic courses that could be taken by either undergraduates or graduates. If a graduate of our undergraduate program decided to go on to a master's, none of the courses already taken had to be repeated. Sometimes we counselled more non-professional courses in the college of arts and science and in education, or even business, or music, or journalism, if these were relevant; at other times more advanced courses in library science.

Our next big innovation was the audiovisual requirement for all who qualified for a library school degree. Something of the audiovisual struggle has already been chronicled. Developing the basic audiovisual course was only less exciting to me than the infiltration of non-print formats and concerns into all other courses. Support for audiovisual instruction in our new dimensional library school library, probably the first Materials Center ever modeled, and the activation of a Graphics Laboratory for the making of media, from exhibits through motion pictures, were the next most exciting innovative achievements of the school.

Perhaps in order of triumphal satisfactions the program of library use instruction—undergraduate as well as graduate—came next. There had certainly never been anything like the "500" course before, nor the bibliographic counselling on all theses and dissertations of a graduate school. As we averaged about six sections of "500" classes each term for some 20 years, a rough estimate would total, on the basis of 1,000 each calendar year, some 20,000 graduate students who had been library sophisticated beyond the average of those who have studied in graduate schools of the United States.

Extension at Florida State was something of an epic. In these same 20 years—1947-1967—at least 10,000 students were introduced to the elements of library science in their home communities. Mostly, these students were teachers working toward the validation of their certificates, or toward advanced degrees. But there were also many homemakers. In that period, regular faculty members from the library school visited teaching centers in 37 counties in Florida, from Pensacola in the extreme northwest to Key West in the southeast, just 90 miles from Havana, Cuba. Two full time extension teachers each taught three classes every term. If the distance permitted, the teachers drove their own car to each of the three centers each week. If the distances were great, teachers flew to Their teaching centers. One year, Louise Galloway, one of our most devoted extension teachers, flew 40,000 miles to her classes from September to June, and Eastern Airlines featured a full length picture of her on their magazine cover.

The extension teacher's schedule was a strenuous one, but more than ordinarily rewarding. A typical term might include a Tuesday class in Tampa; Wednesday in Sarasota; Thursday in West Palm Beach. This would enable the teacher to return to campus some time Friday. The week-end would enable the teacher to finish grading student work, and prepare for the following week, as well as attend our monthly faculty meeting. The weekend also provided opportunity for conference with resident faculty colleagues, and renewal of association with the school.

The triumphs were many in those 21 years at Florida State as dean of its library school. They were made possible by what is of first importance to any school's life—faculty and students. Agnes Gregory in Children's Literature and Sara Srygley in School Librarianship, and I designed the school's beginning in that pre-opening year 1946-47. They are two of the most creative teachers I have ever known. Both of them have always stirred their students to extend themselves. In the summer of 1947, Robert Clapp became our fourth full time faculty member. He had been a straight A student at Peabody Library School, after a Phi Beta Kappa bachelor's degree at Vanderbilt. He, too, is still in the FSU Library School where he has over these past 25 years instilled a sense of intellectual responsibility in students to go along with sensitive understanding of library technical processes, of academic librarianship, of library administration. For many years he served as assistant dean. His high standards and refusal to compromise with contemporary tendencies to laxness have given him a reputation for discipline, with some students, but great respect and high regard by all. He was my right hand man for years, and helped me weigh many of my enthusiasms. We sometimes differed on major decisions. Perhaps our greatest difference was on the timing for the beginning of our doctoral program, which was, as a consequence, delayed by the university until after my retirement. However, Bob was not as responsible for this delay as the new graduate school dean, who felt quite insecure himself about the scope of a library science doctorate, interposed obstacle after obstacle. The doctorate came in a rush after my retirement and is prospering. I believe that Bob and I, and other members of our faculty, laid the foundation for this degree with our many hours of hard work on the design.

Of the faculty members that followed our 1947 cadre, Ruth Rockwood became key at a number of points. In both cataloging and in public librarianship she absorbed students to the point where they wanted to probe beyond requirements. Student after student came to volunteer how Dr. Rockwood made the hard subject of cataloging easy to understand. Others would say frankly, when she was off campus, we will wait for her return before taking cataloging. One whole year she was a Fulbright Fellow in Thailand and recruited many outstanding students from that country.

These thumbnail sketches of an incomparable faculty do not begin to indicate the inspiration each gave to me in the direction of an innovative library school. Sarah Reed came along next and for some eight years she epitomized the great teacher to her students and to her colleagues. Day or night, Sarah was on hand to listen to students' concerns, and to counsel unselfishly. In my way I expressed my appreciation to Sarah for the delectable cookies she baked for all of us, as if it were the real reason I had invited her to serve on our faculty. Her leaving was a real sacrifice in more than one way. Right at the opening of the academic year in September, Dave Clift called from ALA headquarters to ask if I would release Sarah on short notice to become secretary of the Committee on Accreditation. It was an honor to Sarah and to the school. But with her deep sense of loyalty to the school and to me she refused to leave on short notice, until I called her into my office and half sternly and half mockingly asked, "Am I still your boss, as you have called me on occasion?" When she answered affirmatively, I said "I order you to report to Dave Clift as quickly as you can board a flight for Chicago."

How can I begin to do justice to all of that 14-member incomparable faculty. Whatever other specifications ALA has written into standards, they are all meaningless without the people who are the faculty and the students, and later the alumni. When on the last visit of COA, Jack Dalton asked me "what do you consider strongest in the Florida State University Library School?" I responded instantly, "The faculty." After the visiting committee had spent some days they wrote in their report, "The Faculty is even better than the Dean realizes." With apology to them I say a word about the others. Gerald Jahoda, recommended by Ralph Shaw, helped me effect that modulation between traditional Reference and Information Science beyond my fondest hopes. Because of his understanding, I escaped the trauma of the audiovisual integration, earlier. John Goudeau revitalized our academic librarianship offerings when he came to us from his directorship of the New Orleans Louisiana State University. I had known John Milford Goudeau as far back as our common efforts right after World War II to gain ALA recognition for our respective, new, Library schools—Kent State and Florida State. There is Mary Alice Hunt and there is Bill Quinly, two audiovisualists with the advantage of library science to help them understand the integration I desired. But the other audiovisual teachers, Otis McBride, Myles Ritchie, and the late Harold Moreland helped in their own way to build audiovisual understandings into the preparation of librarians and teachers.

There have been several librarians of our library school library who caught the vision of the Materials Center concept and helped us implement a new education for librarianship at least two decades before the 1969 Media Standards were ratified. The earliest was Bess Daughtry, author of that first manual on integrated cataloging of all formats. A second was Audrey Newman who became state supervisor of school libraries in Florida. No librarian has surpassed in devotion Helen Danford, who has been Librarian of our Materials Center longest of all.

At Peabody, I had Anne Greer as executive secretary for eleven years. It is Marguerite Sellars at Florida State who has virtually committed her life to the School. If there were a union it would excommunicate her. She arrives at work at least an hour and a half before the building is open; has the coffee urn started so that students can be greeted with a cup of coffee before they go off to their first class. Incidentally, she directs a staff of four assistant secretaries, mimeographs school publications in formats that would make any commercial printer drool, maintains impeccable files of student records and correspondence; is the flawless budget keeper; and has saved the life of this dean countless times. I daresay my successor, Harold Goldstein, would amen, "ditto."

This has been a heart rather than a head chronicle of a life in Library Education. Therefore it should close with love for at least two generations of library school students, if not three. Because before I retired several students introduced themselves to me: "You not only taught my mother, but my grandmother." Since I have headed an ALA accredited school about as long as any one now alive, my list of students would run into thousands. I am very proud of them, of their achievements all over the world, as far away as distant Thailand, Tasmania, and Taiwan, and many nearer places abroad and at home. Sentimental memories of families that began in library school, of momentous decisions in the lives of individuals, of crises and tragedies troop through my mind every time I reread the volume of letters presented to me upon my retirement. I owe my students every word that was so graciously written into the Beta Phi Mu Award of 1967 "for distinguished service to education for librarianship."

18. Testament

Quest for Quiet began my decision for librarianship. The mystical lure of quiet must close this manuscript. Perhaps I can make this lure most tangible by writing that I have always liked to dream. My imagination has always seemed to want to repudiate "telling it like it is." There was always present somewhere inside a picture of something more beautiful than anything that surrounded me physically. Try as hard as I would to suppress this dreaming, to please my parents who worried about the way I used to lose myself in another world, I would reluctantly and forcibly return myself to the here and now. Chores around the house and the later necessity of making a living forced me out of my day dreams. Yet I would persist in imagining what was really happening on "Mulberry Street."

Of all places on this earth, libraries encouraged me to meditate and dream. In the quiet of reading room or stack I would eliminate all who wanted to tell it like it is on this imperfect planet, and lose myself in what George Dawson had once called books—"the diary of the human race." In between readings, I would meditate, and then dream. Hours, and sometimes a whole day, would melt away like this, and then I would look up and find a brother or sister standing by my table and saying, "Where have you been. Mother is worried to death about you."

Perhaps this dreaming is very dangerous, as some teachers and child psychologists might contend. I know that ancient China was criticized by some historians and critics of civilizations as having lived too much in the world of dreams. As a student of history, I agree nations have appeared to prosper when there was a balance between physical action and spiritual meditation. If ancient China suffered from an overbalance in meditation, I sometimes wonder whether we in the contemporary United States are not declining from an over-accent on where the physical action is.

In the library quiet that lured and awed me I was drawn most to reading in the supernatural. As I indicated in the opening chapter, I kept reading the fairy tale classics to an age so late that the Toledo librarians worried over me. Then the Greek, Roman, and Norse myths took hold and would not let go of my imagination. After that, ghosts and folklore; writers like Poe and Jules Verne spell-bound me. I did not yet know that there was already a vast occult literature; and when I did discover it, I hid my reading from my college professors, especially in the sciences, some of whom I felt would hold that against me in grading. Then I met a physicist who openly boasted of a home library in science fiction. I heard him respond to a colleague's iconoclasm one day, "Why not? Science is stranger than fiction."

That there could be a place for the supernatural in any world as agnostic as science never occurred to me until one day at Peabody in 1935. Psychologist Joe Moore, collaborator on the Peabody Library Information Tests, and close friend, introduced me to a new book sensation in psychology, and a deck of cards. It was the famous *Extrasensory Perception* by Joseph Banks Rhine, published the year before, long before any reference book had yet begun to define ESP as *awareness or knowledge of something without the use of the known sense organs*. Yet this was exactly that mystical something I was experiencing in library quiet that had attracted me to the profession of librarianship.

All of this concern really has its beginning in our Holy Bible, which I have read with perhaps some different stirrings from what preachers have often sought to encourage. Nor have I been quite able to communicate my deepest concerns to my Sunday School classes at First Baptist Church, although they have been college freshmen or sophmores these past 20 years or so. On occasion when I have led the discussion of our Wednesday night Sunday School Teachers' meeting I have been tempted; but always I have turned to the more comfortable consideration of the upcoming Sunday lesson, or to a discussion of Reference sources in religion for classes. The nearest I have come to sharing what troubled me is at the International Christian Leadership breakfast Wednesday morning.

For 18 years now, the Tallahassee chapter has met one morning a week at seven-thirty. Following the usual format, we begin with a prayer, have breakfast, and then one of us leads in a discussion of a contemporary problem and how a Christian would solve it. The group was founded by the present Chief Justice of the Florida Supreme Court and includes men of several Christian denominations.

When my turn came around, about once every two or three months, I have frequently browsed in aspects of my deepest concern—immortality; the meaning of death; the estrasensory. This wonderful group of men has been most patient, most understanding, perhaps more sympathetic than many of my colleagues in both town and gown.

What has troubled me both in church and out is a reluctance to probe the meaning of death and the possibility of life after. I have sensed this reluctance in even my reading of the Old and New Testaments. This was confirmed in some of the commentaries, and even in the fine article on parapsychology by Gardner Murphy, which I prompted for *Collier's Encyclopedia*. I have pondered the words in that article, many times, that "Judaism and Christianity have in general been hostile to traffic with spirits and to the paranormal as a whole."

Why should this be? Certainly the Resurrection is a confirmation for Christians of the truth of immortality. Nor is the Old Testament without its supernaturals. I would expect science to be much more reluctant about the supernatural than religion. But strangely enough some scientists have been largely responsible for overcoming the taboo that the Judeo-Christian, if not some of the oriental religions, have put upon "trafficking" in the supernatural.

As the extrasensory world opened to me in the library quiet, I went through a sequence of concentrations. Telepathy, first, intrigued me, especially as Gerry and I discovered quite early in our married life that frequently we were thinking about the same thing at the same time, for no apparent reason. Time and again we would try to retrace the antecedents of these telepathic communications to the obvious assumption that when two people live together intimately they are bound to develop similar references. This proved true in many cases; but surprisingly not in many other instances, when for no reason at all the same extraneous subject would come into our thoughts simultaneously.

As our years increased, we began trying to discuss the meaning of death as rationally as possible. We recalled that part of the marriage vow "until death do us part" with much concern. We agreed that if God, or a genii (as in the fairy tales) should come to us with an offer of one wish it would be that we might go together, so that the survivor would not have to suffer the supreme anguish of life. As we approach our 43rd anniversary, we sometimes attempt to relieve our concern with what is now referred to as the activist's amendment of the vow to "until three years do us part."

If our pragmatism suggests I should be ashamed to reveal my impracticalities, I would counter with one of the poems I liked at Fisk, and that one of my students sent me recently. Our climate being what it is, I suppose I should remind that the poet is Black.

DREAMS
By Langston Hughes

Hold fast to dreams
For if dreams die
Life is a broken-winged bird
That cannot fly.

Hold fast to dreams
For when dreams go
Life is a barren field
Frozen with snow.

At home the other night I met the words of the great Carl Gustave Jung as I was reviewing an article for *Collier's Encyclopedia* (volume 13, page 670):

I am convinced that the investigation of the Psyche is the science of the future . . . It is the science we need most, for it is gradually becoming apparent that the greatest danger to man is neither famine, nor earthquakes, nor microbes, nor cancer, but himself.

This I believe. Inside of us is the answer to the riddle of the universe. We must search deep down if we would know who we are, the meaning of life and death, those imponderables of existence that haunt our every living moment, whether we admit it or not. The climate for such concern with ultimates I am convinced is Quiet. Because so much of our world is committed to noise only proximates can be found there. In libraries is the quiet prelude to ultimates. That is the mystical reason why I believe I made my decision for librarianship.

A Selection of Writings by Louis Shores

ORIGINS OF THE AMERICAN COLLEGE LIBRARY, 1638-1800 (1934, 1935, 1963, 1966, 1972)
BASIC REFERENCE BOOKS (1937, 1939)
KNOW YOUR ENCYCLOPEDIA (1937)
HIGHWAYS IN THE SKY: The Story of the AACS (1947)
BASIC REFERENCE SOURCES (1954, 1972)
INSTRUCTIONAL MATERIALS (1960)
AROUND THE LIBRARY WORLD IN 76 DAYS: An Essay in Comparative Librarianship (1967)
REFERENCE BOOKS FOR JUNIOR COLLEGES (1960)
MARK HOPKINS' LOG AND OTHER ESSAYS (1965)
LIBRARY-COLLEGE USA: Essays on a Prototype for an American Higher Education (1970)
THE LIBRARY AUTHOR (1971)
LOOKING FORWARD TO 1999 (1972)
LIBRARY EDUCATION (1972)
AUDIOVISUAL LIBRARIANSHIP: The Crusade for Media Unity, 1946-69 (1973)
REFERENCE ART AND INFORMATION SCIENCE (1975)

A selection of books co-authored and edited by Louis Shores
Bibliographies and Summaries in Education to July 1935 (with W. S. Monroe, 1936)
Best Methods of Study (with Samuel Smith, 1938, 1951, 1955, 1958)
General Education: A University Program in Action (with W. H. Stickler and Paul Stoakes, 1950)
Challenges to Librarianship (1935)
Books-Libraries-Librarians (with John David Marshall and Wayne Shirley, 1955)
The Library-College (with Robert Jordan and John Harvey, 1966)
Collier's Encyclopedia: Advisory Editor, 1946-60; Editor-in-Chief, 1960-

Index

Academic Librarianship, 11 ff
Accession book, 34
Accreditation, 202
Adelaide, 135
Administration, 27-28
Africa, 125
Afrikaans, 129, 132
Agra, 73
Aiea, 147
Air University, 75
Alger, Horatio, 7
ALA (American Library Association), 26 ff
 -American Library History Round Table, 26, 152, 232, 253-55, 258-60, 288
American Mercury, 228
Anderson, Hans Christian, 4
Annual Lecture, 93, 106 ff
Ansley, Charles, 181
Antioch College, 200, 208
Apartheid, 127, 132
Appian Way, 124
Arithmetic, 4
Armed Forces, 54 ff, 81
Armed Forces Librarian, 81
Armed Peace Force, 75
Army, 56 ff, 215
AACS, Army Airways Communications System, 215 ff
Around the World Mission, 136
Art, 96, 273 ff
Articulation, 202, 280
Asia, 125
AALS (Association of American Library Schools), 257
ASLIB, 90 ff
ACRL (Association of College and Research Libraries), 257, 260
Athens, 125
Audiovisualism, 103, 211 ff
Audiovisual Librarianship, 223 ff

Australia, 118, 125, 134
Australian National University, 138
Authority, 182-83
Autobiography, 4-5
Autonomous courses, 200

Bachelor degree, 19
Bangkok, 143
Baptist Church, 296
Barnes & Noble, 175
Bartlett, Richard, 233
Baseball, 7 ff
Basic Reference, 24, 94, 140, 162 ff, 286, 289
Baskin, Sam, 210
Basra, 79
Beethoven, 15
Belfast, 108
"Best Methods of Study" 283
Bible, 296
"Bibliographic incest," 163
Bibliotheque Nationale, 95, 123
Birla Temple, 73
Birmingham, England, 99
Bishop, William Warner, 33-34, 233
Blackburn, Robert, 185
Black-White, 100, 153 ff
Book selection, 32-33
Bookmobile,
 -British, 89 ff
Books, 13 ff
Bootstrap, 75
Bradford, Gamaliel, 90
Brady, St. Elmo, 29 ff
Branscomb, Harvie, 210
Breasted, James Harvey, 175-76
Britannic, 109 ff
Brewer, *Historic Notebook*, 168
Britannica Encyclopaedia, 116, 173
Britannica Junior, 173 ff
British National Bibliography, 84
BOR (British Other Ranks), 73 ff

301

British Reference, 88 ff
Brown, Charles Harvey, 54 ff, 103, 254
Brown, Ray Francis, 29
Brown University, 229-30
Bryant, Douglas, 102
Buffalo, N.Y., 3
Bullseye, 58
Burma, 263
Butler, Pierce, 163

Cambridge University, 89 ff
Campbell, Doak S., 75, 203, 283, 289
Canberra, 138
Canberra, Major Address, 138, 140
Cape of Good Hope, 128
Cape Town, 126, 128, 130
Carlyle, Thomas, 195 ff
Carnegie Corporation, 33 ff
Carroll, John, 189
Casani, Santos, 113
Cataloging, 22
Cavin, Loutrell, 79
Censorship, 41 ff, 166
Certification, 221
Challenges to Librarianship, 103
Chambers, Whitaker, 25
Chambers's Encyclopaedia, 116-17
Change, 231
Chaucer House, 53, 84, 102
Cheney, Frances Neel, 56
Chicago, 41 ff
Chicago, University, Graduate Library School, 224 ff
China, -Burma, -India Theatre, 71 ff, 263
Civil War, 157
Clapp, Robert, 80, 291
Clapp, Verner, 103
Classification, 22, 85
Clayton, Howard, 211
Cleveland, Ohio, 3 ff,
   -Public Library 3 ff, 17 ff,
   -School 4 ff
Clothes, 45
Cluster Colleges, 209-10
Cobh, 109
College, 11 ff
CCNY, 20 ff (College of the City of New York)
Collier's Encyclopedia, 53, 75, 112, 114, 118, 120, 127, 133, 134, 140, 161 ff
Collins, LeRoy, 7
Collison, Robert L., 111
Colon Classification, 86 ff
Colosseum, 124
Columbia, 21 ff, 229
Columbia Encyclopedia, 181
Commencement, 24 ff
Communism, 15-16, 41, 271 ff
Comparative Education, 52 ff
Comparative Librarianship, 51 ff, 87, 112, 145-6, 165, 239, 247
Compton, F. E., 174
Compton's Pictured Encyclopedia, 174 ff
Conas, 71 ff
Conciliation, 154 ff
Confrontation, 126-34, 155 ff
Confidential Reference, 88, 92
"Congressional Set", 240
Conscientious Objector, 61
Conservatism, 271 ff
Constants, 225 ff, 298
Continuous Revision, 191
Control Tower, 71
Cookbooks, 45 ff
Cosmopolitan Atlas, 191
Courtship, 41 ff
Copeland, Emily, 157
Copenhagen, 121
Couch, W. T., 191, 271
Cousins, Norman, 152
Crabb, Alfred Leland, 28
Criticism, 274
Crusades, 154 ff
Cry the Beloved Country, 162
Cryptography, 59 ff, 71
Cultural Exchange, 87
Cunningham, Eileen, 288
Current Reference Books, 170, 286, 289
Curriculum, 224
Currier, Theodore, 29 ff
Curtis, Florence Rising, 27

Dale, Edgar, 103
Dalton, Jack, 76
Daub, 59 ff
Dartmouth College, 229
Dean of Library School, 291

Death, 297
Debating, 15 ff, 37 ff
DeBernardis, Amo, 217
Decimal Classification, 22 ff
Delhi, 71 ff
Demiashkevich, M. J., 51
Demonstrators, 105, 136
Dempsey, Jack, 151
Denmark, 118
Deutsches Bucherverzeichnis, 123
Deutsches Bibliographie, 123
Dewey, John, 6
Dewey, Melvil, 22
Dictionaries, 169
Disciplines, 206
Dissertation, 230
Ditzion, Sidney, 233
Doctoral Program, 284
Documentary Films, 218
Documentation, 90
Downs, Robert Bingham, 76
Drama, 274 ff
Dreaming, 294-5
"Dreams," by Langston Hughes, 297
Drexel Institute, 210
Dublin, 108 ff
Dudley, Lavinia P., 268
Duhamel, Maurice, 80
Durban, 131

Economics, 11-12
Einstein, Albert, 231
Encyclopedia, 113, 116, 289
Encyclopedia Overview, 199
Encyclopedics, 175 ff
Encyclopedist, 171 ff
"Eleven-Plus Examination," 117
England, 83 ff
English Language, 169
Essentialism, 5
Evangelisms, 151 ff
Evans, Luther, 102, 103, 111
Experimental Colleges, 205 ff
Extension, 220
Extension at Florida State University, 291
ESP (Extra sensory perception), 297

Fairweather, Jane, 124-5
Fairy Tales, 3 ff

Farman, Ivan, 125
Fielding, Henry, 13
Fisk University, 24, 29 ff, 153 ff
 -Jubilee Singers, 29 ff
Florida, 102
Florida A & M University, 157
FASL (Florida Association of School Librarians), 221 ff
FAVA (Florida Audiovisual Association,) 221 ff
Florida Education Association, 223
Florida Library Association, 111, 265-8
Florida State University, 5, 75, 212, 289
Fontaine, Everett, 191
Food, 45, 95, 97
Football, 35-36
Ford, Charles, 268
Format Classification, 214 ff
Fort Hamilton, 60-61
Four-letter Words, 270
Fourth R., 165
France, 118
Francis, Sir Frank, 120, 138
Frankfurt, 122
Franklin, John Hope, 38 ff
Free Inquiry, 164
Freedom to Read, 41
Fukuda, Miss Naomi, 143, 145
Fulbright Fellowship, 53, 62 ff

Galloway, Louise, 291
Gandhi, 73
Garfield, Eugene, 163
General Education, 283-4
Generic Book, 80, 211 ff, 280
Geraldine, 42 ff, 61, 82
Gerould, James Thayer, 227
Germany, 118
Gestalt, 207 ff
Glasgow, 102 ff
Gleason, Eliza Atkins, 35
Goodwill Ambassador, 119
Graneek, 108, 135
Graphics, 216
"The Great Depression", 286
Gregory, Agnes, 80, 290
Grolier, 189
GCA, (Ground Control Approach) 72
Guantanamo, 65

Guide to Historical Literature, 233
Guide to Reference Books, 120

Haeckel, Ernest, 110, 274
Hagel, Ray, 193
Hall, Mary E., 281
Hampton Institute, 27
Hampton Roads, 60 ff
Harlem, 25, 154
Halsey, William, 130
Harvard Classics, 200
Harvard University, 227 ff, 229
Harvey, John, 210
Hawaii, 146
Hawaiian Library Association, 148
Hawaii, University of, 147
Health, 178
Henne, Frances, 103
Heidkamp, Herb, 127
Henderson, John, 271 ff
Here and Now, 294
Hero, 197
Heroes and Hero Worship, 196
Highways in the Sky, 74
Hippie, 180
Hirschberg, Herbert S., 9-10
History, 225 ff
Hitch-hike, 18 ff
Hitler, Adolph, 52, 61
Hoban, Charles, 217
Hobart, 135-6
Homemaking, 44 ff
Hong Kong, 142
Honolulu, 147
How To Use Your Library, 175
Howard University, 25-26
Hughes, Langston, 297
Hunt, Mary Alice, 80
Huxley, Aldous, 53, 114 ff
Huxley, Julian, 115

Immelman, Rene, 126, 129
Independent Study, 89
India, 242, 263
Indian Ocean, 69 ff
Information, 88
Information Science, 90, 92, 138
Innovation, 210 ff
Innsbruck, 97
Inquiry, 166

Instruction, 185
Instructional Materials, 170, 215
Instructional Materials Specialist, 221 ff
Integration, 156 ff
Intellectual Freedom, 41, 233, 269 ff
Intellectual Responsibility, 239 ff
Intellectual Warfare, 96-97
Intelligence Analysis, 74
International, 118
ICL (International Christian Leadership), 296
Iowa State University, 254
Iran, 70
Iraq, 70 ff
Ireland, 108 ff
Irish Free Press, 108
Isolationism, 55
Italian Seminars, 104 ff
Italy, 97 ff, 104 ff, 118

Jahoda, Gerald, 92, 293
Jamestown, N.D., College, 210
Japan, 118, 138, 143, 146
Jesse, William, 84, 263
Jesus, 184
Johannesburg, 126, 131
Johnson, B. Lamar, 210
Johnson C. Smith University, 160 ff
Johnson, Charles Spurgeon, 127, 154 ff
Johnson, Walter, 8
Joint University Library, 54 ff
Jones, Henrik, 99
Jones, Thomas Elsa, 25 ff, 29
Jordan, Robert, 197
Journal of Library History, 26, 234 ff, 256
Joyce, James, 109
Jung, Carl, 297

Kane, *Famous First Facts*, 203
Keats, John, 277
Keio University, 144
Kells, Book of, 108
Kenya, 125
KWIC (Key Word in Context), 90
Keyserling, Herman, 167
Kingery, Robert, 184
Kipling, Rudyard, 10, 254 ("finest story in the World")

Kirk, Russell, 271
Know Your Encyclopedia, 175
Koran, 73
Kunitz, Stanley, 170

Lacy, Dan, 103
Lake, Erie, 17
Lang, Andrew, 3
Lapu Lapu, 141
Larson, ole, 212
Learning, 4 ff
 -by doing, 4 ff
Learning Resource Center, 233, 249
 (see also Library; Materials Center)
Learning Today, 211
Leeds, 99-100
Lehrer, Tom, 272
Lester, Robert, 54
Lewis, Leora, 174, 177
Leyte Gulf, 141
Liberal, 273
Liberty Ships, 66 ff
Librarian, 41 ff, 221 ff
Librarianship, 23, 41
Library, 1, 5
Library Architecture, 154 ff, 202
Library Arts, 199
Library Association, 90, 93
Library-College, 12, 89, 101, 152, 195 ff, 240, 248-9
Library-College Associates, Inc., 211
Library-College Charter, 210
Library-College Journal, 211
Library Communities, 12
Library Education, 294
Library of Congress, 22
 -Classification, 22, 26, 111
Library Education, 21, 227 ff
 -for Librarianship, 91, 277 ff
Library Education Division, 278
Library History, 152, 224 ff
Library History Seminars, 233
Library Journal, 170
Library Science, 289
Library Use, 21, 282
Listening Post, 218
Literary Criticism, 274 ff
Literature of Reference, 164 ff
London, 83 ff, 120, 130
London, University,

-School of Librarianship, 90
Love, 40 ff

McArthur, Douglas, 141
McBride, Otis, 55-56, 80, 290
McDermott, Marian, 147
McGill University, 172
McLuhan, Marshall, 214
Macmillan, Inc., 192
MacPherson, Harriet Dorothea, 22
Magnetic tape, 218
Magnolia, Mass. Conference, 210
Mahar, Mary Helen, 89 ff
Malcles, Louis-Noelle, 125
Manley, Marian, 233
Manuscripts, 119
Marinelli, Anne, 104 ff
Marriage, 43 ff
Marshall, John David, 233
Marx, Karl, 15 ff, 25, 270
Master degree, 20-21
 -thesis, 20
Materialistic Interpretation of History, 271
Materials Center, 216, 290
Matlock Bath, 115 ff
Maxwell Air Force Base, 76 ff
Media, 211 ff
Media Clinics, 222 ff
Media Standards, 212
Media Unity, 211 ff, 221
Medical Librarianship, 288
Medium Fair, 222
Medium School, 246-50
Meditation, 110, 295
Meharry Medical College Library, 288
Melbourne, 136
Melbourne, University of, 136
Mencken, H. L., 6, 228
Merchant Marine, 62 ff
Merritt, Leroy, 258
Metcalf, Harlan, 182
Metcalf, Keyes, 233
Metcalfe, John, 139
Metropolitan Library Association, 242
Metropolitan Opera, 59-60
Miami Beach, 57
Michigan, 56
Midlands, 98 ff

Milam, Carl, 179
Minorities, 25, 153 ff
Mobile service, 89 ff
Mohrhardt, Foster, 233
Mongoose, 72
Moore, Joe, 295
Mosque, 73
Mother, 3
Motion Picture, 213
Mudge Citation, 169
Mudge, Isadore Gilbert, 21-22, 167
"Mulberry Street", 294
Mumford, Quincy, 138
Municipal Universities, 20-21, 201, 226
Murphy, Fred, 189
Murphy, Gardner, 296
Music, 14 ff, 19-20
Mythology, 6 ff

Nairobi, 125
Nashville, Tennessee, 24, 28 ff, 54
National Diet Library, 144
NEA Journal, (National Education Association), 212
National Library Week, 152
Navy, 66 ff, 78
Negro Education, 12 ff
Negro Magazines, 157
Negro Press, 156-57
Nehru, 73
Netherlands, 104-5
New College, Sarasota, 208
New Delhi, 71 ff
New England Town Meeting, 242-43
New South Wales, University of, 139
New York City, 17 ff
New York Herald-Tribune Books, 172
New York Times, 172
Newness, 231
Newsboy, 7 ff
Norris, Frank, 276
North, 155 ff
North, Stafford, 210
Northwestern University, 39
Novel, 13-14
Nyasaland, 126

Oahu, 145
Obscenity, 41, 270

Occult, 115 ff
Odysseys, 49 ff
Oklahoma Christian College, 210
Omnibus, 211
One Race, 153 ff
One World, 75
Oral History, 235 ff
Organization Librarian, 252 ff
 -British, 92 ff
 -Southeastern Library Assn., 158
Origins of the American College Library, 74, 202, 225 ff
Orne, Jerrold, 77 ff
Orwell, George, 278
Oxford University, 89

Pacific University, 208-9
Pacifism, 74
Page, 9 ff
Pageant of America, 36
Palm Beach, 59
Palmer, Bernard, 84
Panama Canal, 66 ff
Paris, 94 ff, 104, 123
Parsons College, 208
Party, 54-55
Paton, Alan, 126, 132, 162, 277
Peabody College, 51, 54, 172, 215, 281 ff, 285, 288-89
Peabody Journal of Education, 173, 215
Peabody Library Information Tests, 175, 281
Peace, 74 ff
Pearl Harbor, 55, 147
Penchanters, 37
Penelope Barker, 61 ff
Pennsylvania, University of, 229
Peripheries, 278 ff
Persian Gulf, 69-70
Perth, 134
Philip, Duke of Edinburgh, 93
Philippine Library Association, 140
Philippine Library Association, Major address, 140
Philippines, 118, 140
Philosophy, 95, 107, 231
Physics, 10-11
Piano, 14 ff
Pictures, 213

Piggot, Mary, 91, 108
Pinto, Olga, 125
Poetry, 10-11
Poole's Index, 107
Poole, William Frederick, 233
Port of Embarkation, 59 ff
Powell, Ben, 233
Powell, Lawrence Clark, 233
Pragmatism, 279
Prejudice, 151 ff
Pretoria, 132
Pretoria, University of, 133
Princeton University, 227 ff
Progressive Education, 51
Prohibition, 38-39
Projectors, 216
Prostitution, 182
Public Librarianship, 8 ff
Public Library, 240-4, 254, 259
Public Library,
 -Delhi, 74
 -New York, 17 ff, 154
 -Toledo, 9 ff
Public Library Inquiry, 41
Pubs, 83
Pulitzer Prize, 275

Quest for Quiet, 294-5, 298
Quiet, 278, 298
"Quiet Force, The", 140, 148

Radin, Paul, 29 ff
Rand McNally, 191
Ranganathan, 86 ff, 102
Ranke, Leopold von, 230
Rathbone, Josephine Adams, 233
Reading, 4 ff, 12 ff
Reading Interests, 157 ff
Realia, 213
Realism vs. Reality, 274 ff
Reality, 274 ff
Red Brick University, 101
Reddick, Laurence Dunbar, 38 ff
Redstone Army Center, 78
Reed, Sara, 292
Reference, 22, 82 ff, 125, 239, 284, 286
Reference Books, 164, 169
Reference-passive, 164
Reference Philosophy, 163, 167
Reference Questions, 100

RSD, (Reference Services Division), ALA, 163, 256, 258
Reference Standards, 117-18
Reference theory, 106, 163, 166
Rhodesia, 125
Reincarnation, 240
Riviera, 98
ROTC (Reserve Officer Training Corps), 75
Richardson, Louise, 290
"Riddle of the Universe", 298
Rider, Fremont, 103
Rockwood, Ruth, 112, 292
Roden, Carl, 233
Rodriquez, Norma, 137
Rollins, Athol, 174 ff
Rome, 97 ff, 124
Rose, Ernestine, 25, 154
Rosicrucians, 242
Ross, Martin, 12 ff, 19
Rothrock, Mary Utopia, 262-3
Royal Library, Denmark, 122
Royal Library School, Denmark, 122
Romulo, Carlos P. General, 141
Rush, N. Orwin, 232
Russian Literature, 14 ff

Salisbury, 125
San Francisco, 130, 148
Santa Cruz, California University, 209
Sarasota, 204
Saturday Review, 152, 172
Scholastics, 175
Schomburg, Arthur, 25, 35
School, 4 ff, 19-20
School Librarian, 244-6
School and Society, 201
School Librarianship, 12, 21, 223
 -British, 89, 281
Scorpion, 72
Scotland, 99, 101 ff
Scott, Sir Walter, 10
Sea, 113
Security, 59 ff
Seduction, 273
Segregation, 38-39, 155 ff
 -abroad, 159 ff
SELA (Southeastern Library Assn.), 263-5
Sellars, Marguerite, 293

Sinclair, Upton, 268
Sex, 40 ff, 121, 270 ff, 272
Shane, M. L., 215
Sharr, 135
Shaw, Ralph, 147, 204, 262
Shaw List, 34 ff
Sheehan, Sister Helen, 197
Shelf list, 34
Shirley, Wayne, 103, 231
Sinclair, Upton, 15, 156, 276
Sister, 3-4
Socialism, 272
Smith, Ralph, 179
Smut, 272
South, 24, 27 ff, 101, 154-55
South Africa, 118, 126
South Africa, Republic of, 133-4
South China Sea, 140
Southeastern Library Association, 111, 158
Spain, Frances, 143
SCOR (Special Committee on Re-organization), 260-2
Special Librarianship, 12 ff, 21, 78, 251-2
Spelling, 4
Sports, 96
Srygley, Sara, 80, 290
Staccato, 278
Stacks, 154 ff
State Library, Hawaii, 146
Steinbeck, John, 276
Sterling Memorial Library, 228
SAC (Strategic Air Command), 78
Stickler, W. Hugh, 207 ff
Stroven, Doctor, 147
Strozier, Robert, 194
Struther, Jan, 278
Subscription Books Bulletin, 92, 171
Sunday School, 296
Supernatural, 295
Sydney, 139
Sydney, important address, 139
Symphony, 19-20

Taj Mahal, 73
Tape Recorder, 218
Tasmania, 137
Tauber, Maurice, 76
Teaching, 19, 175 ff

Teaching With Books, 210
Tennessee Valley Authority Pioneer Regional Library Service, 263
Theology, 160
Third Activities Committee, 165
Thomas, Marcel, 123, 125
Tibet, 242
The Tinder Box, 4
Tokyo, 143
Toledo, 8 ff, 153
Toldeo, University of, 11 ff
Tolstoy, 13 ff
Tower Stack, 154-55, 228
Towne, Jackson, 271
Transatlantic, 82 ff
Transparency Overlay, 186
Travel, 46
True University, 196
Tyler, Helen and Steve, 57
Typhoon, 68 ff

U-Boats, 59 ff
Ultimates, 240
Underdog Complex, 151
Undergraduate Education, 152
United Kingdom, 82 ff, 118
United Nations
   -Hammerskjold Library, 119
U.S. Air Force, 53, 75
USIS (U.S. Information Services), 96
U.S. Supreme Court, 155

Vanderbilt University, 54
   -Medical School Library, 288
Van Hoesen, Henry Bartlett, 229
Vatican, 98
Vegetarianism, 86
Verwoerd Government, 129
Video History, 236
Vladimirov, Vladimir, 119

Wakulla Springs Colloquium, 206 ff
Wales, 98 ff
Walford, A. J., 117-18, 120, 125
Waples, Douglas, 224
War Changes, 56
Washington, D.C., 26, 75
Weedon's Encyclopedia, 173
Wells, Jack, 84
Welsford, Percy, 84 ff, 93, 103

Western Australia, University of, 135
Western Reserve University, 26
What Is Art, 273
Wheelock, Eleazar, 229
White, Sir Harold, 138
Whitehead, Alfred, 231
Wight, E. A., 56, 179
Wilkie, Wendell, 75
William and Mary College, 226 ff
Williams, Edward Christopher, 25-26
Williamsburg, 226 ff
Williamson, C. C., 21 ff
Willingdon Airport, 71 ff
Wilna, University of, 119
Wilson Bulletin, 170
Wilson, Halsey, 170, 233

Wilson, Louis Round, 54 ff, 103, 233
Wilson, Woodrow, 227-28
Women, 40 ff
Working Party, 92
Wranglers, 37
Woman's Home Companion, 191
Wray, 135-7
Wright, Edward Allen, 288-9
Wylie, Philip, 239, 268

Yale University, 228-29
Yoga, 242
Yust, Walter, 268

Zachert, Martha Jane, 235 ff

Z
720
S53
A35

DEC 9 1976